ISSUES IN PHYSICAL EDUCATION

Issues in Physical Education

Edited by

Neil Armstrong and Andrew Sparkes

CASSELL

Cassell Educational Limited
Villiers House
41/47 Strand
London WC2N 5JE

First published 1991

British Library Cataloguing in Publication Data
Issues in physical education.
  1. Great Britain. Schools. Curriculum: Physical education
  I. Armstrong, Neil II. Sparkes, Andrew
  613.7071041

ISBN 0 304 32413 2 (hardback)
     0 304 32432 9 (paperback)

Typeset by Fakenham Photosetting Limited, Fakenham, Norfolk
Printed and bound in Great Britain by
Dotesios Limited, Trowbridge, Wiltshire

Contents

Contributors

Dr Neil Armstrong
Reader in Exercise Science
Director of the PEA Research Centre
University of Exeter

Dr Stuart Biddle
Lecturer in Education
Associate Director of the PEA Research
  Centre
University of Exeter

Sue Bray
Lecturer in Education
University of Exeter

Geoffrey Meek
Lecturer in Education
University of Exeter

Sue Thomas
Lecturer in Education
University of Exeter

Dr Andrew Sparkes
Lecturer in Education
Associate Director of the PEA
  Research Centre
University of Exeter

Dr Kenneth Fox
Lecturer in Education
Associate Director of the PEA
  Research Centre
University of Exeter

Peter Drewett
Lecturer in Education
University of Exeter

Carole Raymond
Lecturer in Education
University of Exeter

Bryan Woods
Lecturer in Education
University of Exeter

Preface

When we were approached by Professor Wragg, Director of the Exeter School of Education, and Naomi Roth of Cassell we were delighted to accept the challenge of addressing some of the major issues in physical education as we enter the 1990s. Having accepted the task we recognized how immense it was. Should we attempt to cover everything or focus on specific issues only? After considerable thought we opted for the latter, based upon the expertise and interest available at Exeter. As such, we have taken selected issues to consider in detail and this needs to be recognized when reading the book as a whole. This is not to imply that there is a lack of interest in other issues but rather that within the limitations of one volume we could only do justice to a few.

The first part of the book focuses our attention on a range of curricular issues. In the second section we have chosen to consider in detail issues relating to health because this has emerged as a major focus of our research in recent years within both the School of Education and the Physical Education Association of Great Britain and Northern Ireland Research Centre.

In the Curriculum Issues section, since many of the contributions in this book suggest changes in the way in which we approach a range of issues in physical education (PE), it is appropriate that the first three chapters focus on curriculum change. In Chapter 1, Andrew Sparkes explores the paradox often faced in schools—that involves impressions of stability and yet change, of diversity and yet sameness. Andrew begins by discussing the differences between real and superficial change and then he considers the manner in which various perspectives shape the ways in which the process of change is addressed in schools. Throughout the analysis the complexities of the change process are emphasized and the centrality of teachers within this process is highlighted. In Chapter 2, Andrew takes us into the world of the school to look at the process of curriculum change within a PE department. Drawing on case study material he allows us to see change through the eyes of the physical educators involved. His findings indicate that change should not be viewed as a neutral process and that teachers will perceive the costs and rewards of change in different ways depending upon the perspective they hold. Andrew suggests that if losers are a fundamental reality in the change process then attempts to innovate will meet with limited success unless this reality is recognized, and collectively explored in a sensitive and supportive manner, by those involved in the changes themselves.

In Chapter 3, Carole Raymond develops the theme of curriculum change and suggests that all PE teachers need to engage in various forms of management work if they are to play a central role in the process of change within schools and thereby gain a sense of control over the direction their subject takes in the future. Carole outlines some of the factors that influence the process of change and highlights the need for a systematic approach to management that is sensitive to the needs of those involved. It is argued that the abilities to communicate effectively and to cope with conflict are crucial skills in relation to curriculum change and that these should form part of the management skills vocabulary of all teachers.

The issue considered in Chapter 4 is that of equality in schools. Here, Sue Thomas focuses upon gender in order to outline a range of conceptual and practical problems associated with the promotion of equality for girls and boys in PE. Various strategies are discussed in relation to forms of pedagogy, content, organization, and assessment procedures that impact upon the achievement of equality. Sue suggests that this is no easy task but argues that it is a key issue that PE teachers need to address in the future.

In a similar vein, Geoff Meek in Chapter 5 considers the mainstreaming of disabled pupils into PE lessons. He outlines a model that indicates the facilitators required to initiate and sustain mainstreaming, such an important process for every child regardless of ability. In relation to this issue and the promotion of equal opportunity through PE, Geoff suggests that particular teaching perspectives are more appropriate than others. He advocates the acceptance of an all-encompassing participation model for both curricular and extra-curricular activities in order to enhance the introduction and success of mainstreaming.

In Chapter 6 Stuart Biddle turns his attention to the issue of motivation and achievement. He begins by summarizing the major findings of studies that have investigated the attributions that people make after they have had successful and unsuccessful experiences in sport and PE. Stuart then considers the implications of these findings for PE teachers and highlights the consequences of attributions in relation to failure and attribution retraining.

Peter Drewett, in Chapter 7, outlines the evolution of several approaches to assessment in PE with particular reference to examinations and profiling. Within the context of the National Curriculum a range of tensions and problems associated with these forms of assessment are highlighted. Peter goes on to focus on the debate surrounding the purposes of formative and summative assessment and mentions the difficulties of making valid and reliable judgements in relation to the psychomotor, cognitive, and affective domains.

Chapter 8 opens the section on Health Issues. Here Ken Fox attempts to unravel some of the complexities involved in the definitions of fitness and health. He analyses the development of the health-related fitness movement and makes the case for the adoption of a broader health perspective if physical education is to establish itself in the promotion of public health.

Neil Armstrong, in Chapter 9, focuses on the available research into British children's health-related physical activity. Drawing on his own data he demonstrates that children have surprisingly low levels of habitual physical activity and that many children seldom experience the intensity and duration of physical activity associated with health-related outcomes. He discusses the importance of adopting an active lifestyle during childhood and concludes by briefly exploring the role of the physical education teacher in promoting health-related physical activity.

Stuart Biddle's contribution in Chapter 10 develops Neil's chapter and discusses methods of promoting health-related physical activity in the curriculum. He addresses both individual strategies for behaviour change and interventions at institutional level. Stuart argues that a radical shift in emphasis from the product of exercise outcomes to the process of exercise participation is required by teachers before activity levels will change and the associated health benefits become apparent.

Sue Bray reviews the development of physical education in primary schools in England throughout the twentieth century in Chapter 11. She emphasizes the health focus in physical education and recognizes the changes in social conditions which have influenced the physical education curriculum. She expresses her concern over the fact that most health-related initiatives have focused on the secondary phase of education and offers ways of introducing health-related aspects of physical education into the primary curriculum.

Many children suffer from chronic illness and it is inevitable that physical education teachers will have to cope with children affected by bronchial asthma, diabetes or epilepsy. In Chapter 12 Bryan Woods reviews the incidence, aetiology, and treatment of these conditions and discusses the implications for the physical education teacher. He analyses the potential dangers that may be associated with acute exercise-induced episodes and concludes his chapter with practical advice for physical educators.

In the final chapter of the book Andrew Sparkes takes a critical look at the health-related fitness movement. He attempts to stimulate debate by focusing upon the process of problem-setting as it has developed within the traditional, educational, and radical strands of this movement. Andrew suggests that problem-setting is a form of social editing that eliminates a range of possible problems from consideration while foregrounding others that become the focus of attention for the development of solutions. His consideration of the nature of problem-setting indicates that no single approach or perspective is able to provide the 'answer' to the many complex issues of health since all approaches to this issue have their blind spots, their strengths and weaknesses, so that each frames the problem in different ways and advocates different solutions. Andrew concludes that there is much to be gained in the future by those involved in the HRF movement adopting a more holistic and reflective stance regarding the process and products of problem-setting in order to gain a greater awareness of the inevitable selectivity inherent in their own views and the views of others so that each can be subjected to critical evaluation.

Chapter 1

Curriculum Change: On Gaining a Sense of Perspective

Andrew C. Sparkes

It has become almost a truism to say that the only permanent thing in this world is change. In recent years there has been an influx of new ideas into the physical education (PE) curriculum, such as the Games For Understanding approach, Health-Related Fitness, and new forms of assessment. There seems to be a great deal going on in PE and more changes are likely to occur in the future prompted by the Education Reform Act of 1988. As Evans (1986) argues, 'In Britain today, the physical education curriculum is in a state of flux. For many PE teachers, as for their academic counterparts, the practices of decades have suddenly become quite problematic rather than acceptable features of their teaching and curriculum' (p. 1). However, there is another truism in educational circles which suggests that the 'more things change the more things stay the same'. For instance, recent studies that have focused on the PE curriculum[1] would seem to confirm the views of Whitehead and Hendry in 1976 that, give or take the odd bit of educational gymnastics or dance, 'the content of the secondary school curriculum seems not to have changed as radically as many have believed' (p. 41).

The problem of change is not specific to the subject area of PE. Schools and teachers in many other countries appear to be extremely resistant to real change as the following comments from around the world indicate. From Sweden, Tangerud and Wallin (1986) note, 'When schools are seen from a long-range vantage point, it can be said that by and large they have not changed fundamentally over some decades ... schools seem to change in appearance but not much in depth' (p. 45). From North America, House (1979) claims, 'The most remarkable feature of the educational system is its capacity for continuity and stability in the face of efforts at change ... We are confounded by the inability of innovations to transform the schools' (pp. 9–10). From Italy, Rosario (1986) believes, 'Reactive and resistant mechanisms function to preserve school behaviour in a context of innovation and change' (p. 35). Finally, in Britain the situation is summed up well by Evans (1985) who contends that comprehensive teaching and mixed-ability grouping in particular, 'is replete with both innovation without change, and change without innovation. Stratification, social division, inequality of educational opportunity stand largely unscathed, despite the hustle and bustle of curricular activity which on the surface suggests that substantial educational innovation is afoot' (p. 147). Essentially, as Rudduck (1986) notes:

> We are left with a paradoxical impression of stability and yet change, of diversity and yet sameness. We can try to explain this paradox by distinguishing between change which affects the deep structures of schooling, and developments which alter day to day practice but not always the way teachers and students *think* about learning. We may have learned how to introduce new content and materials into the curriculum but it seems that we are not so adept at changing the process of teaching and learning: too often the new content is conveyed in the baggage of traditional pedagogy.   (p. 6)

In this chapter I want to explore aspects of this paradox. Initially, my focus is on the issue of real as opposed to superficial change. Following this, several perspectives that have shaped the ways in which we address the problems of change in schools are considered. By examining the images that each perspective holds regarding teachers, an attempt is made to highlight the potential of each to bring about real change. My intention throughout is to emphasize the centrality of the teacher as an active agent in the complexities of the change process.

SUPERFICIAL VERSUS REAL CHANGE

Change is an extremely complex *process* and not just a simple end *product*. As indicated earlier, despite the hustle and bustle that creates an appearance of change on the surface, we are often left with the feeling that not much has changed at a deeper level. That is, superficial change—as opposed to real change—has prevailed. If we are to talk of *real* change rather than *superficial* or *surface* change, then we must view innovations as a multi-layered and multi-dimensional process. As part of this dynamic process real change would need to involve transformations within the three dimensions indicated in Figure 1.1.[2]

Having adopted a curriculum package, some teachers may then develop new teaching styles and strategies, but then again they might not. Adopting a package is easier for teachers than changing their practices in the gymnasium. Even if changes do take place in their practices this does not mean that teachers will necessarily challenge or begin to change the ideologies and beliefs that inform their educational practices in the gymnasium and their relationships with children. However, as Figure 1.1. suggests, if we are to talk of real change then a key dimension for consideration is the transformation of the beliefs, values, and ideologies held by teachers that inform their pedagogical assumptions and practices. These lie at the heart of real change and without such transformations we have innovation without change. As Kirk (1988) realizes, 'Innovation refers to new or original practices and ideas in particular contexts, but does not imply that *change* necessarily takes place. It is possible to present an innovation that embodies some new idea without this ever bringing about any genuine change in what people think or do' (p. 83).

Here, the case studies by Evans *et al.* (1987) of several PE departments who 'innovated' by introducing mixed-sex grouping provide some important insights. Their findings suggest that mixed-sex grouping is an innovation that can be accomplished with relative ease in an organizational sense. However, they emphasize that teaching in mixed-sex classes is not enough in itself to violate the reality of teachers (who are

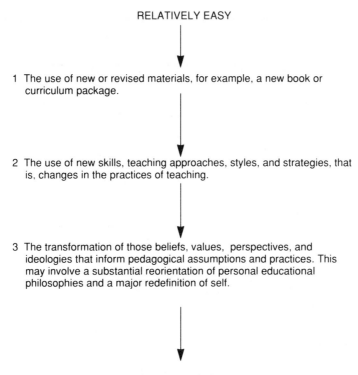

RELATIVELY EASY

1 The use of new or revised materials, for example, a new book or curriculum package.

2 The use of new skills, teaching approaches, styles, and strategies, that is, changes in the practices of teaching.

3 The transformation of those beliefs, values, perspectives, and ideologies that inform pedagogical assumptions and practices. This may involve a substantial reorientation of personal educational philosophies and a major redefinition of self.

EXTREMELY DIFFICULT

Figure 1.1 *Dimensions of change* (based on Fullan, 1982, p. 30).

weakly trained with strong subject and gender specific identities) so that the mental barriers of *imagined* differences between boys and girls are challenged. This view is supported by Scraton (1986, 1990) who argues that rather than challenging teachers' assumptions concerning the gender ideologies of physicality, motherhood, and sexuality, mixed-sex grouping—adopted without any attempt to raise the consciousness of teachers and pupils regarding the significance of gender issues—can often serve to reinforce and reproduce these ideologies in the gymnasium for both teachers and pupils alike.

The same could be said of the introduction of mixed-ability *grouping* in many schools. This organizational change can be adopted in a school without ever bringing about a shift to mixed-ability *teaching*, since many teachers find it difficult to change their beliefs regarding the nature of 'ability' in children. Some will continue to believe that children are limited in what they can learn by a genetically 'fixed' amount of intelligence. Others, at the opposite end of a continuum, will continue to believe that the environment has the greatest impact on the learning process. These beliefs about ability will strongly influence the ways in which teachers interact with children in the gymnasium, and this has significant implications in terms of the learning experiences of children since the *form* of communication is as important as the *content* of the curriculum.

As Figure 1.1 indicates, real change involves transformations in the ways that people think and feel about the world around them. As we move to the deeper dimensions of change the process becomes much more difficult and problematic since a substantial redefinition of self may be required. Nias (1989) distinguishes between the 'situational self' and the 'substantial self'. The former concerns those social identities that change with time, place, and role; in Goffman's (1959) terms it involves the multiple selves that we learn to present to others depending upon the situation. In contrast, the latter refers to the most highly prized aspects of our self-concept and the attitudes and values which are salient to them. This inner core is protected from challenges, is persistently defined, and is highly resistant to change. While Nias (1989) warns against a completely static view of the self she comments, 'To be sure the substantial self is hard to reach even by reflexive activity (e.g. introspection and self-examination), and is well defended and difficult to change, in part because people develop situationally specific strategies to protect themselves from the need to alter the ways in which they perceive themselves' (p. 21). Clearly, it is not easy for people, even if they are willing, to change their thinking and behaviour significantly. However, this is exactly what is at stake in implementing educational changes. This is true of all real curriculum change because as Woods (1984) argues,

> a curriculum area is a vibrant, human process lived out in the rough and tumble, give and take, joys and despairs, plots and counter-plots of a teacher's life. It is not simply a body of knowledge or a set of skills; nor simply a result of group activity . . . to some extent at least, individuals can and do chart their own courses, and can engage with the curriculum at a deeper personal level.   (p. 260)

Therefore, real change can be threatening and stressful for the teachers involved and this important fact cannot be overlooked by those who wish to bring about changes in our schools. This issue needs to be borne in mind throughout the following sections which provide a selective focus upon several perspectives that have shaped the ways in which the problems of educational change have been addressed.

THE TECHNOLOGICAL PERSPECTIVE

The technological perspective identified by House (1979) emerged powerfully in the post-Sputnik era and dominated many attempts to bring about changes in schools during the late 1960s and early 1970s.[3] Involved were large-scale, centrally funded, National Curriculum projects which utilized a Research–Development–Diffusion approach to change. While there are many versions of this approach the source of the innovation tended to lie with small, expert and well-resourced teams, often based in institutions of higher education or government agencies, who researched and developed curriculum packages that were then disseminated to schools where, it was assumed, adoption and implementation by teachers would take place according to procedural guidelines specified within the curriculum package. As such, the main focus of the technological perspective was on knowledge as a product, and this knowledge was to be controlled by scientists and scholars working outside of schools who would then transfer it in a top-down fashion to teachers in schools. In considering this approach Lawson (1990) comments, 'Objective or value free knowledge is transported from researchers and their work organizations to practitioners in theirs.

The exchange is primarily one way, with the practitioner being a more or less passive adopter' (p. 164).

More recently, according to Acker (1990), many of the initiatives spawned by the Educational Reform Act of 1988 are following a similar approach, encouraging a focus on the innovation itself and the means by which it is implemented: 'For example, the Statutory Orders represent, almost by definition, a technological approach. They contain the programme by which teachers are to bring about ends set by others' (p. 259). Acker acknowledges the claims made in 1989 by the National Curriculum Council (NCC) that the National Curriculum is, 'not a strait-jacket' (p. 1), but suggests that an iron hand can be glimpsed behind the velvet glove since the NCC (1989) make it clear that the National Curriculum is, 'non-negotiable as a framework for every school' (p. 3), that 'more rigorous methods of curriculum planning and evaluation will be necessary' (p. 6), and that 'continuity is no longer an optional issue in planning the curriculum' (p. 9). Finally, Acker draws attention to the prescriptions contained in several of the NCC documents, such as, 'Schools will need to . . .'; 'It is essential to . . .'. Others have also commented upon such issues and Gurney (1989) notes:

> Unfortunately teachers seem to have very little say in relation to major educational change; never has this issue been so critical as at the present time of the Educational Reform Bill. At a time when the collective energies of teachers have been exhausted by action surrounding pay and conditions, when we are immersed, not feeling properly prepared, in major examination reform, the timing of further and controversial reform has ensured that the effect of critical debate is minimised.   (p. 15)

In recent years government legislation has provided a major thrust to the adoption of many innovations in schools. This thrust has developed in a climate of economic recession characterized by intense competition for scarce educational resources. In the context of the National Curriculum and the emergence of the local financial management of schools, many innovations have been forced upon schools and departments. As a consequence, they have very often been adopted more as a means of survival rather than for any deeply held beliefs concerning the value of the proposed changes which have been imposed in a top-down fashion by outside 'experts'. In view of this Fullan (1982) notes:

> Bureaucratically speaking, then, the political and symbolic value of adoption for schools is often of greater significance than the educational merit and the time and cost necessary for implementation follow-through. But note that the symbolic value is not unimportant. Such adoptions may be necessary for political survival, may be the necessary first steps which set the preconditions for real change in practice, or may represent the only change possible in certain situations.   (p. 51)

While such forced adoptions may be preconditions for change, in practice we need to be wary of their negative impact upon teachers. As Gurney (1989) reminds us, 'Imposed change can be disastrous' (p. 27). Since there seem to be indicators that the technological perspective is re-emerging in a thinly disguised form then it might be worthwhile mentioning some of the weaknesses identified with this approach when it was utilized in the 1960s and 1970s.

1   The assumption was made that the innovation was necessarily good.
2   The innovation was seen as the sole prerogative of the researcher, developer, and

administrator. The receiver (teacher) was seen as essentially passive and the ideal was the 'teacher-proof' curriculum package that would be adopted for use. There was little if any public ownership of meaning and the teachers rarely, if ever, felt in control of the innovation process.

3   It centred on grand strategies for planned innovation which did not focus upon *specific* human problems. Rather, they offered a set of facts and theories which were seen to generate useful products and services, which as innovations were then ready to anyone who might find them useful.

4   The focus was on the individual; organizational variables were overlooked.

5   There was a concentration on materials rather than pedagogies. The assumption was made that new curriculum materials could be relied upon to initiate and sustain new patterns of teaching and learning.

6   The assumption was made that similarities amongst classrooms and schools were more important than dissimilarities, and that what works well in one school will automatically work well in another. Therefore, the approach lacked versatility.

Not surprisingly, Kirk (1990) comments that those initiatives contained within the technological perspective had very little success in achieving the goal of planned educational change. In particular he suggests, 'their attempts to exclude teachers from the development process proved to be naïve; in order for programmes to work in specific locations, teachers were forced to make changes' (p. 412). Paradoxically, teachers were then blamed for making these changes which were seen as a distortion of the central prescriptions for action which the developers presupposed were clear and unambiguous. According to Darling-Hammond (1990), 'Another reason for such recurrent failure is that teachers' prior learning, beliefs and attitudes are rarely considered as an essential ingredient in the process of teaching itself, much less in the process of change ... The teacher is viewed as a conduit for instructional policy, but not as an actor' (pp. 238–9).

Furthermore, as Rudduck (1986) points out, in its pure form this perspective 'was arrogantly simplistic and somewhat neglectful of the school's sense of its own identity ... The ownership of meaning remained with its originators. Many teachers felt as though they were puppets dangling from the threads of someone else's invention' (p. 9). Lawson (1990) reinforces this point and argues that this approach failed because it did not take into account 'the behavioural, cultural, and political realities of work practices and the ways in which these contour conceptions of, and actions in relation to, various kinds of knowledge' (p. 164). The culture of the school, the classroom context, and the personal meanings of those involved in the change are, to all intents and purposes, ignored or simply not seen as major issues for consideration. However, teachers do have a major impact on how an innovation is received and Richardson (1990) comments:

> teachers exercise considerable control over the decision of whether and how to implement a change. In addition, because of the situational nature of teaching, there are strong arguments for the notion that teachers should make these decisions. Thus, any change process should both acknowledge this control, and help teachers understand and be held accountable for the pedagogical and moral implications of their decisions.
>
> (p. 13)

By not acknowledging the control that teachers do and should have over changes in their schools and classrooms, the technological perspective contained the seeds of its own destruction. Should it re-emerge in a different form in relation to contemporary government policies as Acker (1990) has suggested, then it remains to be seen as to whether it will meet with any great success in producing change at the *classroom* level.

By considering in detail some of the weaknesses of the technological perspective my intention is not to suggest that curriculum materials produced as kits, packages, and predesigned programmes by government and commercial agencies do not have a part to play in the process of change. As Kirk (1990) comments, 'The pervasiveness of these materials, and the emergence of commercial agencies to produce them, would appear to suggest that teachers find them acceptable, useful, and as desirable aids to their work' (p. 409). Therefore, it would be nonsense to suggest that large-scale curriculum projects are of little value. Indeed, as Rudduck (1986) argues, despite their many weaknesses the departure of such projects can be viewed as an intellectual loss since, 'What was distinctive about them was that their central teams had the time to tackle fundamental curriculum issues in ways that are often beyond the scope of school-based teams whose members have a full teaching load' (p. 11).

Essentially, once it is accepted that teachers will and should adapt material to their own circumstances then curriculum packages and texts can help to initiate changes. As Cohen and Ball (1990) conclude in reviewing several cases in which teachers have changed their practices with the help of such material, 'One moral of this story, then, is that texts and other curriculum materials can be important agents of change ... these agents work only as teachers are able or inclined to let them work' (p. 251). Likewise, Darling-Hammond (1990) recognizes that curriculum materials can act as powerful messengers that can assist teachers to introduce new topics into their lesson. However, she argues that these materials 'can do little about transforming the nature of the classroom environment or the teaching–learning interactions within it' (p. 236). Therefore, it seems clear that curriculum packages can be a useful aid but that by themselves they will not lead to real change in our schools.

THE ECOLOGICAL PERSPECTIVE

An alternative approach to change is the ecological perspective. According to Olsen (1982) this view moves away from framing the teacher as passive, and places an emphasis on the importance of the immediate and complex teaching environment— that is, the 'classroom ecology' as a source of explanation for change. Dreeben (1970) encapsulates this view, in which what teachers do is taken to be a consequence of the 'properties' of their classroom in the following comment, 'The most obvious characteristic of the school is the division into isolated classrooms under the direction of the teacher. This fact in itself determines much of what happens in schools' (p. 51).

This conception of teacher behaviour uses the biological analogy of an ecosystem to characterize the response of the teachers to their environment, and these responses are seen as adaptive in the evolutionary sense. Hence, the 'environment' controls the teacher behaviour in some unexpressed way, with the mind of the teacher being seen as a 'black box' which interprets signals from the environment and responds. Whilst the ecological conception of change acts as an important reminder of the complexity of teachers' working conditions, the *tactics* for change which arise from it are still interventionist as the teacher is manipulated by others who use an 'understanding' of the classroom environment to find ways of gaining teacher compliance with *plans from the outside*. More recently, Webb and Ashton (1987) have extended this perspective to include the teachers' cultural, social, institutional, and personal environment. They suggest that their ecological orientation is concerned with *interventions* that are directed at the *school environment* and that it is not focused narrowly on the personalities and beliefs of individual teachers since this 'individualistic' orientation tends to 'blame' the teacher for the lack of change. However, they remain focused upon the conditions that teachers work in as the main explanation for change, or the lack of it, in schools.

This ecological stance has had a strong influence on those studies that focus on the 'management of change' which have as their goal the *creation of conditions* within the school that get innovations adopted and implemented.[4] A key area of research within this approach has been the headteacher as a 'leader' who is able to influence the environment or climate in a school to a considerable degree. Numerous studies on the role of this individual as an 'active supporter of change' have been carried out which characteristically produces 'guidelines' to assist headteachers in becoming effective *managers of change* in terms of creating and directing efforts in an optimal environment. As a consequence, there have been moves towards 'management training' for headteachers and senior teachers, presumably based upon the assumption that via immersion in some relevant 'theory' the actual practices of the classroom will change accordingly. However, Fullan (1986a) and Hoyle (1986a) warn that such schemes are not simple solutions to producing change in schools, and questions have been raised regarding the common practice of removing headteachers from the staff groups in schools in order to encourage them to collaborate with the same group when they return.

Despite these concerns the ecological perspective has made a major contribution to our thinking in that it forces a recognition of the impact that the working conditions of teachers, and the way schools are organized, can have upon practice in the classroom. As Hargreaves (1984) comments:

> All teaching takes place in a context of opportunity and constraint. Teaching strategies involve attempts at realizing educational goals by taking advantage of appropriate opportunities and coping with, adjusting to, or redefining the constraints. Often, the coping strategies that teachers adopt to deal with contextual contingencies can become so habitual, so routinized, that they seem like coping no more, but worthwhile and valid teaching. In this way, provisional adaptations turn into routine commitments ... *Material circumstances, then, do affect the standard and quality of teaching*, as the HMI have themselves noted in surveys of the effects of public expenditure policies on teaching and learning.
>
> (p. 219; my italics)

In considering the situational constraints that impact upon teachers to maintain routine behaviours, Hargreaves (1984) includes the persistence and extension of 16+ examinations which are to be used as a barometer of teacher success, the continuing high levels of class size and teacher–pupil ratios that make individualized treatment and small-group work difficult, and the declining levels of resources which make experimentation and adjustment of learning tasks to individual needs problematic. To these he adds the inappropriateness of, and deterioration of standards in, school buildings; the unsuitability of compartmentalized classrooms for team-teaching, resource-based learning etc.; and the general discouragement that dilapidated walls and leaking roofs present to teachers who might otherwise take great pride in improving the display and all-round aesthetic environment of their classrooms. These situational constraints structure the possibilities that teachers face in their classrooms, and while Gitlin (1987) is right to point out that they do not *determine* teacher behaviour they certainly have a powerful influence upon it since 'teacher behaviour reflects a compromise between teacher values, ideologies, and the press of school structure' (p. 107).

The ecological perspective also links the teacher into wider political and economic systems that have tremendous powers to shape the basic work conditions of teachers as outlined above. It brings to the fore such contentious issues as professional status and recognition, along with the funding of state education. In doing so it moves away from the teacher-blaming stance of the technological perspective to emphasize the point that if changes are required in the ways that teachers operate, then it is crucial that the constraints and conditions that reinforce prevailing practices are altered. In the present climate such a stance is likely to be politically unattractive since it has major resource implications for the educational system. However, to expect real change without changing the fundamental working conditions of teachers to support any given change is somewhat simplistic.

THE CULTURAL PERSPECTIVE

While curriculum packages can provide useful support for teachers who wish to initiate change, and while the working conditions provide a framework for how any change might develop, the technological and ecological perspectives remain limited in their conceptualization of the change process when taken in isolation. Both are hindered because they remain distant from the meaning of school events as construed by those in the action. As Olsen (1982) comments, both are 'ineffective platforms for change because they lead us to ignore the systems of thought that teachers bring to bear on problems by treating teachers as objects of manipulation. Rather than seek more sophisticated methods of manipulation, we need to find out what those systems of thought are like and to do this we have to pay attention to what insiders tell us' (p. 9). Accordingly, he calls for a humanistic conception of change in schools, which takes change to be a *process* and not simply a product. This would seem to be a crucial step, since as Fullan (1982) notes 'the transformation of subjective realities is the essence of change' (p. 29). Similarly, Gipps (1987) in her work with primary teachers realizes that, 'As well as institutional realities, there are personal realities which must be considered too. What does change mean to the classroom teacher?' (p. 3). This shift of emphasis to the meanings that teachers hold regarding curriculum change is at the heart of the cultural perspective. For Hargreaves (1984):

> In this view, teachers, like other people, are not just bundles of skill, competence and technique; they are creators of meaning, interpreters of the world and all it asks of them. They are people striving for purpose and meaning in circumstances that are usually much less than ideal and which call for constant adjustment, adaptation and redefinition. Once we adopt this view of teachers or any other human being, our starting question is no longer why does he/she *fail* to do X, but why does he/she do Y? What purpose does Y

fulfil for them? Our interest, then, is in how teachers manage to cope with, adapt to and reconstruct their circumstances; it is in what they achieve, not what they fail to achieve.

(p. 216)

More recently, Hargreaves (1989) has re-emphasized the impact of the teaching culture upon change:

> What the teacher thinks, what the teacher believes, what the teacher assumes—all these things have powerful implications for the change process, for the ways in which curriculum policy is translated into curriculum practice. Some of these patterns of thinking, belief and assumption are so widely shared among the community of teachers that they amount to what might be called a broad occupational culture of teaching. This culture of teaching, I shall argue, seriously inhibits practical curriculum change at school and class-room level.
>
> (p. 54)

Despite a range of definitions being available for the term 'culture', Feiman-Nemser and Floden (1986) point out that many of the studies that have focused on culture have made the assumption that it provides a common base of knowledge, values and norms for action that people grow into and come to take as 'the natural way of life'. Reinforcing this point Erickson (1987) comments, 'Culture, considered as bits of knowledge and as conceptual structures, defines options because it shapes what we think is possible. Most fundamentally it is ontological—it defines what *is* in the world, what exists and what does not' (p. 19). In relation to this I have suggested (see Sparkes, 1989, 1991) that culture is a 'tool kit' of symbols, stories, rituals and world views which people may use in numerous configurations to solve different kinds of problems. From within their cultural tool kit teachers select differing pieces for constructing certain lines of action in specific situations.

In reacting to similar constraints, dilemmas, and concerns certain tools become defined as appropriate and successful within a culture. These tools are then selected for use over others in the teacher's tool kit. The constant use of a limited set of tools over time ensures that their application and operation becomes routinized and taken for granted. As a consequence of this process various 'sacred norms' such as presentism, conservatism, and individualism (cf. Corbett *et al.*, 1987) are created that are pervasive within the wider occupational culture of teaching.[5] Having said this, we should be wary of viewing the culture of teaching as monolithic since in reality it is fragmented. Indeed, the tool kit metaphor fractures the notion of a singular culture since different tool kits will contain different combinations of tools and various groups within the teaching profession will have access to a range of particular kits. As Feiman-Nemser and Floden (1986) realize:

> The assumption of cultural uniformity is, however, untenable. Teachers differ in age, experience, social and cultural background, gender, marital status, subject matter, wisdom, and ability. The schools in which they work also differ in many ways, as do the groups of students they teach. All these may lead to differences in the teaching culture.
>
> (p. 507)

In view of this Acker (1990) differentiates between the wider culture, that of the occupation, and of segments within it such as primary and secondary teaching which have substantial effects in shaping teacher beliefs about how children should be treated and childhood understood. Drawing on the work of Nias *et al.* (1989) she uses the term *organizational culture* to describe the specific variations of the occupational culture that are developed within specific institutions. Acker acknowledges that the headteacher's philosophy is a crucial source of variation from one school to the next, particularly in primary schools. However, she notes:

> Yet it is not the *only* determinant. Others include the size of the school, the age range, the type of children and community served, the physical setting and resources available to the school ... The innovation process in an inner city school with difficult children and a mobile set of teachers may be quite different from what happens in a stable working class school, or in a rural school with two teachers, or in a school in an affluent neighbourhood with ample resources and extensive parental participation. The various teacher cultures predate and mediate any government initiatives. They influence the technical process of implementation and the extent to which teachers define innovation as deskilling or professionalising their work.
>
> (pp. 261–2)

In a very real sense each school has its own inherent culture and its own relationships among teachers, children, senior management, governors etc. Therefore, when newcomers to a school first arrive (a probationary teacher or a newly appointed experienced teacher) they enter much more than a building. They enter a culture of teaching that has evolved in response to specific local circumstances and the wider cultural values of the society that together establish what is the appropriate teaching role. In order to function successfully within the school the newcomer must come to terms with this role and the values that sustain it. As Hargreaves (1984) remarks:

> Teaching is certainly a matter of competence. But it is a competence of a particular kind. It is the competence to recognise and enact the rules, procedures and forms of understanding of a particular cultural environment. What is involved is not a *technical* competence to operate in a pre-given, professionally correct and educationally worthwhile way, but *cultural* competence to 'read' and 'pass' in a system with its own specific history, a system once devised and developed to meet a very particular set of social purposes.
>
> (p. 217)

The cultural realities of the school cannot be overlooked since individual teacher change has to take place within this local culture. As Cohen and Ball (1990) argue, 'Although policies regularly announce a new instructional order, the classroom slate is never clean. Whatever novelties policy-makers embrace, teachers must work with residues of the past' (p. 251). Therefore, the cultural context of the school provides possibilities and sets limitations for the change process. Limitations are set up by the routinized coping strategies that teachers actively and creatively develop as a response to the structural and situational constraints that are imposed upon their conditions of work, which means that once in motion the culture of teaching is reproductive and self-generating. However, possibilities exist because, as was mentioned earlier, the structures of schooling do not totally determine the behaviours and visions of teachers. The tool kit metaphor strongly suggests that teachers are skilful users of culture and not simply 'cultural dopes' who are the passive recipients of the views of dominant groups in society. Teachers, quite simply, are not passive and unreflective vessels into which culture is poured, they are not just cogs in a self-perpetuating machine, rather they are active in defining and redefining their circumstances within it. That is, teachers are both makers and breakers of culture. For Watkins (1985):

> The duality of agency and structure transcends the dualism of voluntarism, in which agents act free from any constraint, and structural determinism, where the conditions not the agents act, through the recognition that institutions are made up of actors who indulge in practices which are both constrained and enabled by those institutions. In this way *human agency can often transcend and overcome the organizational restrictions which*

exercise domination over them. Such practices, while sometimes not being acknowledged by the actors as such, consequently lead to the generation, maintenance or transformation of these institutions.   (p. 29; my italics)

The cultural perspective, by recognizing this dynamic relationship between agency (the ability to make choices and create conditions) and structure (barriers or constraints that restrict options and actions), recognizes that what people have made they can also change. This recognition returns the teacher to the centre stage of the change process and it has been at the heart of many school-based curriculum development activities that have drawn upon and utilized an action research approach with its images of the teacher-as-researcher and the teacher as reflective practitioner.[6] As Forward suggests, action research encourages a critically reflective attitude to teaching and life in schools on the part of teachers so that they can change things. 'Action research involves some type of social or educational intervention and therefore it is only good sense that the practitioners involved should participate ... Action research does not treat people as statistics or objects but regards them as autonomous and responsible participants in the process under investigation' (Forward, 1989, p. 33).

CULTURAL CHANGE AND ACTION RESEARCH

The starting point for bringing about change via action research is the world as individual teachers perceive it and their problems as defined by them within a particular cultural context. Essentially, three basic questions are asked as part of the action research process: What is happening now?; In what sense is this problematic?; What can be done about it? Addressing these questions involves a continuous cycle of reflection and action. Larter (1989) in considering his own struggles to improve his practice over a period of time outlines this cyclic process as follows:

- perceiving problems in my practice, relating to some of my educational values not being realised;
- imagining solutions to these problems;
- planning courses of action and acting in the direction of such plans;
- observing and gathering data as the plan is acted upon;
- reflecting upon the action and the data;
- modifying problems in the light of findings;
- imagining solutions to problems.   (pp. 44–45)

Besides locating the teacher at the centre of the change process another important principle of action research is that it is *collaborative* (cf. Chambers, 1983; Kemmis and Henry, 1984). This collaboration can be of various kinds, such as between teachers within the same school, between teachers in different schools, between teachers and advisors, between teachers and lecturers in institutes of higher education, or a combination of all of these. A good example of school-based collaborative action research is provided by Oldroyd and Tiller (1987). Their work is chosen because it involves collaboration between the university sector and a school that explicitly set out to challenge the teaching culture.

The basic stance adopted by Oldroyd and Tiller (1987) was that any understanding of the unique culture of a school takes time and energy which calls for a reorientation of the role of outside expert who must come to terms with the teaching culture from within. Therefore, one of the authors (Tom Tiller), a seconded university lecturer, joined the staff at Priory School in Weston-Super-Mare as a 'researcher-consultant-in-residence'. This role was chosen with a view to going native in order to understand the cultural uniqueness of the school and to assist the staff, through existing channels, to develop an action research approach in order to help them deepen their critical awareness of school processes and individual actions. As Oldroyd and Tiller comment:

> The basic assumption behind this enterprise in school improvement is that competence can be increased when teachers reflect deeply about their actions and situations as a prelude to modifying both. This involves bringing the meanings of actors in the complex social milieu of the school and classroom out into the open where these messages can be examined and shared.   (p. 16)

Importantly, the researcher-consultant-in-residence was able to introduce the group of teachers, who chose to work together, to a variety of methods (diaries, tracking pupils, meta-communication) for illuminating the perspectives of actors (both teachers and pupils) on their own actions in relation to the cultural contexts in which they occurred. Furthermore, he was able to introduce concepts to deepen the analysis of these perspectives by introducing substantive reading to certain members of the group who then fed it back into discussions so that the teachers were able to move beyond naïve description.

Gradually, the teachers as a group began to question the different realities that existed in the school, examples being the official school aims, and the experiences of pupils and their own experiences as teachers. They began to reflect about the actions, contexts and meanings which propelled them into the 'glass roof' of their own experience. This allowed them to discern barriers (glass walls) not normally visible at ground level and thereby identify possible space for new forms of action. The glass walls that formed the barriers to change—namely, technical-material (facilities and funds etc.), socio-psychological values (the perceptions and priorities of other teachers etc.), and political-power (decision-making power of headteachers etc.)—were identified and challenged. In a very real sense they gained the conceptual tools that allowed them to see with the eyes of a stranger so as to fracture their daily routine practices.

This form of collaborative school-based action research, along with the other forms of collaboration mentioned earlier, has great potential for empowering teachers to explore and change their school cultures. Talking about his own critical reflections on past action and his struggle to improve the process of education, Larter (1989) notes the liberating experience with regard to his professional life: 'Essentially, I think this is because I realise that the impetus for change lies with me, not forgetting the influence that students and colleagues will have, through discussion and a shared approach to the events under scrutiny' (p. 42). Importantly, Larter emphasizes that by engaging in the self-reflective transformation of practice and by attempting to bring practice under self-reflective control through a commitment to rationality, truth, truthfulness and rightness, he became critical of the ideological and institutional conditions that denied his attempts to bring about such control.

Here, as Gurney (1989) argues, we can see that action research implies that change grows outwards from the individual in ever-increasing circles which involve the whole school, the governing body, and the local educational authority. That is, change moves upwards in the opposite direction to the normal hierarchy of change. In view of this, Gurney comments, 'action research can have very powerful political implications and this potential power strengthens the value of the paradigm' (p. 27). This potential is related to the manner in which action research encourages critical reflection that involves critical thought and empowerment. According to Berlak and Berlak (1987):

> Critical thought is a process of freeing oneself from dependence upon taken-for-granted ways of viewing and acting in the world, and seriously entertaining and evaluating alternative possibilities ... To evaluate alternative courses of action we must see connections—connections among everyday events, patterns of behaviour, and cultural, social, political, and economic forces. In a phrase, it is to see the relationship of 'micro' to 'macro' ... Empowerment implies contributing to the shaping of society, rather than being subjected to the power of others. It goes beyond critical thought and includes a readiness to act with others to bring about the social conditions that one has chosen through a process of collaborative, critical inquiry. Action requires courage, but it also requires the possession of knowledge and skills necessary to change the situation—a classroom, a school, or any other arena of human activity.   (pp. 169–70)

Having talked of the potential of action research to bring about change we need to be wary of viewing this approach as the panacea for all the problems of educational change. For example, Rudduck (1986) comments, 'School-based curriculum development sounds good ... But it's damn difficult to do it well' (p. 11). She goes on to argue that while this approach to change can produce local relevance it is this very intimacy that can create its own problems. 'The price of local relevance may be, given the conditions under which teachers have in the past had to attempt school-based curriculum development, either a lack of pedagogic coherence and rigour, or an unwitting conservatism' (p. 11). Also, as Smyth (1989) recognizes, within action research there is the in-built presumption that teachers and students 'will necessarily want to become self-aware and act in ways that promote their own interests and those of their students in preference to the forces of dogma and irrationality that blind them to the nature of reality. This of course may be quite an erroneous assumption' (p. 8).

School-based innovations initiated by teachers engaging in action research also has to confront the power structures within any given school whereby various individuals and groups have differential access to power resources.[7] Since action research implies change it has the potential to challenge the *status quo* and thereby threaten the vested interests of many. As Gurney (1989) argues, 'Change involving a group of teachers is acceptable to "authority" provided it complies with given policy. Change which challenges existing structures or invites others to justify their practice, in institutions not conversant with research-based development, is not welcome' (p. 27). Therefore, within the micropolitical matrix of school life teachers attempting to effect change in the dominant culture may have much to lose—for example, their promotion prospects may be damaged. In view of this McAleer and McAleavy (1989) comment, 'Whether teachers can be instruments of institutional change is another matter and, indeed, given the professional risks, whether teachers would wish to undertake such a task is a matter of doubt' (p. 217).

Finally, it needs to be recognized that it is not only the school hierarchy that can be threatened by the challenge to the values embedded in the daily routines of the school. Other teachers can also feel threatened and feel that their professional competencies are undermined. In this sense, Gurney (1989) notes, 'Change within an individual classroom may be fairly acceptable to others provided it does not impinge upon them' (p. 27). Therefore, changes in schools initiated by teachers engaged in action research are not necessarily any less conflict- or tension-ridden than changes initiated from other sources. This is because they too are acted out within schools and departments that are best viewed as arenas of struggle, contexts in which power is unevenly distributed and in which there are likely to be ideological differences and conflicts of interest. As such, teacher-initiated change involving action research is no easy task. Indeed, there is no easy way to bring about real change in schools

COMMENT

The perspectives that have been considered each have strengths and weaknesses. Each has contributed to our understanding of the change process in schools. We are now more aware that change in schools is not a simple mechanical process that can be driven by outside experts. Nor is change activated and sustained by the mere introduction of a curriculum package. It has been recognized that the working conditions of teachers are important in restricting or encouraging change, but that altering these conditions is not enough in itself. Finally, conceptualizing change as a cultural problem has emphasized the importance of context and the creation of shared meanings within working groups of teachers. As a consequence, the task is not to choose which is the 'best' perspective but to learn from the collective insights that they provide so that we can address change in a more sensitive manner in the future. As Rudduck (1986) argues, 'What we need now is to use the understanding won from these experiences in a new synthesis of initiatives—a partnership where we can be sensitive to the problems that change poses at a personal as well as a professional level for those involved' (p. 11).

Such a synthesis will not be easy. However, there are indicators that new forms of thinking regarding change are emerging that draw upon a range of perspectives. For example, Darling-Hammond (1990), in reviewing recent case studies of policy implementation with regard to curriculum reform in the USA, talks of an emerging paradigm for policy analysis: 'one that attends to policy conditions and contexts, the nature of teaching, and the process of change' (p. 233). She goes on to suggest that what is interesting about this new approach is the way in which policy initiatives are looked at with a pedagogical eye that locates and interprets classroom events in the context of a wide array of possible curriculum goals and teaching alternatives which illuminates the choices forgone as well as the decisions made by teachers. In short, policy analysts have begun to recognize and value the central role of teachers in bringing about change. For Darling-Hammond

> the process of change is slow and difficult. It requires perseverance, and it requires investments in those things that allow teachers, as change agents, to grapple with transformations of ideas and behaviour: time for learning about, looking at, discussing, struggling with, trying out, constructing, and reconstructing new ways of thinking and teaching. (p. 240)

That those within the curriculum reform movement are talking in such a way is encouraging. More and more it is recognized that whether innovation is planned on a large scale or is teacher-initiated, the process is complex, risky, and defies the production of simplistic formulas that can be imposed to guarantee real changes in what teachers think and do. As Fullan (1982) argues, change is never a wholly rational or fully predictable process, and we should not seek ready made guidelines but rather struggle to understand and modify events which are intrinsically complicated, difficult to pin down, and ever-changing. However, as we struggle with these uncertainties and complexities we can rest assured that it is teachers who ultimately act as the gatekeepers of change in our schools. It is teachers who decide to change their practices or challenge their deep underlying philosophies. It is they who are the critical mediators of change in action. Essentially, Fullan (1982) reminds us, 'Educational change depends on what teachers do and think—it's as simple and complex at that' (p. 107). However we approach change in the future this simple fact remains and we ignore it at our peril.

NOTES

1   For recent studies of the content of the PE curriculum see Branford (1987), Hill (1986), and the PEA (1987).
2   Figure 1.1 is clearly an oversimplification of the complexities of change in practice. Its purpose is simply to highlight some of the qualitative dimensions that are involved.
3   The technological perspective, along with various other models of change, is reviewed in greater detail by Hord (1987), Kirk (1988), Nicholls (1983), and Raggat (1983). While House (1979) sees the political perspective as separate and distinct from the others I have chosen not to consider this perspective in isolation in this chapter because for me all the perspectives are inherently political.
4   For reviews of the management of change see Hoyle (1986a, 1986b), Fullan (1986a, 1986b), and Nicholls (1983).
5   Presentism, conservatism, and individualism are discussed in greater detail by Gitlin (1987), Andy Hargreaves (1989), David Hargreaves (1982), and Sparkes (Chapter 13 in this volume).
6   The image of the teacher as researcher and as reflective practitioner has its roots in the works of Dewey (1933), Pinar (1975), Stenhouse (1975, 1983), and Schon (1983, 1987). Some possibilities and problems associated with critical reflection and curriculum change are discussed by Sparkes (1991).
7   Issues of power within schools and departments involved in change have been focused on by Bell (1986), Rudduck and Wilcox (1988), Sparkes (1990a, 1990b, 1990c, 1990d, 1990e).

REFERENCES

Acker, S. (1990) Teachers' culture in an English primary school. *British Journal of Sociology of Education* **11**, 257–73.
Bell, L. (1986) Managing to survive in secondary school physical education. In J. Evans (ed.), *Physical Education, Sport and Schooling: Studies in the Sociology of Physical Education*, pp. 95–111. London: Falmer Press.
Berlak, K. and Berlak H. (1987) Teachers working with teachers to transform schools. In J. Smyth (ed.), *Educating Teachers: Changing the Nature of Pedagogical Knowledge*, pp. 169–78. London: Falmer Press.
Branford, C. (1987) The physical education curriculum for boys in a local education authority. Unpublished M.Phil. thesis, Loughborough University of Technology.

Chambers, P. (1983) Democratization and pragmatism in educational research. *British Educational Research Journal* **9**, 21–5.

Cohen, D. and Ball, D. (1990) Relations between policy and practice: a commentary. *Educational Evaluation and Policy Analysis* **12**, 249–56.

Corbett, H., Firestone, W., and Rossman, G. (1987) Resistance to planned change and the sacred in school cultures. *Educational Administration Quarterly* **23**, 36–59.

Darling-Hammond, L. (1990) Instructional policy into practice: 'The power of the bottom over the top'. *Educational Evaluation and Policy Analysis* **12**, 233–41.

Dewey, J. (1933) *How We Think: A Restatement of the Relation of Reflective Thinking to Educational Practice*. Chicago: Henry Regnery Co.

Dreeben, R. (1970) *The Nature of Teaching: Schools and the Work of Teachers*. Glenview: Scott Foresman.

Erickson, F. (1987) Conceptions of school culture: an overview. *Educational Administration Quarterly* **23**, 11–24.

Evans, J. (1985) *Teaching in Transition: The Challenge of Mixed Ability Grouping*. Milton Keynes: Open University Press.

Evans, J. (1986) Introduction: 'Personal troubles and public issues'. Studies in the sociology of physical education. In J. Evans (ed.), *Physical Education, Sport and Schooling: Studies in the Sociology of Physical Education*, pp. 1–10. London: Falmer Press.

Evans, J., Lopez, S., Duncan, M., and Evans, M. (1987) Some thoughts on the political and pedagogical implications of mixed-sex groupings in the physical education curriculum. *British Educational Research Journal* **13**, 59–71.

Feiman-Nemser, S. and Floden, R. (1986) The cultures of teaching. In M. Wittrock (ed.), *Handbook of Research on Teaching*, pp. 505–26. London: Collier Macmillan.

Forward, D. (1989) A guide to action research. In P. Lomax (ed.), *The Management of Change*, pp. 29–39. Clevedon: Multilingual Matters Ltd.

Fullan, M. (1982) *The Meaning of Educational Change*. New York: Teachers College Press.

Fullan, M. (1986a) Improving the implementation of educational change. *School Organization* **6**, 321–6.

Fullan, M. (1986b) The management of change. In E. Hoyle and A. McMahon (eds), *World Yearbook of Education—The Management of Schools*, pp. 73–86. London: Kogan Page.

Gipps, C. (1987) Bringing about change in primary schools: the case of special needs. Paper presented at the British Educational Research Association Conference, Manchester, September.

Gitlin, A. (1987) Common school structures and teacher behaviour. In J. Smyth (ed.), *Educating Teachers: Changing the Nature of Pedagogical Knowledge*, pp. 107–19. London: Falmer Press.

Goffman, E. (1959) *The Presentation of Self in Everyday Life*. New York: Anchor Books.

Gurney, M. (1989) Implementor or innovator? A teacher's challenge to the restrictive paradigm of traditional research. In P. Lomax (ed.), *The Management of Change*, pp. 13–28. Clevedon: Multilingual Matters Ltd.

Hargreaves, A. (1984) Teaching quality: a sociological analysis. *Journal of Curriculum Studies* **20**, 211–31.

Hargreaves, A. (1989) *Curriculum and Assessment Reform*. Milton Keynes: Open University Press.

Hargreaves, D. (1982) *The Challenge of the Comprehensive School*. London: Routledge & Kegan Paul.

Hill, C. (1986) An analysis of the physical education curriculum in a local education authority. Unpublished M.Phil. thesis, Loughborough University of Technology.

Hord, S. (1987) *Evaluating Educational Innovation*. London: Croom Helm.

House, E. (1979) Technology versus craft: a ten year perspective on innovation. *Journal of Curriculum Studies* **1**, 1–15.

Hoyle, E. (1986a) The management of schools: theory and practice. In E. Hoyle and A. McMahon (eds), *World Yearbook of Education—The Management of Schools*, pp. 13–26. London: Kogan Page.

Hoyle, E. (1986b) *The Politics of School Management*. London: Hodder & Stoughton.

Kemmis, S. and Henry, C. (1984) *A Point by Point Guide to Action Research for Teachers.* Deakin: Deakin University Press.

Kirk, D. (1988) *Physical Educational and Curriculum Study—A Critical Introduction.* London: Croom Helm.

Kirk, D. (1990) School knowledge and the curriculum package-as-text. *Journal of Curriculum Studies* **22**, 409–25.

Larter, A. (1989) A question of dialectics. In P. Lomax (ed.), *The Management of Change*, pp. 40–6. Clevedon: Multilingual Matters Ltd.

Lawson, H. (1990) Beyond positivism: research, practice, and undergraduate professional education. *Quest* **42**, 161–83.

McAleer, J. and McAleavy, G. (1989) Action research: paradigm for individual development or organisational change in further education. *Educational Management and Administration* **17**, 214–24.

National Curriculum Council (1989) *A Framework for the Primary Curriculum.* York: NCC.

Nias, J. (1989) *Primary Teachers Talking: A Study of Teaching as Work.* London: Routledge.

Nias, J., Southworth, G., and Yeomans, R. (1989) *Staff Relations in the Primary School.* London: Cassell.

Nicholls, A. (1983) *Managing Educational Innovations.* London: George Allen & Unwin.

Oldroyd, D. and Tiller, T.(1987) Change from within: an account of school-based collaborative action research in an English secondary school. *Journal of Education for Teaching* **12**, 13–27.

Olsen, J. (1982) Classroom knowledge and curriculum change: an introduction. In J. Olsen (ed.), *Innovation in the Science Curriculum*, pp. 3–33. London: Croom Helm.

Physical Education Association (PEA) of Great Britain and Northern Ireland (1987) Report of a Commission of Enquiry, *Physical Education in Schools.* London: Ling Publishing House.

Pinar, W. (ed.) (1975) *Curriculum Theorizing: The Reconceptualists.* Berkeley, CA: McCutchan.

Raggatt, P. (1983) *The Process of Change.* Unit 26, Block 4, *Curriculum Innovation.* Milton Keynes: Open University Press.

Richardson, V. (1990) Significant and worthwhile change in teaching practice. *Educational Researcher* **19**, 10–18.

Rosario, J. (1986) Excellence, school culture and lessons in futility. *Journal of Curriculum Studies* **18**, 31–44.

Rudduck, J. (1986) *Understanding Curriculum Change.* Sheffield: USDE Papers in Education.

Rudduck, J. and Wilcox, B. (1988) Issues of ownership and partnership in school-centred innovation: the Sheffield experience. *Research Papers in Education* **3**, 157–79.

Schon, D. (1983) *The Reflective Practitioner.* London: Temple Smith.

Schon, D. (1987) *Educating the Reflective Practitioner.* San Francisco, CA: Jossey-Bass.

Scraton, S. (1986) Images of femininity and the teaching of girls' physical education. In J. Evans (ed.), *Physical Education, Sport and Schooling: Studies in the Sociology of Physical Education*, pp. 71–94. London: Falmer Press.

Scraton, S. (1990) *Gender and Physical Education.* Deakin: Deakin University Press.

Smyth, J. (1989) Developing and sustaining critical reflection in teacher education. *Journal of Teacher Education* **40**, 2–9.

Sparkes, A. (1989) Culture and ideology in physical education. In T. Templin and P. Schempp (eds), *Socialization into Physical Education: Learning to Teach*, pp. 315–38. Indianapolis, IN: Benchmark Press.

Sparkes, A. (1990a) Power, domination and resistance in the process of teacher-initiated innovation. *Research Papers in Education* **5**, 59–84.

Sparkes, A. (1990b) Winners, losers and the myth of rational change in physical education: towards an understanding of interests and power in innovation. In D. Kirk and R. Tinning (eds), *Physical Education, Curriculum and Culture: Critical Issues in the Contemporary Crisis*, pp. 193–224. London: Falmer Press.

Sparkes, A. (1990c) *Curriculum Change and Physical Education: Towards a Micropolitical Understanding.* Deakin: Deakin University Press.

Sparkes, A. (1990d) The changing nature of teachers' work: reflecting on governor power in different historical periods. *Physical Education Review* **13**(1) 39–47.

Sparkes, A. (1990e) The emerging relationship between physical education teachers and school governors: a sociological analysis. *Physical Education Review* **13**(2), 128–37.

Sparkes, A. (1991) The culture of teaching, critical reflection, and change: possibilities and problems. *Educational Management and Administration* **19**, 4–19.

Stenhouse, L. (1975) *An Introduction to Curriculum Research and Development*. London: Heinemann.

Stenhouse, L. (1983) *Authority, Education and Emancipation*. London: Heinemann.

Tangerud, H. and Wallin, E. (1986) Values and contextual factors in school improvement. *Journal of Curriculum Studies* **18**, 45–61.

Watkins, P. (1985) *Agency and Structure: Dialectics in the Administration of Education*. Deakin: Deakin University Press.

Webb, R. and Ashton, P. (1987) Teacher motivation and the conditions of teaching: a call for ecological reform. In S. Walker and L. Barton (eds), *Changing Policies, Changing Teachers*, pp. 22–40. Milton Keynes: Open University Press.

Whitehead, N. and Hendry, L. (1976) *Teaching Physical Education in England*. London: Lepus Books.

Woods, P. (1984) Teacher, self and curriculum. In I. Goodson and S. Ball (eds), *Defining the Curriculum: Histories and Ethnographies*, pp. 239–61. London: Falmer Press.

Chapter 2

Exploring the Subjective Dimension of Curriculum Change[1]

Andrew C. Sparkes

In the previous chapter various perspectives regarding the change process in schools were considered and the complexities of real change highlighted. The chapter concluded that teachers are the central actors in this process since it is they who are the critical mediators of change in action. Taking this as the starting point, this chapter draws upon case study material to take us inside the world of the school to look at a teacher-initiated innovation through the eyes of the physical education (PE) teachers involved.[2] By adopting such a stance we can see that curriculum change has personal meanings for those involved, with this colouring their view of, and reaction to, any innovation. Gaining an awareness of this subjective dimension is important since it challenges the often-held belief (e.g. see Williams, 1986) that teacher resistance to innovation is in some way pathological and replaces it with the view that such resistance (as well as acceptance) is part of the intelligent action of teachers in the context of their working lives. By focusing upon the emergent concerns of this group of PE teachers in relation to their teaching perspectives I want to highlight the differential costs and rewards that are available to teachers when change occurs. In doing so I hope to indicate that losers as well as winners are a fundamental reality in the process of innovation. Essentially, as Ball (1987) reminds us:

> Innovations are rarely neutral. They tend to advance or enhance the position of certain groups and disadvantage or damage the position of others. Innovations can threaten the self-interests of participants by undermining established identities, by deskilling and therefore reducing job satisfaction. By introducing new working practices which replace established and cherished ways of working, they threaten individual self concepts. Vested interests may also be under threat: innovations not infrequently involve the redistribution of resources, the restructuring of job allocations and redirection of lines of information flow. The career prospects of individuals or groups may be curtailed or fundamentally diverted. (p. 32)

Clearly, innovating in schools is an extremely complex affair which will affect various individuals and groups in different ways.[3] Some will define themselves as winners and some as losers in the process; this means that rarely can change be introduced without some form of overt or covert conflict (see Sparkes, 1986, 1990).

Winners will be those people who perceive themselves as currently experiencing more gains than losses from the changes or who anticipate doing so in the foreseeable future. In contrast, the losers perceive the losses (potential or actual) to outweigh the gains. In addition, there will be some teachers who are 'sideliners' (Roskies *et al.*, 1988) who do not define themselves as either winners or losers in the process because they are unsure if the changes are positive or negative for them, or they do not consider the changes personally relevant to their lives. For example, a temporary teacher, a supply teacher, a teacher about to retire, or a teacher about to move to a post in a new school may hold this view.

All *real* change, according to Marris (1986), involves loss, anxiety and struggle. Likewise, Kanter (1985) argues that even those who define themselves as winners and who look forward to new opportunities can experience loss—loss of the past, loss of routines and comforts, loss of traditions that were believed important, and perhaps the loss of relationships that had become close over time. This is an important point because those who initiate innovations often assume that the changes introduced will be to the benefit of all involved. These individuals, who often hold high status positions in the school or organization, are prone to view the change process through 'rose coloured glasses' and this leads them to perceive more curriculum satisfaction and group decision-making involvement than their low status colleagues. As Brady (1985) points out, this status variable has a major educational implication:

> If those in authority have a more idealized picture of curriculum functioning in the school, this view might conceivably *limit their perception of staff discontent in curriculum matters, and act as a brake on further change.* Such a finding further underlines the need for those structures in schools which facilitate continuous dialogue amongst all staff whatever the position they occupy in the hierarchy. (p. 267; my italics)

To ignore the differential costs and rewards for those involved in innovation is to ignore the reality of life in schools and the world that teachers are confronted with in their daily working lives. It also acts against the 'practicality ethic' of teachers which Doyle and Ponder (1977–78) summarize as follows:

> In the normal course of school events teachers receive a variety of messages intended to modify and improve their practice ... the term 'practical' is used frequently and consistently to label statements about classroom practices . . . *This labelling represents an evaluative process which is the central ingredient in the initial decision teachers make regarding the implementation of a proposed change in classroom procedure.* (p. 2; my italics)

For teachers working with children in the gymnasium, swimming pool, classroom, or out on the games field only those messages which are perceived to be practical will be allowed, albeit tentatively at first, into the teaching plans. The practicality of any proposal being judged in relation to the following criteria:

1   Does the change potentially address a need? Will the students be interested? Will they learn?
2   How clear is the change in terms of what the teacher will have to do? Does the proposal for change possess procedural clarity?
3   How will it affect the teacher personally in terms of time, energy, new skill, sense

of excitement and competence, and interference with existing goal priorities? What are the personal costs and rewards involved?

Utilizing such criteria, it is not surprising that many teachers define a host of proposals for change as frivolous because they simply do not address issues of boundedness, psychic rewards, time scheduling, student disruption, interpersonal support, and so forth (see Lortie, 1975). As Richardson (1990) found in her study of a programme for change in relation to classroom reading, several changes were adopted and tried out in the classroom but then dropped because they didn't 'work' for the teacher. She notes that 'working' for the teachers in her study meant that 'the activities did not violate the teacher's beliefs about teaching and learning; they also engaged the students, permitted control over students felt necessary by the teacher, and helped teachers respond to system-level demands such as high test scores' (p. 14). Importantly, Richardson emphasizes that rarely was the adoption of some aspect of change by the teacher related to the original scholarly theory of the researchers who wished to initiate change: 'The filtering of a research-based practice through the teacher's personality and/or belief system seemed to alter the practice quite dramatically, such that it could no longer really be viewed as the same practice' (p. 15).

Often, as House (1974) argues, there is little reason for teachers to believe in change since it often involves high personal costs and few incentives to make such an investment worthwhile. He notes, 'Innovations are acts of faith. They require that one believe that they will ultimately bear fruit and be worth the personal investment, often without the hope of immediate return' (p. 73). Yet far too often innovatory proposals are justified in esoteric and abstract terms, such as, 'improving the quality of life' or 'benefiting society'. However, in their discussions with science teachers being introduced to an integrated science approach, Brown and MacIntyre (1982) found that the teachers rarely considered the 'concerns of society' or the 'nature of science' when focusing upon the innovation. They suggest:

> Their attention was given primarily to questions of whether or not the innovations provided the opportunity and conditions for the teacher to do an effective and satisfying job. Would their training and competence be adequate? Would the substance of the innovation reflect their own specialisms, skills and interests and so be rewarding to teach? To what extent were they being asked to put considerable effort into changing their familiar and preferred ways of teaching in order to achieve something they did not regard as valuable? (p. 11)

What this makes clear is that each individual teacher will subjectively assess the ratio of investment to return for themselves in relation to their own value system. As Fullan (1982) comments, 'teachers are often more concerned about how the change will affect them personally, in terms of their in-classroom and extra-classroom work, than they are about a description of the goals and supposed benefits of the program' (p. 28). Should the costs outweigh the rewards then teachers will quite sensibly resist change or, at best, hedge their bets and make minor investments that allow superficial changes to be introduced that do not disturb teacher ideologies, values, beliefs and practices. Consequently, we need to gain a greater understanding of this subjective assessment and become more aware of what the change means to the teachers in their own terms so that changes can be negotiated in such a way as to take the subjective realities of teachers into account. Should these realities be ignored then it is likely that superficial rather than real change will prevail.

TEACHING PERSPECTIVES AND INNOVATION

In order to gain a more detailed understanding of how teachers subjectively assess their position with regard to the change process it is useful to have some insights into what it is that teachers find rewarding in their work. Feiman-Nemser and Floden (1986) in their consideration of the extrinsic and intrinsic rewards associated with teaching suggest that the latter—that is, student learning and attachment, collegial stimulation and support, the 'glow' of service, and the craft pride generated by evidence of successful teaching—are what make the job worthwhile for the majority of teachers. This may sound rather idealistic in view of the industrial conflict and unrest that has characterized the teaching profession in recent years. However, the work of Templin *et al.* (forthcoming) strongly suggests that positive interaction with pupils and colleagues remains one of the major satisfactions for physical education teachers in England and North America. Similarly, Poppleton and Riseborough (1988) conclude that the most powerful predictors of job satisfaction amongst the teachers in their study were the perceived quality of their classroom relationships and the degree of opportunity and challenge experienced in their work. As Poppleton (1988) observes, 'there are also aspects of teaching which are generally accepted as sources of major satisfaction, and these all belong in the classroom' (p. 15).

This is not to imply that all teachers will define the classroom as their major source of satisfaction. Just as it is inappropriate to view the cultures of teaching as homogeneous, so it is also inappropriate to suggest that teachers as an occupational group define the rewards and costs of teaching in similar ways. Several studies have indicated that rewards and costs may vary significantly with the age, experience, present career position, and gender of teachers.[4] In addition, teachers do not exist purely within the confines of the school and Morgan (1986) points to the struggles that teachers are involved in when they attempt to balance their interests in terms of 'doing the job' (task), their long and short-term career aspirations, and their personal values and life-circumstances beyond the school gates. Therefore, what is rewarding to one teacher at a certain point in time may well become defined as a cost at a later date as the life circumstances of the individual change (see Sparkes, 1988a). In reality, of course, any major innovation will entail a large number of more or less simultaneous changes. This point is made clear in the work of Roskies *et al.* (1988) who focus on the process of technological change in industry. They note:

> From the workers' point of view, moreover, it is highly unlikely that these changes will only affect a single aspect of the individual's job, and even more unlikely that all those affected will view the consequences in the same light. In fact, any large scale transformation is sufficiently complex and ambiguous that for the individuals concerned it is perhaps best viewed in classic stress terms, that is, as a situation of potential challenge, threat or harm in which the outcome is both uncertain and important to the individual's welfare. The emotional importance of the situation makes it necessary for the individual to assess its meaning for him or her, but the ambiguity and differential impact of change are likely to highlight individual differences both in what is perceived and how it is interpreted. (p. 124)

Likewise, Oliver *et al.* (1988) are quick to emphasize that it should not be assumed that all teachers will respond to incentives in a similar fashion, regardless of personal idiosyncrasies, since they will perceive and value rewards in different ways. It very much depends upon the perspective of the teacher. Becker *et al.* (1961) use the term 'perspective' to refer to a:

> coordinated set of ideas and actions a person uses in dealing with some problematic situation, or refer to a person's ordinary way of thinking and feeling about and acting in such a situation. These thoughts and actions are coordinated in the sense that the actions flow reasonably, from the actor's point of view, from the ideas contained in the perspective.   (pp. 34–7)

Consequently, teacher 'A' may define a change as rewarding whilst researcher 'B' sees the same change as a high-cost exercise. Furthermore, if a teacher changes her or his perspective then what was originally defined as a high-cost exercise might be redefined as very rewarding. For example, during my own research into a teacher-initiated innovation within a physical education department at a large English co-educational comprehensive school called Branstown, I became aware that there were two contrasting and competing perspectives operating within the PE department. The two perspectives identified—which were dimensional rather than dichotomous two-member typologies (see Hammersley, 1977)—were the 'sporting' and the 'idealist'. The former tends to be elitist, traditional, meritocratic, subject-centred, and concerned with the maintenance of standards via the production of winning school teams. The latter tends to be egalitarian, child-centred, progressive, and concerned with the personal and social development of pupils via self-paced individual activities.

Teaching perspectives are both constituted by, and composites of, ideologies, beliefs, values, and knowledge forms, about what should be included in the curriculum and how it should be taught. At Branstown school, the contrasting perspectives contained different views of both subject paradigm and subject pedagogy (see Ball and Lacey, 1984). The former refers to the appropriate content of a subject while the latter relates to the systems of ideas and procedures for the organization of learning under specific institutional conditions. The study of Branstown school indicates clearly that different perspectives can exist within the same subject subculture, and within the same department, which ensures that a given innovation will mean different things to different people. To illustrate this point I would like to consider briefly a few of the emergent concerns that arose within the department in relation to certain aspects of the teacher-initiated innovations.

CONTROL

Teaching is an extremely difficult and complex task and the school day is hectic with so many things to do and so little time to get them done in. Consequently, attempting to initiate or cope with change can be an added source of stress in the daily working lives of teachers. According to Fullan (1982) the teaching environment is characterized by the following:

1   Multidimensionality—the classroom is a crowded place with several functions to be carried out (discipline, giving out equipment, instructing, relationships etc.).

2 Simultaneity—interacting with one pupil while monitoring others, preparing the next question or practice, directing simultaneous groups etc.

3 Unpredictability—anything can happen, what works well with one pupil does not motivate another, a well planned lesson can go wrong, equipment can malfunction, the weather can change etc. (p. 27)

The environment described above is potentially very stressful unless conditions are controlled in some way. Consequently, teachers expend a great deal of time and energy in attempting to control their immediate environment (which includes both pupils and other teachers) in order to produce the predictability that will enhance order and reduce stress. As Denscombe (1985) points out:

Classroom control is an essential feature of teaching yet . . . it is not something which can be taken for granted. Teachers certainly enter the classroom with the official authority to control but, in practice, they still have to *win* that control rather than assume it exists or simply hope to enforce it as a right. For the most part, control is something which has to be achieved, worked for and frequently re-established during the course of the working day. (p. 10)

A range of strategies that teachers develop to maintain control have been identified (see Denscombe, 1985; Pollard, 1985; Woods, 1979). Over time these become routinized. Changes in routine necessitate further costly investments of time and energy to stabilize the environment once again. As one of the PE teachers who had a strong sporting perspective commented[5]

When I first came here it was bloody awful. I didn't know what hit me. I'd say that the whole of my first year in the school, perhaps more, was devoted to getting control in my lessons. I didn't smile for the first term and basically I was a real bastard, but I had to show them where the line was and who was the boss, what my standards were and how far they could go. I didn't like doing it but now, five years on, things are much easier because of it, they really are. Control is not a problem for me now. The kids know me and how far they can go, and I know them and we have a great relationship. We have a laugh, but if it goes too far I can quickly get them back where I want them. I'm still dead strict with the first years, so that they know where they stand with me.

This teacher, along with others in the PE department at Branstown school who held a sporting perspective, believed that one of the proposed changes which involved changing the organization of their games lessons from streaming by ability to mixed-ability would produce control problems. That is, it would destabilize the routines that they had worked so hard to develop with specific groups of children. In particular, they anticipated control problems from high-ability pupils who were not usually a source of stress for them, because in mixed-ability lessons they believed these children would not be 'stretched' and would get bored. For these teachers the change to mixed-ability groupings was a high-cost exercise. In contrast, those holding the idealist perspective, whilst maintaining a concern for control in lessons, felt that mixed-ability lessons would assist in maintaining classroom control and defined the change as rewarding. As one of them commented:

When I take the girls for hockey I find it easy to work with the top group for a variety of reasons, but equally it's very difficult when you have to take a group that is all low ability; that's a real strain for me because they mess about so much. In lots of ways I would prefer it if they were mixed because then the less able could work with the more able and I feel this would stop them messing about. The good kids are good anyway and perhaps this would rub off on the others.

COMPETENCE

This has two components. First, there is 'technical' competence which centres upon the ability of the individual teacher to perform a physical skill; an example is the execution of a lay-up shot in basketball. Very often physical educators choose not to demonstrate a skill in their lessons and use able pupils to provide a model for the rest of the class to approximate. However, there appears to be a measure of psychological safety in knowing that they could demonstrate should the need arise. In addition, for those holding a strong sporting perspective the ability to perform physical skills to a high level formed a central aspect of their identity which revolved around the image of competent sportsperson and able performer. As one of them pointed out, 'If you can't do it then you shouldn't be in there teaching it.'

One aspect of the innovation meant that the male members of the department would have to teach more educational gymnastics lessons as part of the boys' curriculum. Several of these teachers held strong sporting perspectives and the introduction of this activity to the curriculum constituted a direct threat to their conception of self as capable sportsperson and able performer. One of the PE teachers, who was an excellent games player but who defined himself as less than able in gymnastics, explained how this affected his confidence to teach the latter:

> I think it's probably because I feel more comfortable [in games]. I can't demonstrate much in gymnastics because I'm not much of a gymnast. I can demonstrate the fairly easy things but there is no way that I can demonstrate anything that is difficult because I probably couldn't do it [laughs]. I'll probably land on my head [laughs].

The same teacher felt even more insecure when it came to the teaching of educational gymnastics. He, along with several other male colleagues who held the sporting perspective, was a very capable games player but did not feel confident in his ability to demonstrate the relevant skills to children in an educational gymnastics lesson. To relearn the necessary skills was defined as a a high-cost exercise and it is interesting to note how several of these teachers utilized their teacher autonomy within the confines of the gymnasium to transform educational gymnastics into Olympic gymnastics, a discipline in which they were able to demonstrate a range of closed skills and so maintain their sense of self as competent performer. In contrast, the department head who wished to initiate the shift towards more educational gymnastics for the boys was a very capable gymnast. His initial teacher education programme had prepared him well in this area and in his first teaching post he had learnt a great deal from his departmental head regarding educational gymnastics. In this sense, he felt secure and confident in teaching these activities.

The second form of competence is 'procedural' and revolves around the question of 'how do I teach it to children?' Here, teachers have to make the difficult conceptual transformation from abstract ideas contained in the 'discursive' mode of consciousness to actualities that are mediated within the 'practical' mode of consciousness (see Cole, 1985). This is the often-cited gap between theory and practice. For instance, several of those holding the sporting perspective were able to discuss at an abstract level some of the themes involved in educational gymnastics such as flight, rotation, and weight bearing etc. However, they were unsure as to how these concepts should be operationalized in a lesson and unsure about the way to explain these concepts to children.

As a younger member of the department commented, 'I think I grasp some of the ideas behind ed gym but my real problem is how to get those ideas across to the kids. The ideas are there, it's just that I struggle to put it into words in a way that they can understand.'

This kind of transformation is often hindered by a lack of procedural clarity regarding the nature of an innovation and what its implications are for practice. Consequently, teachers often are left with a sense of 'false clarity' or 'painful unclarity'. According to Fullan (1982) the former occurs when teachers *think* they have changed 'but have only assimilated the superficial trappings of the new practice' (p. 28). The latter is experienced when 'unclear innovations are attempted under conditions which do not support the development of the subjective meaning of the change' (p. 28). Both of these act to ensure that little, if any, change takes place in classroom practice.

ACHIEVEMENT

It would appear that teachers in general have a strong achievement orientation, and Kirk (1986) notes, 'In a fundamental sense, the idea of teaching presupposes a concept of achievement or success. In other words, to teach is to attempt to achieve some goal; to be ineffective is to fail to teach' (p. 169). However, teachers seem to lack a technical culture and often do not see themselves as sharing a viable, generalized body of knowledge. Consequently, as Lortie (1975) suggests, this can lead to ambiguity and a lack of direction which causes teachers to be unsure of the influence they actually have on the children in their lessons. This orientates many physical educators to assess their pedagogical impact predominantly in terms of the following achievement criteria: attainment, effort, and enjoyment (see Sparkes, 1989). All these provide visible end products which confirm, to both teachers and pupils, that the teacher is 'achieving' and they are used in combination during lessons with different kinds of pupils to maintain the teacher's sense of self. For instance, with high-ability pupils all three achievement criteria can be matched but with low-ability groups the main criteria become those of enjoyment and effort only—that is, perceived pupil ability influences the achievement criteria that are utilized in any given lesson.

At Branstown school those physical educators who held the sporting perspective favoured lesson organizations where they maintained contact with the most able pupils—that is, where pupils were streamed by ability. Here their conceptions of self as 'good teacher' were most readily reinforced since all of the achievement criteria were matched by the able children. In particular, with a group of able pupils the attainment criterion which related to the production of observable and accountable physical skills was possible. Several who held the strong sporting perspective believed they were only 'really teaching' when they were with a top group of elite pupils and felt that during their contact time with the less able they were 'merely' childminding which clearly undermined their conception of self as 'professionals'. As one member of the department in her probationary year commented:

> I have a top group for first years. That's quite nice. It gives you a chance to work with the team players ... Also you can move much faster. Where the bottom groups are still dribbling or hitting, with the top group you are working out a system of taking corners,

something very complicated ... So, I think it [the introduction of mixed-ability] would slow down the progress you made.

For those holding the sporting perspective, working with skilled pupils in the top group was defined as a high-credit encounter that provided the maximum returns for their expenditure of energy. In contrast, their contacts with groups of low-ability pupils tended to be defined as debit encounters since they required a high expenditure of the teacher's energy for little return with regard to the attainment criterion. Not surprisingly, the introduction of mixed-ability groupings in place of streaming by ability in games lessons was seen by these teachers as a high-cost exercise because the presence of low-ability pupils would reduce their capacity to match the three achievement criteria simultaneously. In particular, it would significantly reduce their capacity to produce high-level physical skills in a lesson with the children and this denied them the satisfaction they gained from matching the attainment criterion that provided them with visible evidence that they were 'good' teachers.

In contrast, those holding the idealist perspective saw the maintenance of the 'top group' streamed system in games as a high-cost activity. This form of organization acted as a direct threat to their sense of self as 'good teacher' and these teachers found great satisfaction from working with the less able children in a mixed-ability setting. For the departmental head, contacts with low-ability pupils were defined as high-credit encounters while contacts with the top group were seen as debit situations because he felt that the more able children would achieve success with little help from the teacher. With this teacher, 'real' teaching took place in a mixed-ability context and especially in contacts with low-ability pupils where he was most able to experience himself as 'good' teacher. He noted:

> I experience more satisfaction, there is more success, and I feel a lot better when I come out of a gymnastics lesson, when I have seen a few kids' faces when they have done something for the first time and they are not the good ones. Now that means more to me than seeing the teams win a football or rugby match.

STATUS

Status is an important issue within the teaching profession, and within the subject subculture of physical education it is almost an obsession (see Sparkes *et al.*, 1990). This concern over status is noted by Hoyle (1986) who comments, 'As a profession, teaching is prone to status concerns and, within teaching, physical educationists are particularly prone to pondering status issues' (p. 43). Status is important in schools because status means strength and strength means bargaining power for the limited resources available in the school. Pollard (1982) points out that:

> At an institutional level finite resources are available, thus setting parameters for activities in school, and these are much dependent on the particular policies or patterns of allocation which exist in each school. These will reflect the institutional bias, in particular the influence of the headteacher, and the relative power and negotiating skills of staff as they bid for resources.   (p. 32)

Consequently, Goodson (1984) believes that the higher the status of the subject, the higher the resources and the better the prospects for the teachers involved in terms of staffing ratios, higher salaries, higher capitation allowances, more graded posts and better career prospects. Therefore, the struggle for status is essentially a battle over the material resources of each subject teacher and subject community. It is clear that not all subjects in schools are ascribed equal status (see Hoyle, 1986). The vast majority of schools reflect the mental–manual distinction that is legitimized in the wider society (Braverman, 1974) and this means that academic subjects generally enjoy a higher status than practical ones.

It is not surprising to find that in the physical education department at Branstown school *all* the teachers, regardless of their perspective, believed that their subject was seen by other members of staff as being marginal to the instrumental aims of the school. Accordingly, in terms of the subject status hierarchy that operated implicitly in the school, they felt that they were at the bottom of the heap along with the other 'practical' subjects such as art and music. All were in agreement that status went to the academic subjects like maths and science. The probationary teacher in the department expressed her views as follows:

> Low status in the school would be how the hierarchy views the subject. So if they were planning a curriculum, what subject might they slot in last. They put in their five maths, and their five French, and they've got one space left, 'Oh, we'll give it to PE'. If you're given a scale point in the school, looking around at the departments, who would you give it to first? It wouldn't be PE it would be an academic subject.

However, what did differ with regard to perspective was the manner in which attempts were made to enhance the status of the subject within the school. Those holding the sporting perspective tended to utilize an elitist strategy which relied on the visible and public display of sporting excellence via the production of successful school teams. To achieve these ends both curricular and extra-curricular time was often devoted to the improvement of sporting performance in the major team games. Reflecting back on his experiences with the rugby teams when he was first appointed at Branstown school one of the teachers noted:

> When I started teaching I fell on my feet in so much as the first team I took won every game of the season ... For people to look and say, 'Oh, the first and second years are doing well, who's taking them?' I mean it could have been bloody King Kong, it wouldn't have made any difference, they would still have won. But as a new teacher that gave me a lift because people would say, 'It's really going well, keep it up, well done'. That surely has got to be a smaller version of the PE department. If you can produce successful school sides and get a good reputation, then people will look to the PE department and say, 'Well done, congratulations'.

In contrast, the idealist perspective was anti-elitist and concerned to promote mass participation amongst pupils. The teachers holding this perspective believed that the best way for physical education to gain status within the school was for it to justify itself in relation to the broader educational aims and objectives of the school curriculum as provided by local and national policy documents. Consequently, they stressed the need to focus attention upon the educationally worthwhile experiences that were made available to all children in their physical education lessons during the course of the normal working day. For these teachers subject status could only be enhanced if the case was argued in educational terms. Indeed, they believed that the elitist strategy adopted by those holding the sporting perspective, particularly with its emphasis upon extra-curricular sport and inter-school competition, actually worked against the subject gaining recognition in the school. The department head certainly believed that such a strategy would not impress the school hierarchy and in particular the head-teacher, 'He's a chap that thinks, he goes right back to basics and says, "What is your subject doing for the child?" . . . He really doesn't want to know what the 1st XV or the 1st XI are doing. He wants to know what you are doing and how it affects the child.' The same teacher commented:

> There has been a strong emphasis on games within the school and it's going to take time to get away from that, and get people away from the idea that we simply produce good teams and PE is just about games . . . If we are going to justify the subject we are going to have to justify it more in terms of what we are doing in the overall subject, rather than what we are doing in games . . . The right people to influence are the ones who will sit down and listen to the educational implications of what you are trying to do in PE for *all* the kids.

COMMITMENT

According to Nias (1981) the term 'commitment' has been ascribed many meanings and she warns that to conflate them 'is to obscure differences in motivations among teachers, and to run the risk of confusing idealistic and/or highly contentious perform-ance of the teaching role with length of service' (p. 182). Building upon the conceptual framework provided by Nias, I have focused elsewhere (see Sparkes, 1988a) upon the ebb and flow of commitment within the innovative process at Branstown school. The categories considered were: commitment as caring, commitment as involvement (the expenditure of time and energy), commitment as career continuance (or 'getting on' in teaching), commitment and critical incidents, and commitment and the attribution of motives. The dynamic interplay between these forms of commitment and the manner in which they appear to be intimately linked to the other teacher concerns discussed so far bears testimony to the extremely complex nature of change within schools and departments.

The interactive nature of the various forms of commitment also highlights the dangers of divorcing the lives of teachers in schools from their personal lives beyond the school gates. For example, several critical incidents involving serious injuries, sustained while playing rugby at weekends, influenced one of the male members of the physical education department at Branstown school to reduce his commitment to the subject and department in order to develop a career line within the pastoral system. Other events that strongly influenced this decision included a divorce, the birth of a first child, a strong sense of self as a competent performer which would be negated if he was unable to demonstrate in lessons, and a disliking for the innovations that were being proposed in his department. In a very real sense this teacher defined himself as a loser in the process of department innovation and so transferred his allegiances elsewhere to those areas of school life where he believed he would be a winner.

BECOMING AWARE OF LOSSES AND GAINS

The details provided of the PE department at Branstown school indicate that it is possible, depending upon the perspective of the individual, for some teachers to define themselves as winners, some as losers, and others as sideliners in the process of innovation. The dynamic interplay of costs and rewards in relation to life in and out of school is complex and defies the imposition of simplistic formulas upon the dynamics of an individual's world. Despite this complexity it would seem that an awareness of, and an ability to communicate about, the individual costs and rewards of any innovation is an essential aspect of promoting departmental change in schools. As a consequence, it becomes critical that the working environment is structured in such a way as to be supportive of teachers and to encourage open and honest dialogue between department members. Encouraging this form of dialogue is a necessary first step in allowing those who are involved in the process of innovation to become aware of the perspectives of others and the manner in which costs and rewards are defined differently from within contrasting frameworks.

Initially, to assist this process it might be worthwhile for the departmental head, even though she or he might not be the initiator of the innovation, to engage the other members of the department in confidential interviews on a one-to-one basis in order to gain access to their concerns and anxieties regarding the proposals for change. It needs to be emphasized that if, within this process, departmental heads should wish their colleagues to be open and honest, then they themselves need to be open and honest about the costs and rewards for them in relation to the innovation. Where possible, as part of this interactive process, a series of departmental discussions should be negotiated in which uninterrupted time is set aside so that the private concerns and worries of individual teachers are able to be made public by the teachers themselves. This sharing of concerns and worries enables those involved to create a collective response to innovation that incorporates both the losers and winners by allowing each to gain some sense of ownership regarding the process of change.

The process of negotiation that has been described is clearly time-consuming. However, teachers need to be given this time and space in order to realize that they have problems in common regarding change that may best be overcome in a collective fashion rather than dealt with as private burdens. This collective response would need to incorporate a recognition of the individual differences and needs that exist within the department and these would have to be addressed within the change process itself. It is important that teachers become aware, as a group, that there will be losers amongst them for whom the high costs of change are not worth paying. Furthermore, it needs to be recognized that the costs and rewards of innovation might not be spread consistently throughout the school or department.

Losers will exist and they may experience a high degree of alienation that will require the development of supportive structures in the school to sustain their commitment and provide a set of reassuring values. Once aware of this the group can begin to develop strategies to support such colleagues. For example, in terms of helping to reskill individuals who are concerned about their procedural competence in a particular activity, it might be possible to arrange their timetable so that they can team-teach with a colleague who feels confident in this activity. Visits might be arranged to other schools nearby to draw upon and learn from the expertise of their staff so that a network of support is developed within the locality. Likewise, in-service courses could be arranged or people with particular expertise could be invited to the school to share their ideas with the department. Which avenue is explored to support colleagues will be a group decision whereby each member is involved in the process of innovation throughout. Consequently, curriculum change needs to be seen in its broadest sense and with this in mind Watson (1986) suggests:

> It is important, therefore, that over time the school be managed in such a way that, if burdens of change are inevitable and discriminatory, the burden does not always discriminate against the same group. Indeed, on occasion it may well be appropriate to link two innovations in such a way that those who lose through one change will nevertheless benefit through a different innovation. (p. 105)

If 'losers' are a fundamental political reality then it would appear self-evident that attempts to innovate will not meet with success unless this reality is recognized and collectively explored by those involved. This being the case it would be inappropriate to mislead teachers into believing that they will all be winners initially, for 'management integrity' is an essential element in the management process (cf. Peters and Austin, 1985). In addition, Liker *et al.* (1987) believe the following to be important issues in the management of change. First, the 'victims' of structural change should not be blamed for their negative attitudes and these should not simply be classified as 'resistance to change' (see also Roskies *et al.*, 1988). To do so is to compound the problems and anxieties inherent in the process of change by denying the legitimacy of the loser's worries, or worst of all, to deny that these worries even exist. Second, in focusing upon the 'new' it is insensitive and illogical to forget the 'old' completely. Third, those initiating change should avoid symbolic participation—that is, they should not attempt to create the illusion of participatory democracy in terms of the decision-making process etc. if they have no intention of relinquishing control over this process. Individuals will be rightly critical of participation that lacks substance and clearly this approach will not assist in those involved gaining a sense of ownership of the change process (see also Rudduck, 1988). Finally, Liker *et al.* (1987) emphasize that the old culture should not be destroyed without taking substantial time to build another in its place. For instance, in their study of technological innovation they illustrate how one company's old paternalistic management culture was rapidly destroyed with a view to creating a new corporate culture more compatible with the demands of advanced manufacturing technology. However, transforming cultures is a notoriously difficult enterprise and they found no evidence that the old culture had in fact been replaced by a new coherent set of values and beliefs. Indeed, Roskies *et al.* (1988) imply that this 'people change' is the most difficult and uncertain aspect of innovating.

Clearly, the interactive matrix of perceived costs and rewards plays a significant part in the process of innovation. Unfortunately, as Webb and Ashton (1987) realize, the intrinsic forms of reward that substantiate the majority of teachers in their work have been greatly reduced in recent years and this has led to a lowering of morale in the teaching profession. On the same pessimistic theme, Cole (1984) believes that teachers are now entering an era which will be characterized by a crisis of a kind, and of a degree, that they have not previously known. In view of the diminishing rewards in teaching for many people the process of innovation may become even more precarious and complex than it already is. One thing that we can be sure of is that an awareness of the costs and rewards for the teachers involved will continue to provide not only insights into the lives of teachers, but also an understanding of the problems and worries they have to cope with as part of the process of innovation in schools.

NOTES

1 This chapter draws substantially upon a paper entitled 'Towards an understanding of the personal costs and rewards involved in teacher-initiated innovations' that was published in *Educational Management and Administration* **17**(3), summer 1989, 100–8. I am grateful to Michael Locke for his editorial permission to use this material.
2 This involved a three-year case study of teacher-initiated innovation that was instigated in the PE department of Branstown school when a new departmental head was appointed. During the first year of the study I adopted the role of researcher-participant, while in the second and third year I utilized interviews and documentary sources to explore the meanings that the PE teachers involved associated with the change process. Further details of this study are available in Sparkes (1986, 1987a, 1987b,1988a, 1988b, 1990)
3 For examples see Ball (1981, 1985), Riseborough (1981), Roskies *et al.* (1988), and Sparkes (1987a).
4 Examples of how teachers experience change differently are provided by Poppleton *et al.* (1987), Poppleton (1988), Poppleton and Riseborough (1988), Riseborough (1986), and Sikes *et al.* (1985).
5 Unless otherwise indicated all quotations from the PE teachers at Branstown school are taken from interview transcripts.

REFERENCES

Ball, S. (1981) *Beachside Comprehensive*, Cambridge: Cambridge University Press.
Ball, S. (1985) School politics, teachers' careers and educational change: a case study of becoming a comprehensive school. In L. Barton and S. Walter (eds), *Education and Social Change*, pp. 29–61. London: Croom Helm.
Ball, S (1987) *The Micro-Politics of the School: Towards a Theory of School Organization*. London: Methuen.
Ball, S. and Lacey, C. (1984) Subject disciplines as the opportunity for group action: a measured critique of subject sub-cultures. In A. Hargreaves and P. Woods (eds), *Classrooms and Staffrooms*, pp. 232–44. Milton Keynes: Open University Press.
Becker, H., Geer, B., Hughes, E., and Strauss, A. (1961) *Boys in White*. Chicago: University of Chicago Press.
Brady, L. (1985) Status in school based curriculum development. *Journal of Educational Administration* XXIII, 219–28.
Braverman, H. (1974) *Labour and Monopoly Capital: The Degradation of Work in the Twentieth Century*. London: Routledge & Kegan Paul.
Brown, S. and McIntyre, D. (1982) Costs and rewards of innovation: taking account of the teachers' viewpoint. In J. Olsen (ed.), *Innovation in the Science Curriculum*, pp. 107–39. London: Croom Helm.
Cole, M. (1984) Teaching till two thousand: teachers' consciousness in times of crisis. In L. Barton and S. Walker (eds), *Social Crisis and Educational Research*, pp. 48–74. London: Croom Helm.
Cole, M. (1985) 'The tender trap?' Commitment and consciousness in entrants to teaching. In S. Ball and I. Goodson (eds), *Teachers' Lives and Careers*, pp. 89–104. London: Falmer Press.
Denscombe, M. (1985) *Classroom Control: A Sociological Perspective*. London: George Allen & Unwin.
Doyle, W. and Ponder, G. (1977–78) The practicality ethic in teacher decision making. *Interchange* **8**, 1–12.
Feiman-Nemser, S. and Floden, R. (1986) The cultures of teaching. In M. Wittrock (ed.), *Handbook of Research on Teaching*, pp. 505–26. London: Collier Macmillan.

Fullan, M. (1982) *The Meaning of Educational Change*. New York: Teachers College Press.

Goodson, I. (1984) Beyond the subject monolith: subject traditions and sub-cultures. In P. Harling (ed.), *New Directions in Educational Leadership*, pp. 325–41. London: Falmer Press.

Hammersley, M. (1977) *Teacher Perspectives*. Open University Course E202, *School and Society*. Milton Keynes: Open University Press.

House, E. (1974) *The Politics of Educational Innovation*. New York: McCutchan.

Hoyle, E. (1986) Curriculum development in physical education 1966–1985. In *Trends and Developments in Physical Education. Proceedings of the VIII Commonwealth and International Conference on Sport, Physical Education, Dance, Recreation and Health*. London: E. & F. N. Spon, pp. 35–48.

Kanter, R. (1985) Managing the human side of change. *Management Review* **74**, 52–9.

Kirk, D. (1986) Health related fitness as an innovation in the physical education curriculum. In J. Evans (ed.) *Physical Education, Sport and Schooling: Studies in the Sociology of Physical Education*, pp. 167–81. London: Falmer Press.

Liker, J., Roitman, D., and Roskies, E. (1987) Changing everything all at once: work life and technological change. *Sloan Management Review* **28**, 19–47.

Lortie, D. (1975) *Schoolteacher: A Sociological Study*. Chicago: University of Chicago Press.

Marris, P. (1986) *Loss and Change*. London: Routledge & Kegan Paul.

Morgan, G. (1986) *Images of Organization*. London: Sage.

Nias, J. (1981) 'Commitment' and motivation in primary school teachers. *Educational Review* **33**, 181–90.

Oliver, B., Bibik, J., Chandler, J., and Lane, S. (1988) Teacher development and job incentives: a psychological view. *Journal of Teaching in Physical Education* **7**, 121–31.

Peters, T. and Austin, N. (1985) *The Passion for Excellence*. New York: Random House.

Pollard, A. (1982) A model of classroom coping strategies. *British Journal of Sociology of Education* **3**, 19–37.

Pollard. A. (1985) *The Social World of the Primary School*. Eastbourne: Holt, Rinehart & Winston.

Poppleton, P. (1988) Teacher professional satisfaction: its implications for secondary education and teacher education. *Cambridge Journal of Education* **18**, 5–16.

Poppleton, P., Deas, R., Pullin, R., and Thompson, D. (1987) The experience of teaching in 'disadvantaged' areas in the United Kingdom and the U.S.A. *Comparative Education* **23**, 303–25.

Poppleton, P. and Riseborough, G. (1988) Teaching in the UK in the mid–1980s: secondary teachers' perception of their working conditions, roles, classroom practices and work satisfactions. Paper presented at the American Educational Research Association Conference, New Orleans, USA, April.

Richardson, V. (1990) Significant and worthwhile change in teaching practice. *Educational Researcher* **19**, 10–18.

Riseborough, G. (1981) Teachers' careers and comprehensive schooling: an empirical study. *Sociology* **15**, 325–81.

Riseborough, G. (1986) 'Know-alls', 'whizz kids', and the crisis of schooling. Paper presented at the British Educational Research Association, Bristol, September.

Roskies, E., Liker, J., and Roitman, D.(1988) Winners and losers: employee perceptions of their company's technological transformation. *Journal of Organizational Behaviour* **19**, 123–37.

Rudduck, J. (1988) The ownership of change as a basis for teachers' professional learning. In J. Calderhead (ed.), *Teachers' Professional Learning*, pp. 205–22. London: Falmer Press.

Sikes, P., Measor, L., and Woods, P. (1985) *Teachers' Careers: Crises and Continuities*. London: Falmer Press.

Sparkes, A. (1986) Strangers and structures in the process of innovation. In J. Evans (ed.), *Physical Education, Sport and Schooling: Studies in the Sociology of Physical Education*, pp. 183–93. London: Falmer Press.

Sparkes, A. (1987a) The genesis of an innovation: a case study of emergent concerns and micropolitical solutions. Unpublished Ph.D. thesis, Loughborough University of Technology.

Sparkes, A. (1987b) Strategies rhetoric: a constraint in changing the practice of teachers. *British Journal of Sociology of Education* **8**, 37–54.

Sparkes, A. (1988a) Strands of commitment within the process of teacher-initiated innovation. *Educational Review* **40**, 301–17.

Sparkes, A. (1988b) The micropolitics of innovation in the physical education curriculum. In J. Evans (ed.), *Teachers, Teaching and Control in the Physical Education Curriculum: Studies in the Sociology of Physical Education*, pp. 157–77. London: Falmer Press.

Sparkes, A. (1989) The achievement orientation and its influence upon innovation in physical education. *Physical Education Review* **12**, 36–43.

Sparkes, A. (1990) Power, domination and resistance in the process of teacher-initiated innovation. *Research Papers in Education* **5**, 59–84.

Sparkes, A., Templin, T., and Schempp, P. (1990) The problematic nature of a career in a marginal subject: some implications for teacher education programmes. *Journal of Education for Teaching* **16**, 3–28.

Templin, T., Sparkes, A., and Schempp, P. (forthcoming) *Physical Education Teachers: A Cross Cultural Career Analysis*. Indianapolis: Benchmark Press.

Watson, L. (1986) The 'loser' and the management of change. *School Organization* **6**, 101–6.

Webb, R. and Ashton, P. (1987) Teacher motivation and the conditions of teaching: a call for ecological reform. In S. Walker and L. Barton (eds), *Changing Policies, Changing Teachers*, pp. 22–40. Milton Keynes: Open University Press.

Williams, D. (1986) Managing change—a case study. *School Organization* **6**, 123–29.

Woods, P. (1979) *The Divided School*. London: Routledge & Kegan Paul.

Chapter 3

The Management of Change in Physical Education

Carole W. Raymond

The past decade has witnessed unprecedented efforts to initiate change in our schools. In the United Kingdom the drive towards innovation was particularly forceful and teachers faced a bombardment of change for which few were adequately prepared. It is not surprising, therefore, that many found it difficult to 'keep up' during this turbulent time and have experienced all the anxieties and uncertainties of trying to survive a whirlwind. Not unnaturally, a certain amount of reluctance to change emerged, stimulating much thought and research into the whole process of change and successful implementation.

Change is usually associated with development, progression, renewal, reform and innovation and, as such, can be considered to be with us all the time. It may be intentional and systematic or a form of unintentional drift. It can involve a whole school or just a small part, a department or an individual. It can be major or minor, voluntary or imposed, originate internally or externally, be threatening or non-threatening, it might even be exciting. What is clear, as the previous chapters have indicated, is that the process of change is not an easy one for most of those involved. Contemporary attempts to conceptualize change in physical education (PE) suggest that many teachers are especially resilient to real change, and the significance of the environment in which change takes place along with the involvement of those implicated in the change process have been identified as areas in need of consideration (Sparkes, 1990, Chapter 1 this volume; Kirk, 1988).

My intention in this chapter is to acknowledge the issues raised in the earlier chapters and confirm that the whole process of change is highly complex and difficult, involving the interaction of several variables, social, political, economic, personal and organizational. Nevertheless some change is inevitable, even though it is often out of our control. Bearing this in mind I propose to adopt a positive stance and offer for debate the notion that all teachers should develop a range of management skills that might enhance their contribution to assist the process of change. In pursuit of this I shall begin with a brief review of various literature, supplementing this with findings from my own research that involved a case study of a group of physical educators working in higher education, in order to highlight some common issues considered to hinder change (see Raymond, 1989). The discussion then focuses on the nature of management work in schools in order to consider a selection of specific management skills that are central to the management of change and which all teachers should be encouraged to develop.

FACTORS INFLUENCING THE PROCESS OF CHANGE

Regardless of the theory employed to analyse and understand the change process, the level of success or failure is dependent on the positive interaction of various processes and in particular on the degree of adoption by recipients. Fullan (1982) is just one of many writers who refer to the change as a series of processes. In his early work he considered three broad phases: initiation, implementation and institutionalization.

The initiation phase involves the emergence of a need for change embracing a review of the current situation—what is happening and what is problematic—leading to a vision of where we want to be and why and how this can be achieved. Uncertainty and reluctance to engage in this early phase is likely to result in a 'non starter' atmosphere. The implementation stage refers to the 'front line' activity consisting of the alteration from existing practice to some new or revised forms of practice. In examining any proposed curriculum or policy change, implementation is involved when a person or group of people attempt to use a new or revised programme for the first time. The process is clearly multi-dimensional with a possible three aspects of change at stake: use of new or revised materials, possible use of new teaching approaches (e.g. teaching strategies) and the possible incorporation of new or revised beliefs (e.g. philosophical assumptions and beliefs underlying the particular approach). Institutionalization refers to the behavioural and attitudinal change resulting in total and ongoing commitment. At this stage the change is considered successful if it becomes embedded into the fabric of everyday life and is linked with classroom practice.

The middle phase of implementation is considered crucial. When discussing the significance of this phase, Fullan (1982) describes it as none other than 'a process of learning and resocialization over a period of time involving people and relations among people in order to alter practice' (p. 254). Adults in schools are identified as the main learners; therefore, understanding how adults learn and under what conditions is essential for designing and carrying out the process of change. Many teachers, often main-scale, may be required not only to change behaviour and practice but ultimately to hold new beliefs and understanding (Sparkes, 1987). In relation to this, Wragg (1984) suggests that if an awareness of exactly what is to change can be generated then its implementation can be tackled deliberately and in an informed manner by the teachers involved.

Investigating curriculum development Brown (1980) concluded that any attempt at educational reform is only likely to be successful if teachers are willing and able to accept new ideas about their own work and implement them in their teaching. Willingness is seen to be related to incentives—the rewards and costs (Sparkes, Chapter 2 this volume) or gains and losses (Berg and Ostergren, 1977)—with the correct balance of pressure and support considered essential to generate commitment. 'Ability', defined as a mix of new knowledge and understanding plus the acquisition of attitudes and skills specific to the change programme, is considered equally important yet is largely neglected, there being a tendency to assume that teachers are competent in a multitude of domains and, therefore, have acquired all the skills that might be called for in any given situation. This may not be the case and often teachers are reluctant to admit that they need help to learn new knowledge, skills and attitudes. House (1974) and Sarason (1971) identified the existence of school norms promoting individualism and non-interference with fellow teachers thus reinforcing the likelihood that teachers will grapple with their professional and instructional concerns alone and in isolation from others. Likewise, Fullan (1982) found it unusual for teachers to discuss their work with colleagues and there was little attempt by them to build what he considered a collegial, technical culture with an analytic orientation towards their work. A similar problem was appreciated by Elton (1987) who was concerned with the lack of attention given to the re-education of academics in higher education. This is by no means applicable to all teachers in schools and higher education but certainly exists and has enormous implications if 'real' change is to be achieved.

If teachers, already coping with a multifaceted role and other numerous pressures, are faced with organizational and curriculum change in a way that sees them ill-prepared and ill-equipped then conflict, tensions and anxieties will emerge. In supporting the importance of ability as a prerequisite for change, Constable (1986) has discussed the need to generate a framework for change that systematically raised an awareness of potential problem areas which may be experienced by those expected to stage implementation. She believes that difficulties are often confused with failure and that those involved must expect initial problems, seeing the difficulties as a normal stage of the process, to be explored and solved, taking time, practice and skill. What emerges is the need to appreciate and anticipate problems thus enabling the provision of suitable outlets for the fears that the prospect of change evokes in some people— fears of not being able to cope, that one's sense of competence will be eroded and one's occupational identity challenged and threatened. These need to be considered as genuine concerns which magnify themselves as a threat to some individuals, creating resistance during what may emerge as a period of role crisis (Hopkins, 1985) and loss of self concept (Gray, 1980). In a number of studies investigating effective practice in industry, change has been conceived as equally problematic and Peters (1989) identifies aspects of mutual trust and the development of the full human potential of those involved in the change process as essential for coping with a 'world turned upside down'.

The importance of the teacher at the centre of the change process cannot be denied yet consideration must also be given to the social and organizational context in which the actor and the activity exist (Davies and Morgan, 1982; Sparkes, 1990, Chapter 1 this volume). This incorporates a number of aspects related to school climate and culture (Torrington and Weightman, 1989). Climate refers to how members perceive themselves in relation to others and the prevailing norms that operate within organizations (Wideen, 1985). This notion of climate is problematic and has been challenged by various writers, such as Greenfield (1978) who, in recognizing the complexities of the climate/culture issue, denies the existence of organizational consensus, stability and order. He suggests that organizational values do not exist as an entity in themselves but only as the value system of dominant individuals that is based on differential access to resources of power (see also Gray, 1980; Hovle, 1982, 1986).

Similar issues emerged from my own research involving the study of a group of physical educators in an institution of higher education who were faced with change associated with an expansion programme over which they had little initial control. The source of change was external; a government initiative to increase student undergraduate numbers. Originating from a general interest into how the department would cope with an influx of additional students the study progressively focused on how staff perceived the change and the implications of implementation for them. Data were collected from nine members of staff and eight students over a period of six months, utilizing the techniques of semi-structured interviews, naturalistic observations and documentary analysis.

The immediate positive reactions to the expansion programme from several staff included feelings of job security and opportunity, both at the individual and departmental level, with a period of growth preferred to that of contraction. In spite of the general support for expansion, staff and students interviewed had reservations about how it was going to change the current situation. Concerns focused on the ability of the department to implement and manage the change, in particular whether the programme of events had been carefully 'thought through' by both senior management and departmental staff. Uncertainties about the purpose of the expansion were expressed and how and why it came about. In all, knowledge and understanding regarding the reasons for change were limited due to the lack of information the staff received coupled with their lack of involvement in the initiation phase. A *fait accompli* attitude emerged with little discussion on the consequences of growth for staffing, curriculum, resources and facilities. As one of the staff commented

> It was externally imposed, we just took it in a sense, an *ad hoc* reaction and knee jerk by the school . . . alright in response to higher authority. But if you remember we've always been pushed along these roads without possibly full discussion and certainly not full contemplation, otherwise we wouldn't be struggling the way we are.

Reference to the lack of discussion was reinforced by another respondent who considered the group was 'swept along'. Apparent in staff comments was an undercurrent of dissatisfaction with the prevailing departmental climate, which related to a lack of formal philosophy, feelings of insecurity, lack of confidence, conflict, poor communication and a lack of focus and vision. Such feelings were associated with the problem of role complexity and the demands made upon staff to fulfil a multifaceted contract which included teaching, research and administrative activities. Furthermore, the group tended to work in isolation, with individuals pursuing their own interests and resisting collaboration. As one respondent commented: 'We [Physical Education staff] tend to be a little protective of our own things [course, projects etc.] and we do tend to hide ourselves away.' There was suggestion of a need for 'openness and professional criticism' by one interviewee who then attributed the difficulty of creating such a climate to 'the nature of physical education people being sensitive to criticism'.

Further aspects of 'climate' referred to by the staff included the lack of regular interactions between colleagues, some staff stating that they saw very little of each other: 'Each person seems to be isolated in their own way and no one really knows what anyone else is doing.' Or as another respondent recalled: 'We don't cooperate enough. We don't talk to one another. We don't spend time with one another. It's always going to be difficult with such a large staff.' Physical Education staff meetings were identified as a key time for communication and interaction yet these tended to be organized around long agendas that involved between 15 and 22 items including a mixture of administration and policy matters. This resulted in 'hurried' procedures, with constant reference to time limitations that curtailed any lengthy exploratory discussions.

Other evidence suggesting a less than positive climate for change included two individuals who independently portrayed themselves as 'second-class citizens'. Each expressed these feelings based on a variety of experiences. One example related to an event when all departmental staff were called to a staff meeting concerned with the short-listing of candidates for a new staff appointment. At this meeting the chairperson invited each member of staff to indicate their preferred five applicants. However, one staff member was bypassed in this process and on leaving the meeting commented, 'Now I know how important I am.' A second example referred to an aggregate of experiences which left another member of staff feeling unwilling to contribute to general staff meeting discussions because, 'You know they [certain members of staff] won't take any notice of you. Therefore, you don't think it is worthwhile. It depends on individuals really, some listen.' The same teacher[1] also expressed concern that new inexperienced members of staff did not receive support from experienced colleagues on starting their appointment, 'Some help, but with others you get blown apart, all you get is criticism after criticism. I'm not interested in that. I want some cooperation and help, not to be told what I don't know. I already know what I don't know and don't need to be told about it. I need advice.' Such a statement raises the issue of interdepartmental relationships and the complexity of the real situation in which some staff are sensitive, others insensitive, some collaborative and others individualistic. In this particular case the two teachers who experienced a feeling of 'second-class citizenship' were also the less experienced staff members and unlike their colleagues, who were all in full-time tenured positions, were on two-year contracts. Whilst the contractual expectations made full demands on their time they felt far from fully involved in the overall decision-making processes that were open to other members of staff.

During the study the data collected indicated that the department had no written philosophy and this emerged as a concern which might hinder the process of change. Several staff commented on this: 'I don't think the Physical Education Department knows where it is going'; 'I am aware of a philosophy, I hesitate to state a department philosophy'; 'Well, I don't know that the department as a whole has a philosophy. It would probably be difficult to articulate anyhow'. Support for a collective philosophy was identified by a fourth respondent who noted:

> It's [a collective philosophy] helpful because if there is no consensus you're going to get conflict, which is the situation we're in at the moment. There are not shared understandings of what we are supposed to be here for. Until we actually appreciate each other's situation and are seen to, in a genuine way, then there will always be this problem.

The implication here is that a departmental philosophy could well assist group functioning and understanding. The principal reason for the lack of such a philosophy was attributed to the structure of the department which functioned as a democratic group with a chairperson assuming departmental administrative responsibility for a period of three years. At the time of the study coordinating a collective philosophy was not considered part of the role of the chairperson.

In searching for information regarding the planning and management of change, documents of departmental meetings revealed attempts to make administrative structural adjustments. Examples include the introduction of a year-tutor system to facilitate record keeping for large student numbers and the delegation of departmental duties in order to share the anticipated increased administration load. The distribution of 'jobs' was reported to be on the basis of 'Whose turn is it?' or on a 'Would you like to do it?' basis. Initially this procedure was adopted with administrative ease for it was considered by some that 'jobs are jobs' with little prestige, status or reward. Nevertheless, in reality some staff—along with many students and external parties—perceived some jobs as having more status and prestige; hence what was seen to be a simple administrative exercise did in fact generate some conflict due to the perceived hierarchy of positions.

The approach to planning was generally considered to be weak and unsystematic. This was 'blamed' on the management practices reflected in the internal governance structure in that the department worked within the school, within the faculty, within the institution. The physical education group perceived themselves as almost powerless when it came to 'big' decisions, e.g. increases in student numbers in which the important negotiations were conducted outside of the PE group. Frustrations with the structures were evident in more than one instance. As one physical educator commented 'at the end of the day you are going to be told by somebody, decisions are being made up above anyway'. However, problems were not only structural and hierarchical but also lateral, which according to one teacher involved 'a lack of coordination and willingness of people [subject staff] to work together; to make collective decisions'. This was tied up with the institution's norm of perpetuating a tutor's professional autonomy thus suggesting the opportunity to virtually 'do one's own thing'. The evidence suggests a struggle between the desirability of collective staff responsibilities and collegiality, and the concept of preserving tutor autonomy.

To conclude, my investigation revealed a number of departmental weaknesses affecting its ability to cope with the changes that accompanied the expansion programme. An interpretation of the data relating to how the staff felt they could 'improve' the process revealed several needs:

1 To *understand the change*. Advocacy for change was not in short supply. The origins, purpose and aims of the change were crucial if a willingness to participate in related processes was to be achieved.
2 *Careful and thoughtful planning*. Identifying the key issues and problems in order to prepare appropriate strategies to accommodate both departmental and individual needs.
3 *Clear departmental goals*. An attempt to achieve consensus of purpose in which staff ambiguities are professionally accepted and understood.
4 *Staff development programmes and In-service provision*. Recognize the skills required to cope with change; these may range from disciplinary subject skills to managerial and administrative skills. Establish support systems to alleviate anxieties, insecurities, role conflict and role crisis which may emerge during the change process.

5 *Incentives*. It must be recognized that individuals find change more acceptable if they are to gain from it. Reward structures should be internally created in such areas as the provision of more interesting work, along with the scope to develop personal interests and secondment opportunities. Equally important is the need for all staff to be given the opportunity to meet the requirements for promotion and that the formal reward structures should reflect the broad nature of staff work.

6 *Leadership*. The leadership role is essential and those prepared to assume this role must do so with willingness and possess the necessary abilities to sensitively coordinate and manage both human and material resources.

7 *A positive climate*. This should encompass good communication, integration, relationships and high morale. It will require individuals to accept that a departmental climate is real and powerful and that all must develop an enthusiasm to understand this climate in order to strengthen and support both individual and departmental strengths.

Much of my work reflects the concerns and anxieties identified in earlier literature. The recommended list of needs corresponds well to the findings of Torrington and Weightman (1989) whose work is one of the few large-scale studies on the management and organization of maintained secondary schools in England. It involved 24 schools, 700 days of empirical research, interviews with over 1,000 teachers, attendance at 400 meetings and structured observations of 90 teachers through the varied incidents of their working day. A summary of their findings included:

1 Effective schools deploy time and initiative towards the management of the adults in the school.

2 One of the greatest traditional strengths of school organization is the culture of community that is found. The turbulence of recent years means that great care has to be taken to nurture that culture and particularly to ensure that it is appropriate to the changing organizational structure and mission of the school.

3 All members of school staffs need valuing and rarely have this experience.

4 Various jobs in schools provide their holders with problems of personal credibility in the eyes of their colleagues. Careful attention must be given to the distribution of responsibilities.

5 Management jobs frequently have too great an emphasis on administration instead of management, with the administrative emphasis leading to inefficiencies elsewhere.

6 Organization can often be improved by considering the lay-out of the school and the use of different rooms. The hub of the school is the staffroom, which is the communications centre for staff and children and which provides the best arena for the social interactions and valuing that are so important.

7 Despite a general belief in educational circles that effectiveness is a product of good leadership, with everything depending on the head, they found three different approaches that can produce effectiveness: prescription, leadership and collegiality.   (pp. 10–11)

Torrington and Weightman's (1989) study concluded that those schools that worked best were those that adopted a thorough and thoughtful approach to all aspects of the work of the adults in the school community, thereby creating a supportive network and a combination of firm leadership and decision-making processes in which all teachers felt that their views were represented.[2]

These are important issues that need to be considered if a positive climate for change is to be promoted. The conditions can be influenced by a range of management skills to which I now turn my attention. This next section will briefly look at what management work actually is, with the intention of identifying some key skills relevant to the management of change.

MANAGEMENT

In the past a strategy to help schools cope with change has involved the retraining of headteachers and senior staff in management. These people were often considered to be key change agents with the responsibility for creating certain conditions conducive to change. It is now clear that change does not always emanate from senior staff or remain in their control, but that main-scale teachers are increasingly involved in the initiation and implementation of innovation.[3] It would be reasonable to assume, therefore, that all teachers, albeit at different levels, should be exposed to management work. This was identified by Kirk (1988) who suggested that change leaders will need to develop a special sensitivity with regard to relationships since managing the curriculum involves managing people as well.

Management emerged as one of the catchwords of the 1980s in relation to initiatives to create more effective schools. A recent report of the School Management Task Force (1990), *Developing School Management: The Way Forward*, proposed management development as a crucial process in helping schools achieve their purposes and suggested that all teachers need management education and should receive it on a regular basis. This philosophy pervades my own thinking and has as its impetus a view that ultimately PE teachers, and all other secondary teachers, should manage their own environment and directly participate in departmental and school management activities. Such participation has the potential to contribute to the development of a positive culture in which change may successfully take place.

However, mention 'management training' in some circles and you instantly feel the eyebrows raise and hear the cash tills register. This not unnatural reaction reflects the image of industrial management structures and practices invading education whereby schools function in relation to market economy principles (Apple, 1988). I consider this to be a genuine apprehension but feel it is based on rather a narrow view of management work which is not surprising when one considers the roots of management theory.

Early proponents of scientific management theory called for a systematic study of working practices to derive sound management principles. F. W. Taylor, an influential pioneer during the early years of this century, sought to identify the most efficient means of performance and the most efficient methods of controlling workers. Much of this work was based on personal experiences in factories and foundries and was considered a 'crude' analysis. In the mid-1940s Henri Fayol, a French mining engineer, continued this work developing a more general analysis of organizational development. He classified the fundamental elements of management work as: to forecast, to plan, to organize, to command, to coordinate and to control (Fayol, 1949). These early definitions, although widely recognized and still evident in many areas of industrial practice (perhaps even in some schools), restrict management work to 'directing' and 'controlling' the work that others do.

In close accord with the ideas of Fayol and other classical management writers such as Gulick and Urwick (1937) was the work of Weber (1946), a German sociologist who believed that organizations could best be understood by viewing them as bureaucracies. He concluded that a bureaucracy, with its clear-cut divisions of labour, hierarchical structures of authority, comprehensive systems of rules and regulations, and characterized by impersonal relationships, was the most efficient form of administrative organization. It supported the importance of formal structure to efficient functioning. Such principles appear to be reflected in much of our teaching work, namely the traditional command teaching style adopted by many PE teachers, autocratic leadership, specialization of activities, excessive rules and regulations. The trend of the 1980s was to remove many senior teachers from schools, placing them in management training courses where they were exposed to a 'managerialist' model based on a preoccupation with 'tasks', precise statements of objectives, performance, measurement, individual appraisal, tight financial control and the creation of a corporate image to ensure the organization's ability to achieve a share of the market. Thus, the language of industry permeated schools with headteachers encouraged to devise action plans, set targets, promote programme implementation and develop incentive schemes. It is little wonder that the idea of management in schools is viewed with some scepticism.

Critics of this managerialist model focus on the erosion of the professional school culture in terms of participation and cooperation, in which teachers are reduced to units of production turning out the standardized product or a core curriculum that reflects a deskilling and disempowerment of teachers (Weightman, 1988). Ironically, there is some evidence to suggest that industrialists also appear to be abandoning the narrowness of 'task'-orientated management. A number of studies, including those in the 'excellence series' (Peters and Waterman, 1982; Peters, 1989), have offered clear views of what managers should do to create effective management practices and the move is towards staff development, improved staff relationships, flatter structures, openness and mutual trust. This would appear to be a more sensible way forward if we take notice of the available data on effective schools as portrayed through the eyes of teachers and the concerns raised by various writers trying to understand the process of change. However, we must recognize that schools and organizations do not exist for their teachers, but also have other purposes. Therefore, the balance of management work must reflect both task and people activity. Everard and Morris (1990) offer a definition of management work in its broadest sense. They include:

1   setting direction, aims and objectives;
2   planning *how* progress will be made or a goal achieved;
3   organizing available resources (people, time, materials) so that the goal can be economically achieved in the planned way;
4   controlling the process (i.e. measuring achievement against plan and taking corrective action where appropriate);
5   setting and improving organizational standards.   (p. 4)

In accepting this broad definition we can assume that all teaching jobs contain at least some element of management work. What has tended to happen in schools in the past is that all teachers 'manage' their own classroom activities but unless considered to have a position of responsibility (head of department or senior teacher) they were 'managed' in all other activities. Recent changes in education, particularly the local management of schools and the expectancy of all teachers to manage change, mean that teachers are being increasingly faced with the task of managing other adults—that is, their colleagues. Dean (1985) contends that the development of the ability to undertake such management tasks, and the acquisition of the necessary knowledge and skills, is an extension of the skills a teacher has already started to acquire in the classroom. However, we must not forget that the behaviour which succeeds in the classroom can be quite different to that required with adults. That is, strategies that work with 12-year-olds or adolescents may not work well when used with adults.

Management work

The precise nature of management work will depend on individuals and the context in which they find themselves, but management clearly involves working with people and resources in order to achieve agreed ends amicably and effectively. In this respect, teachers should look towards ways in which they can each develop and gradually acquire the necessary management skills.

Various authors have attempted to define what management work entails. For example, Skinsley (1986) describes the management work of a departmental head in PE as leadership, decision-making and taking, planning, evaluation and assessment, control, informing, representation and resolving priorities. Others provide more comprehensive statements as illustrated in the following based on the work of Dean (1985) and Everard and Morris (1990).

1   *Managing the organization* (interpreted as school/department/classroom)
    - setting aims, objectives, policies, philosophy, ethos;
    - resources, budgeting and finance, buildings, equipment—general and technological;
    - school and department reviews;
    - management structure, teams, subject group facilities;
    - managing the curriculum and learning, curriculum policy, National Curriculum, planning, evaluation and development, timetable.

2   *Managing people*:
    Internally
    - leadership, motivation;
    - communication systems, information dissemination in all directions, seek feedback;
    - decision-making;
    - problem-solving and conflict;
    - conducting meetings;
    - staff recruitment and appraisal;
    - staff development programmes.

Externally
- establish partnerships/relationships with parents, governors, community, local education authority, primary schools;
- represent the school image to outside world, publication materials;
- perceive external environment as a resource looking for sponsorship, cooperation and support.

The extent of management work is endless.[4] During the management of change specific aspects of this work become more significant at the various stages. For example, in endeavouring to implement change the 'change agent' must first look towards initiating some form of overall systematic general plan. This would equate with the teacher's scheme of work providing a loose framework of activities and identifying the various elements of work that need to be done in order to effect the desired change. The example to be used for discussion is an approach offered by Everard and Morris (1990). This has been extensively used by others in both industry and education and is based on the work of Beckard and Harris (1987).

In pursuit of changing practice and attitudes, staff responsible for the change will need to engage in a whole series of management work, planning exercises, meetings, discussions, decision-making and the preparation of documents to name but a few of the activities. The approach presented highlights some of the key stages where management activities become important if change is to be effective (see Figure 3.1). The value of such an approach is to help identify the management work that needs to be done in order to facilitate change. It is not intended as a strait-jacket but is offered as an illustration of the importance of management activities in the total process. The initial stage is that of deciding what change and why. This should involve a review of the demands for change, the nature and characteristics of the proposal and the factors which might affect implementation. At this stage all who are to be affected by the change must have a clear picture of what it will mean for them. The decision to accept the proposal should be based on a dispassionate assessment of its quality and appropriateness.

Once the decision has been made to undertake the change then the next two stages should outline the desired future position and the present situation. The former would involve a construction of the 'ideal' goal—what the staff in the department want, with a clear vision of the direction of the desired change. A review of the present situation would include answers to such questions as 'Where are we now?' 'What is currently working well?' and should highlight salient features in the context of future plans. These two stages may take place in any order and should leave the department with a record of what needs to be done in pursuit of the change. This forms the fourth stage of the process of identifying the gaps and determining what work has to be done. For example, is there likely to be resistance? If so, by whom and can one help to overcome this? Is there a need for in-service and staff development programmes? How can these be provided? Having carefully 'closed the gaps' the fifth stage of the process involves the transition from the present to the future with the actual implementation of the change programme asking and answering the questions 'Who does what by when?', 'How are resources to be allocated?', 'How is commitment to be achieved?'

In the past the early stages (see Figure 3.1, stages 1 to 4) appear to have been the easy part of the process, the crux being implementation. For the change agent this

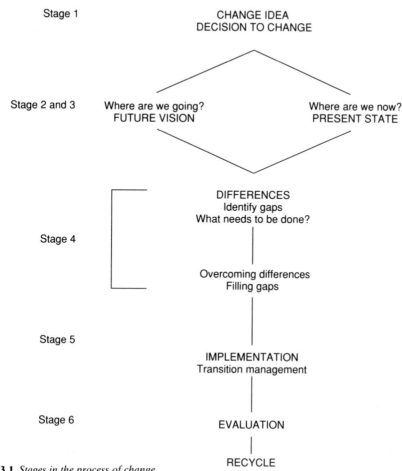

Figure 3.1 *Stages in the process of change.*

involves the transition management stage and it is here that all the real anxieties and apprehensions finally emerge to prevent fulfilment of 'real' change. It is at this stage— and the final stage involving the evaluation and monitoring of the change, whether it was successful and what has been learned—that we need to recognize that implicit in all management work is the art of management skill, involving a combination of personal qualities that the 'change agent' utilizes to achieve agreed ends. If teachers are central in the process of change, as Sparkes has suggested in the previous chapters, then it is not unreasonable to assume that one of the most fundamental skills they require is an ability to manage other people. Management in industry appears to have taken notice of this view and there have been moves to adopt more collaborative and participative styles of management. The new management theorists have drawn from the various sociological and psychological theories on the internal states of organiz- ations. 'Good' management is considered to recognize the importance of people, their diverse personalities, purposes and perceptions. Greenfield (1978) was an early pro- ponent in this field and he advocated that organizations can only be understood through the actions of the people within, suggesting that we must seek to understand their interpretation of the world. This ability to adopt such a phenomenological view must surely be part of the armoury of the change agent involved with managing people. An ability to know and understand the various perspectives and values of the people with whom you are involved. It is the development of this management skill that I consider to be one of the most important to those managing change. Similar skills have already permeated the teacher's work in the gymnasium and on the playing fields, with more teacher sensitivity towards the pupils as opposed to an end product. Such practice should also prevail in the staffroom.

MANAGING PEOPLE

It is now that the 'how' of management work becomes important. This focuses on the specific skills required to conduct management work. Dean (1985) classifies these as presentation, communication, negotiation, leading discussion, decision-making, evaluation, timetabling, organization, planning and administration. Others, such as Everard and Morris (1990) and Manning and Haddock (1989), include several of these in their conception of leadership skills. It would be too great a task to attempt an analysis of each skill.[5] I have, therefore, selected two which I consider are central not only to management work but also to the change process. For me they should be part of every teacher's skill vocabulary and are: (a) the ability to promote effective communication and (b) the ability to cope with conflict.

The ability to promote effective communication

Working with people involves communication and the work of any PE department towards change depends very much on the effectiveness of the communication system. If a department is to develop a positive climate that encourages openness and honesty, then this effectiveness means ensuring that all colleagues involved in the process of change can grow and change together. The key to success here is the development of a commitment to the purpose and permanency of the change. Communication is often looked upon as a mechanical exercise, a means of passing on information to colleagues thereby generating involvement. This sounds a simple exercise, a common-sense activity, and due to this widely used assumption many people underestimate the problems and the importance of the skill involved. Behind all forms of communication are philosophical messages and it is the skill of ensuring that the correct messages are conveyed that makes the effectiveness of the exercise problematic.

Communication in organizations has to be made in all directions, up, down and sideways. The larger the group the more difficult is the task. One can also employ a variety of methods, such as formal and informal, verbal and non-verbal, face-to-face encounters, telephone conversations and written documents. Whatever the method it is not always an easy task to know what you want to say and then be able to say it simply and clearly, particularly in some of the difficult areas associated with change that involve conflicts of interests and ideas. It has to be remembered that all communication is a two-way process involving 'giving' and 'receiving'. Each message given has a meaning based on the giver's understanding and knowledge; equally, the message received will be affected by the recipient's interpretation. One therefore has to consider the nature of the persons involved and judge whether they understand each other. Misunderstandings can easily occur and can act to prohibit and destroy relationships. The effective manager is one who has the ability to recognize these and guard against their repetition by using feedback as a form of 'climate thermometer' (Everard and Morris, 1990).

Verbal and written misunderstandings may be the result of the way in which language is used. For example, the language used may be too technical and require clarity. Less easy situations arise out of distrust, with simple memos and conversations being examined for hidden messages. Stewart (1978) claims that the frequency of such misunderstandings can usually indicate the level of departmental harmony or conflict. However, this may not be a reflection of existing practices but may be a shadow of the past that needs to be overcome. It must also be appreciated that not all teachers will share the same values, attitudes, beliefs and initial commitment to the change process due to a range of powerful influences in their personal histories. Understanding each other's position is crucial and can only be accomplished through interpersonal relationships. Jackson (1977) supports this view and adds that the effect of any particular communication depends largely upon the feelings and attitudes the parties concerned have for one another. As a consequence, managers will inevitably find themselves analysing human personalities and interpersonal relationships. To do this they will require various forms of information and feedback in order to address specific problems as they arise. More importantly, feedback at an accurate level is an essential aspect of monitoring and evaluating the change process itself as it moves through the stages that have been outlined.

Establishing relationships is only part of the way to reaching the ultimate aim of developing a mutual belief in the 'why' of change. The strength of any communication system is measured according to the ability and opportunity for all staff to interact and participate without undue restriction and it is only through such opportunity that staff are able to understand and accept the part that they have to play. It is when this occurs that the manager can consider himself/herself successful. Achieving this requires positive steps to organize regular formal and informal contact through meetings, coffee breaks and lunching together. Most teachers are ambivalent about endless paperwork and meetings, having on the one hand the desire to participate and on the other a reluctance to give up their valuable time. How to achieve the optimum level of involvement must be carefully orchestrated, encouraging people to participate by working together to find and prioritize time. Certain periods of the school year are far busier than others and this must be taken into account during the timetabling of events. For example, 'Baker' days (in-service education of teachers) are ideal opportunities to focus attention on major events. Traditionally these have been largely used for informing and listening or for general administration about the department. However, these days are ideal for looking at envisaged change—involving listening, learning, sharing and doing, reflecting and eventually reviewing the programme.

Active participation does not always naturally emerge from communication and it is the manager's role to structure situations to encourage involvement and effective participation through forms of negotiation and consultation. However, Field (1985) suggests that if teachers engage in such practices then it is essential that discussions are taken seriously, with the view that the majority opinion be accepted even if the proposal is less attractive than the initial statement. Similarly Nias (1980) concludes that sham consultation is worse than no consultation at all and she recognizes that teachers are very good at seeing through such practice. Furthermore, it must be recognized that not all staff want full participation and/or are unused to the process of participation; for these teachers this process would constitute another innovation to be coped with.

In summary, communication is a little more than just meeting in the changing room, sending memos, or putting displays on the notice-board. It is a matter of developing active working relationships which respect each and every person's position and perceptions within the department. This is not easy, for the hectic pace of normal school life can generate many problems and adding a programme of change may well magnify some of these and generate resistance and even conflict. The ability to recognize and overcome such situations is a necessity for teachers.

The ability to cope with conflict

In spite of industrious attempts to develop effective communication and departmental relationships, Torrington and Weightman (1989) argue that it is inevitable that some colleagues will still interpret change as a 'threatening dismantling of a stable order of things, bringing with it a great deal of frightening uncertainty' (p. 85). Others might just refuse to become involved. It is inevitable that various types of difficulty will emerge based on personal and emotional issues, or professional abilities, or a combination of all of these. For example, it is highly unlikely that a conventionally orientated teacher, who enjoys 'doing her/his own thing' is going to immediately welcome the prospect of teaching an integrated project through team teaching with open arms. It is likely that this person will need to engage in some staff development activities with associated counselling and support from colleagues. However, it is not guaranteed that change will automatically follow. Change agents will need the ability to manage difficult people who can appear negative, irritating and impossible to negotiate with. They need to be aware of the various personality types identified by Manning and Haddock (1989) which include: the attacker, egotist, sneak, victim, negator, super-agreeable and non-responsive. By becoming aware of these and by learning to assess, understand and take a genuine interest in each person it is possible to avoid difficult management situations which may hinder the process of change. Essentially, one must anticipate and prepare for the emergence of conflict which can result from attempts to promote change in any school or department.

Conflict is likely to appear in a variety of situations with quite different people. It is not unavoidable, it can be occasionally dangerous, but equally at other times conflict can be valuable. Everard and Morris (1990) refer to two models of conflict. First there is conflict which involves individuals protecting their own interests and who are prepared to support their decision-making at all costs. Second, there is the harmony model which involves a collective responsibility that focuses on individual and group interests with participative decision-making preceding any final outcome. It is the latter framework that I suggest is the most suitable for promoting a climate for change which can be achieved through the ability to recognize and defuse potentially difficult situations.

Many colleagues perceive 'danger' in conflict and this can sometimes be the case if it becomes a 'competitive' conflict where issues of personal glory and ego are at stake. If such a situation becomes overt, with open arguments at meetings, or if coercive strategies are used to gain support for one's views, then tensions will be created that are damaging to the whole notion of collaboration and participation. In a professional environment there must be an element of give and take, a recognition that there are different perspectives involving different attitudes, beliefs and behaviours. It is the role of the change agent to manage the situation in such a way that the energies of staff are directed into more profitable joint activities so that they are able to rise above differences and look towards future achievements. In pursuit of this Everard and Morris (1990) offer a strategy for teachers to consider when faced with conflict situations. This begins with the organization of a meeting with the following principles as a guide for discussion:

1 The parties will talk to each other as openly as possible about the real issues that concern them.
2 They will state their aims, views and feelings openly but calmly, and try to avoid reiteration.
3 They will try to put the conflict into the context of superordinate goals and of the interest of the total organization (a 'helicopter' view). They will look for common goals.
4 They will focus on future action rather than on the events of the past.
5 They will listen carefully to each other's point of view and seek to understand it. To ensure that their understanding of it is correct they may rephrase the other's point of view. However, this must be a genuine attempt at restatement and not a parody of what was said.
6 They will try to avoid moving on to the attack or defence.
7 They will try to build on each other's ideas.
8 They will trust each other's good faith and try to act in good faith.
9 They will plan some clear actions to follow the discussion specifying who will do what by when. (This is extremely important and may easily be forgotten in the euphoria of finding that the other party is not as unreasonable as had been anticipated!)
10 They will set a date and time to review progress and will keep this at all costs.

(pp. 102–3)

Clearly the whole process pivots on the teacher's ability to recognize and confront the conflict situation and employ his/her communication skills to solve it through coalition seeking and negotiation. The importance of developing such skills is supported by contemporary research into schools and organizations that has adopted a micropolitical perspective. This perspective has as its central focus the issues of conflict, power and control in which individuals and groups attempt to extend and promote their own interests at the expense of others. In relation to this Hoyle (1982) describes micropolitics as the 'strategies by which individuals seek to use their resources of power and influence to further their own interests' (p. 88).

Teachers seeking to promote change are more than likely to encounter colleagues competing for control, based on different values, and they will be attempting to resolve the differences while at the same time endeavouring to consolidate a power base. Ball (1987) discusses this as a twin problem of domination and integration, and both Hoyle (1982) and Greenfield (1978) have noted the less pleasant 'darker' side of the micropolitical model in which people draw upon a range of devious tactics in order to control and dominate others. Blase (1988), in studying the use of such approaches by headteachers in American schools, concluded that such behaviour violated teachers' expectations about professional autonomy and status. However, Jones (1988) claims that this interpretation of micropolitical activity is too narrow and suggests that competitive and manipulative behaviour leading to winners and losers is not inevitable. Similarly, Jenkins (1989), in search of a management model for head-teachers in the 1990s, considers:

> High levels of warmth, trust and openness are possible in organizations and manipulative behaviour will in the end be self-defeating. Micro-politics is a reflection of people bringing about their differences and perceptions to the workplace and that politics can be a struggle of reasonable people to get what they consider acceptable to the organization. Micro-political analysis sensitises people to power and the use and abuse of power. Micro-political behaviour is about negotiating around differences, creating tolerance and respect and being sensitive to other people's needs.   (p. 17)

It is this more positive view of micropolitical behaviour, resembling Everard and Morris's 'harmony' approach (1990), that I advocate as the key to managerial success of change in the future.

COMMENTS

Real change is undoubtedly a challenging process and for teachers facing the bombardment of educational change in the 1990s there is a need to look for the means that can help them work collaboratively to appraise and change their practice and school culture. There is no one 'right' strategy but it is clear that the climate in which change takes place is fundamental and is influenced by the form of management involved. The creation of a positive climate cannot be left to chance nor is it the responsibility of just a few teachers. In particular, management work is not the sole responsibility of 'senior' staff. It is time to challenge the idea of a management 'cadre' exercising superior powers and question the assumption that they are the only influential change agents. If physical educators are to genuinely contribute to the future of their pupils' education and preserve their professional influence on the school culture then they must look towards the following:

1 Active involvement in creating a positive climate. This will require recognition of the importance of the more elusive ideographic aspects of school life and in particular those specific to the teachers' culture, understanding that individuals hold different perspectives necessitating an awareness of alternative courses of action, with the ability to evaluate the consequences and consider the implications for their own social world. For to know and understand others with whom you share a working environment is the beginning of trying to understand how best to work together. Inherent in a positive climate is the balance of meeting the needs of individual staff with those of the school and the pupils.
2 Seeking knowledge about what behaviour is considered useful and constructive in bringing about effective change—in particular a focus on the effectiveness of management practice during the change process. Thus, all teachers should engage in a 'participative' management approach, fostering a collegial culture, that involves all members of staff with a shared responsibility.

3   Recent trends in research approaches have sought to promote the notion of reflective practitioner (Schon, 1987; Stenhouse, 1983) and the practitioners' involvement in action research (Carr and Kemmis, 1986; Sparkes, Chapter 1 this volume). Both are attempts to encourage teachers to develop a deeper understanding of their own practice and the interpretation of the intentions of others in the school. In pursuit of developing research activities schools and institutions of higher education should endeavour to establish and promote a partnership for such practice with a view to developing a collective ability to select appropriate strategies toward change. The dissemination and publication of the evidence collated in these research projects is crucial for the future and the usefulness of such knowledge can be extensive, particularly in directing the planning for future programmes and the identification of in-service and staff development needs.

Finally, as teachers come to terms with change as an ongoing, natural and developmental process it is essential that they equip themselves with management skills to ensure that they have some influence and control over the direction of the change. Skills of managing people, the interpersonal relationships developed through effective communication, can only enhance and promote a collaborative trust and a sense of empowerment among teachers. It must be noted, however, that management work is not something that can be fitted into an already hectic schedule. As the American analyst Weick (1985) has commented, 'When organization activity is lived in nine minute bursts, people seldom have the time to reflect on what the bursts mean' (p. 389). If real change is to be negotiated then there is a need to assist teachers to manage change in a secure and supportive culture.

The development of the skills to create such conditions involves the 'manager', whoever it may be, in careful and thoughtful practices. For as Torrington and Weightman (1989) inform us, 'Management is not a box of tricks with a nice drill to suit any eventuality: it is an art that requires clear understanding of issues before the performance can be produced' (p. 11). What we are left with are some extremely complex issues regarding how teachers relate to each other and work with each other in schools. As has been indicated, there is no single 'best' way. However, one thing is for sure, if PE teachers are to survive change and are to have some control over the direction their subject takes in the future, then they must start by making every effort to contribute to the management of the environment in which they work. In the circumstances we find ourselves in as we enter the 1990s it would be professional suicide for physical educators to be indifferent to management issues both within their department and the school as a totality. The future of our subject should be for us to shape and not for others to shape for us.

NOTES

1   For the purpose of discussion the term 'teacher' will be used to refer to physical educators employed in schools and institutions of higher education.
2   For a more detailed example of effective schools see Reid *et al.* (1987).
3   For further case study examples see Ball (1981), Sparkes (1986), Evans *et al.* (1987), Kirk (1988), Torrington and Weightman (1989).
4   See for additional information: Glatter (1988), Bush (1989), Lomax (1989), Davies (1990).

5 See additional examples: Earley and Fletcher-Campbell (1989), Lyons and Stenning (1986), Marland and Hill (1981), and Marland (1986).

REFERENCES

Apple, M. (1988) What reform talk does: creating new inequalities in education. *Educational Administration Quarterly* **24**, 272–81.

Ball, S. (1981) *Beachside Comprehensive: A Case Study of Secondary Schooling.* Cambridge: Cambridge University Press.

Ball, S. (1987) *The Micro-politics of the School.* London: Methuen.

Beckard, R. and Harris, R. (1987) *Organizational Transitions: Managing Complex Change* (2nd edn). Reading, MA: Addison Wesley.

Bell, L. (1986) Managing to survive in secondary school physical education. In J. Evans (ed.), *Physical Education, Sport and Schooling: Studies in the Sociology of Physical Education*, pp. 95–115. London: Falmer Press.

Berg, B. and Ostergren, B. (1977) *Innovation and Innovation Processes in Higher Education.* Stockholm: National Board of Universities and Colleges.

Blase, J. (1988) The politics of favouritism: a qualitative analysis of the teacher's perspective. *Educational Administration Quarterly* **24**, 152–77.

Brown, S. (1980) Key issues in the implementation of innovation in schools. *Curriculum*, spring, 21–39.

Bush, T. (1989) *Managing Education.* Milton Keynes: Open University.

Carr, W. and Kemmis, S. (1986) *Becoming Critical: Education, Knowledge and Action Research.* London: Falmer Press.

Constable, H. (1986) How to succeed in innovation—stop calling inevitable difficulties failure. *Curriculum*, winter, 162–9.

Davies, B. (ed.) (1990) *Education Management for the 1990s.* London: Longman.

Davies, J. and Morgan, A. (1982) The politics of institutional change. In L. Wagner (ed.), *Agenda for Institutional Change in Higher Education.* Guildford, SRHE and NFER–Nelson.

Dean, J. (1985) *Managing the Secondary School.* London: Croom Helm.

Earley, P. and Fletcher-Campbell, F. (1989) *The Time to Manage?* Worcester: NFER–Nelson.

Elton, L. (1987) *Teaching in Higher Education: Appraisal and Training.* London: Kogan Page.

Evans, J., Lopez, S., Duncan, M., and Evans, M. (1987) Some thoughts on the political and pedagogical implications of mixed sex groupings in the physical education curriculum. *British Educational Research Journal* **13**, 59–71.

Everard, B. and Morris, G. (1990) *Effective School Management.* London: Paul Chapman.

Fayol, H. (1949) *General and Industrial Management.* London: Pitman.

Field, D. (1985) Headship in the secondary school. In M. Hughes, P. Ribbins and H. Thomas (eds), *Managing Education: The System and the Institution*, pp. 308–24. London: Holt, Rinehart & Winston.

Fullan, M. (1982) Research into educational innovation. In H. Gray (ed.), *The Management of Educational Institutions: Theory Research and Consultancy*, pp. 245–63. London: Falmer Press.

Glatter, R. (1988) *Understanding School Management.* Milton Keynes: Open University.

Gray, H. (1980) *The Search for More Effective Schools: Problems and Progress on Studies Related to British Schools.* Sheffield: University of Sheffield, Division and Institute of Education.

Greenfield, T. (1978) The decline and fall of science in educational administration. *Interchange* **17**, 157–80.

Gulick, L. and Urwick, L. (1937) *Papers on the Science of Administration.* New York: Columbia University Press.

Hopkins, D. (1985) Drift and the problem of change in Canadian teacher education. In K. Reid and D. Hopkins. *Rethinking Teacher Education*, pp. 107–29. London: Croom Helm.

House, E. (1974) *The Politics of Education Innovation.* Berkeley, CA: McCutchan.

Hoyle, E. (1982) Micropolitics of educational organizations. *Educational Management and Administration* **10**, 87–98.

Hoyle, E. (1986) *The Politics of School Management.* London: Hodder & Stoughton.

Jackson, J. (1977) *The Organization and its Communication Problems.* Harmondsworth: Penguin.

Jenkins, M. (1989) Education managers—paradigms lost. Inaugural lecture delivered at the Polytechnic of Wales, February.

Jones, S. (1988) Organizational politics—only the darker side? *Management Education and Development* **18**, 116–28.

Kirk, D. (1988) Ideology and school-centred innovation: a case study and a critique. *Journal of Curriculum Studies* **20**, 449–64.

Lomax, P. (1989) *Management of Change.* Clevedon: Multilingual Matters Ltd.

Lyons, G. and Stenning, R. (1986) *Managing Staff in Schools: A Handbook.* London: Hutchinson.

Manning, M. and Haddock, P. (1989) *Leadership Skills for Women.* London: Kogan Page.

Marland, M. (1986) *School Management Skills.* London: Heinemann Educational Books.

Marland, M. and Hill, S. (1981) *Departmental Management.* London: Heinemann.

Nias, J. (1980) Leadership styles and job-satisfaction in primary schools. In T. Bush, R. Glatter, J. Goodey and C. Riches (eds), *Approaches to School Management*, pp. 255–73. London: Harper & Row.

Peters, T. (1989) *Thriving on Chaos: Handbook for a Management Revolution.* London: Pan Books.

Peters, T. and Waterman, R. (1982) *In Search of Excellence.* New York: Harper & Row.

Raymond, C. (1989) Perceptions of change in a university department. M.Sc. (Education Management) dissertation. Polytechnic of Wales.

Reid, K., Hopkins, D., and Holly, P. (1987) *Towards Effective Schools.* Oxford: Blackwell.

Sarason, B. (1971) *The Culture of the School and the Problem of Change.* Boston: Allyn & Bacon.

Schon, D. (1987) *Educating the Reflective Practitioner.* London: Jossey-Bass.

School Management Taskforce (1990) *Developing School Management—The Way Forward.* London: DES, HMSO.

Skinsley, M. (1986) The management role of a physical education department. *British Journal of Physical Education* **17**, 186.

Sparkes, A. (1986) Strangers and structures in the process of innovation. In J. Evans (ed.) *Physical Education, Sport and Schooling*, pp. 183–93. London: Falmer Press.

Sparkes, A. (1987) Strategic rhetoric: a constraint in changing the practice of teachers. *British Journal of Sociology of Education* **8**, 37–54.

Sparkes, A. (1990) *Curriculum Change and Physical Education: Towards a Micropolitical Understanding.* Deakin: Deakin University Press.

Stenhouse, L. (1983) The legacy of the curriculum movement. In M. Galton and B. Moon (eds), *Changing Schools, Changing Curriculum*, pp. 346–55. London: Harper & Row.

Stewart, R. (1978) *The Reality of Management.* London: Pan Books.

Torrington, D. and Weightman, J. (1989) *The Reality of School Management.* London: Blackwell.

Weber, M. (1946) *Essays in Sociology.* Oxford: Oxford University Press.

Weick, K. (1985) The significance of corporate culture. In K. Frost (ed.), *Organizational Culture*, pp. 381–89. California: Sage.

Weightman, J. (1988) The managing and organizing balance: collegiality, prescription or leadership? Paper presented at Third BEMAS Research Conference, Cardiff.

Wideen, M. (1985) Characteristics of faculties of education. In D. Hopkins and K. Reid (eds), *Rethinking Teacher Education*, pp. 83–106. London: Croom Helm.

Wragg, E. (1984) *Classroom Teaching Skills.* London: Croom Helm.

Chapter 4

Equality in Physical Education: A Consideration of Key Issues, Concepts, and Strategies

Sue Thomas

In this chapter my intention is to explore the complex issue of equality in physical education (PE). The first part aims to briefly contextualize the issue of equality within a social and educational framework, identifying and discussing some of the diverse and sometimes contradictory interpretations of equality. The second part draws upon many of the conceptual and curricular issues previously identified and examines these in relation to strategies that may potentially provide a greater climate for equality. The practical implications for the PE curriculum are analysed in relation to its organization, content, pedagogy, and assessment.

The conceptual issues and practical ramifications associated with promoting equality in schools have proved problematic for both social and educational reformers. First, from a conceptual point of view there exist fundamentally different and diverse interpretations as to what the notion of equality actually means. Second, in the practical sense, many of the well-intentioned strategies that have evolved to meet the challenge of promoting equality have themselves often unwittingly and inadvertently served to reproduce and perpetuate the underlying dynamics of inequality. Finally, as Williams (1962) suggests, the struggle for equality can often be located within part of a wider political battle over 'access to certain goods' (p. 124) and power.

Equality has featured as an item on the educational agenda since the early 1970s when studies began to identify social class as a key area of educational disadvantage. Since this time, and with the rising interest in the sociology of education, research that has focused on the process of schooling has sensitized those concerned with education to the existence of institutionalized structures and practices that may create and perpetuate inequality, and has also broadened the concept of equality to encompass other disadvantaged groups including girls, ethnic minorities, pupils with special educational needs.[1] Much of this research has illustrated that the path through schooling is by no means a common process. Pupils, both girls and boys, arrive in the classroom or gymnasium differently predisposed and positioned to relate to the curriculum on offer. As Evans (1987) suggests, 'boys and girls do tend to enter PE classrooms differently able to meet the criteria for success and achievement which operate inside them. Years of differential socialisation ensure all too often that this is so' (p. 24). In relation to this Murphy (1989), commenting on gender and the issue of assessment, suggests that socialization differences may account for the different values that pupils may bring to the classroom and the views of relevance that pupils may hold—ones which may encourage them to view and make sense of the world in different ways and 'come to the school with learning styles already developed and with an understanding of what is and is not appropriate for them' (p. 38).

Educational research investigating girls and equality initially focused on the teaching and assessment of science subjects, where the disproportional representation of girls and women following science courses (Smail, 1984) pointed the finger firmly at the social processes operating and occurring within educational institutions. Other studies, for example of Goddard-Spear (1984), showed that the same piece of science writing, when attributed to girls, received lower marks from teachers than when it had been attributed to boys. Such work highlights the pervasive power of gender expectations with their attendant implications for equality. Additionally, numerous classroom interaction studies[2] have indicated that teachers' pedagogical practices are often based on their stereotypical conceptions and expectations of gender-appropriate behaviour which often reinforces, rather than challenges, the inequalities of gender.

Pressure both from educational research and the feminist lobby has been instrumental in bringing the issue of gender and equality in schools into sharp relief as reflected in the setting up of the Equal Opportunities Commission (EOC), in 1976, the inclusion of educational matters in the Sex Discrimination Act (SDA) (1975), the Department of Education and Science (DES) survey *Curricular Differences for Boys and Girls* (1975), and their publication *The School Curriculum* (1981). This latter document suggests that 'the equal treatment of men and women embodied in our law needs to be supported in the curriculum. It is essential to ensure that equal curricular opportunity is genuinely available to both boys and girls' (p. 7). All illustrate the concern for gender equality within education that began to emerge in the mid-1970s and has since been a key feature of educational policy. Indeed, Flintoff (1990) reports an increase in the number of local education authorities (LEAs) issuing policy statements concerning the promotion of equal opportunities. However, she also suggests that at a practical level support for schools has varied between authorities.

POLICY, LEGISLATION, AND INTERPRETATION

The SDA needs to be clarified with regard to its application within the education system. Although, as Williams (1989) has suggested, it prompted examination of all existing curricular provision, it has also been instrumental in the gradual raising of awareness that sexism operates as a barrier to effective teaching and learning. As Carr (1989) states, 'gender issues are, therefore, a matter of professional concern to those who work in the education system' (p. 19). However, over the years its impact and effect in PE has been hindered and limited by the inclusion of special clauses that exempted PE, and PE courses in further and higher education, from complying with its mandate. For example, until the repeal in 1985, section 28 of the SDA exempted PE and its agencies from complying with sections 22, 23 and 25—those which related specifically to educational provision. In effect, it allowed institutes of further and higher education to provide courses for one sex in PE and exempted them from having to provide equal access to both sexes. Such legislation perpetuated the long history of single-sex PE in schools and teacher education, and as Hargreaves (1990) has argued such organization 'provides a practical and ideological foundation for separate sports to continue' (p. 291). In this respect the SDA provided little support for the delivery of PE in the school curriculum, in a non-gender-based way. Following the Education Reform Act (ERA) in 1988, the wording of section 28 has become unclear and the present position is one of ambiguity. Similarly, section 44 is couched in vague and generalized terms which leads Pannick (1983) to suggest that this makes it difficult to mount an effective legal challenge to sex discrimination in school sport.[3] Overall then, and despite a proposed amendment by the EOC in 1986 that section 44 should not apply to school age pupils, these clauses have functioned to legitimize and perpetuate the *status quo* in sport and PE whereby girls are generally denied access and opportunity to participate in competitive sport traditionally played by boys and men. Therefore, the SDA, whilst rendering illegal the more blatant cases of discrimination and inequality within education, still represents a grey area for PE and sport.

In contrast, in the USA—with the passage of Title IX[4] in 1972—equality issues for the sexes appear to have been pursued more vigorously and seriously (Pannick, 1983). For example, PE programmes and courses were *required* to be co-educational (the exception being contact sports), and *required* to provide equal support and opportunity. Whilst this greater level of prescription should not be confused with any assumptions about the degree of success of such changes in resolving gender inequalities, Bain (1990) reports that the effects of Title IX have had a dramatic effect on school PE and teacher education. For example, PE programmes for girls have broadened in response to mixed-sex organization. Equally, many previously separate men's and women's PE departments have merged, perhaps a reflection of the fact that most teacher education courses are now mixed.

The principle of equal access to a broad and balanced curriculum, underpinning the ERA 1988, meets the requirements of the SDA. Both require schools to offer equal access to the same curriculum for girls and boys. Therefore, a curricular subject must be offered to girls and boys on exactly the same terms (Carr, 1989). However, whether intent will be reflected in practice is an issue that both Carr (1989) and Flintoff (1990) have commented upon. As Lees and Scott (1990) argue, 'In practice equal opportunities initiatives very often amount to little more than statements of intent' (p. 334). Furthermore, legislation relating to equality such as that provided by the ERA and the SDA, whilst offering a framework for behaviour, also offers, according to Talbot (1990), a somewhat 'negative interpretation of equality; it tells us what not to do, but fails to help us decide how we should behave towards people in an unequal society' (p. 104). However, legislation *per se* can do little to bring about changes in the attitudes of people, and Carr (1989) suggests that 'stereotyped attitudes and expectations (usually resulting in under-performance) remain a perennial worry. Low expectations and negative attitudes are deeply damaging' (p. 20). Hargreaves (1990) supports this view and offers an explanation when she suggests that liberal feminism has had a tendency to

> overlook the limitations of legal reform and to underestimate the strengths of entrenched resistance to changing attitudes. It is implausible to imagine that genuine equality will result from legal reforms when the power of men over women subtly permeates society or

to think that sport could be changed fundamentally by legislation which embodies gender as an organising principle.   (p. 290)

Thus, while legislation may intend to operate to eliminate unlawful sex discrimination, it cannot, of itself, resolve gender inequalities. Genuine equality for all pupils lies in the practices of the policy-makers, administrators, and those who teach in schools.

THE NOTION OF EQUALITY

Equality, as an issue in PE, needs to be seen in relation to other curricular subjects and in the context of entitlement. That is, equality should be an integral part of good educational practice and not an optional extra (see Flintoff, 1990; EOC, 1989). However, as Evans (1989) suggests, 'the concept and practice of equal opportunities is and has always been highly problematical for social and educational reformers' (p. 85). Byrne (1985) has argued that the 'weakness' of the United Kingdom's attempts to achieve educational equality is located in the difficulty in defining, in educational terms, exactly what is meant by equality. This echoes the sentiments of Benn (1979) who comments, in relation to comprehensive reorganization, that 'it was impossible to ensure equality of opportunity without a definition of those minimum opportunities which should be available to all boys and girls in any school called comprehensive' (cited in Evans, 1990, p. 143). Educational equality as a concept is, therefore, often referentially incomplete and inadequate and thus hinders the achievement of genuine equality. It is, perhaps, because it is rarely made clear what equality refers to (e.g. minimum levels of resourcing, good practice, outcome, access, opportunity) that there has evolved a number of diverse interpretations of the notion.

Williams (1962) suggests that the notion of equality is invoked when the question of 'distribution of, or access to, certain goods' arises (p. 120)—in this case PE and curricular provision. In an attempt to define equality, Byrne (1985) differentiates between *equality*: 'the condition of being equal in quantity, amount, value, intensity etc.' and *equity*: 'the quality of being equal or fair; impartiality' (p. 99). These definitions imply that equality and equity should be viewed as complementary rather than as alternatives. However, the problem remains as to how these concepts relate to curricular practice and provision within PE. There exists, in concept and intent, a number of different perspectives and interpretations of the notion of equality which ultimately shape and frame curricular provision and practice.

CONCERNS OVER EQUALITY ISSUES

It needs to be appreciated that moves towards equality may be met by resistance and viewed 'as tantamount to condoning mediocrity' (Tinning, 1990, p. 14). For example, the restructuring of education along comprehensive school lines in the late 1960s and early 1970s reflected a particular ideological interpretation of equality, yet pockets of resistance then[5] and today perceive such changes as a loss with respect to the lowering of standards. In relation to PE the more contemporary battle and debate over the 'new PE',[6] with its attendant ideology of 'physical education for all', has brought criticism upon the PE profession. This has come mainly from those outside the teaching profession (see Evans, 1989; Thomas, 1989; Sparkes, 1990a, 1990b), the popular press, media, national governing bodies (NGBs) and political sources, but also from sporting agencies such as the Central Council of Physical Recreation (CCPR). As Evans and Clarke (1988) argue, there are those who perceive that 'physical educationalists, like others in the educational world, are so caught up with fashionable egalitarian educational theories and practices that they are failing in their responsibility to the nation's economy, its national identity and sporting prestige' (p. 128).

New and 'trendy' PE policies are accused of threatening the attainment of standards and producing egalitarian mediocrity, representing for some not so much a reappraisal of educational priorities but an inversion of educational values. Essentially, attempts to initiate the process of equalizing, with its accompanying curriculum changes, can be perceived by some as a positive step forward. However, for others, such attempts are regarded as a threat to the *raison d'être* of PE since they are seen as responsible for the supposed declining standards in PE and sport. Hence, resistance to the idea of equality may be seen not so much as the rejection of the ideal of equality, but rather as the rejection of a particular principle of equality and its interpretation. In the case of PE, resistance has been seen to hinge on the belief that standards will fall and as such, may be understood as tension between equality and quality. It is, therefore, easy to see why equality issues are often presented as a polarization between elitist and egalitarian policies.

EQUALITY IN PHYSICAL EDUCATION: CONTRASTING INTERPRETATIONS

Equality of opportunity

This ideal may be understood in the sense of equality of opportunity for everyone in society to secure certain 'goods' and pivots round the question of access to education resources. However, as Talbot (1990) points out, access is not the same as opportunity. This is also emphasized by Williams (1962):

> Suppose that in a certain society great prestige is attached to membership of a warrior class, the duties of which require great physical strength. This class has in the past been recruited from certain wealthy families only but egalitarian reformers achieve a change in the rules, by which warriors are recruited from all sections of the society, on the results of a suitable competition. The effect of this, however, is that the wealthy families still provide virtually all the warriors, because the rest of the populace is so under-nourished by reason of poverty that their physical strength is inferior to that of the wealthy and well nourished. The reformers protest that equality of opportunity has not really been achieved; the wealthy reply that in fact it has, and that the poor now have the opportunity of becoming warriors—it is just bad luck that their characteristics are such that they do not pass the test. 'We are not,' they might say, 'excluding anyone *for* being poor; we exclude people for being weak, and it is unfortunate that those who are poor are also weak.'   (p. 126)

Clearly the concept of equality of opportunity is a complex one. For although equal *access* was offered, in that no one was denied access on the basis of class, the notion of equal opportunity cannot really be seen to exist because the economic, social, and cultural experiences of 'the poor' result in their less than equal opportunity for success. The notion of equality of opportunity in this respect is, therefore, quite hollow. Here, it is possible to draw a parallel with aspects of organizational practice in PE. For example, many schools have sought to provide equal opportunities through the provision of mixed-sex grouping. Unfortunately, as Scraton (1986) suggests, in practice this often means equal access to the 'male domain' (p. 89). She raises the issue that if this is so, then can we really claim to be offering equal opportunity if we ignore, and fail to challenge, the pervasive power of 'well-established differences in socialisation and primary schooling' (p. 89), or the limits imposed by National Governing Body legislation and regulations that restrict girls' access to, or participation in, certain activities in adolescence and adult life? For instance, in athletics in Britain, girls and women may not compete in the hammer, pole vault, triple jump, or steeplechase events. As a consequence, we need to be aware that in some situations (for example year 10 and 11 options) we may be offering equal access to an unequal situation, i.e. offering boys dance or girls football. For ultimately, as Walker (1988) suggests, 'in choosing groups and exercising options, people are not equal' (cited in Talbot, 1990, p. 106).

Equality—the same or equivalent treatment?

Following the previous line of argument it remains difficult to substantiate claims regarding equality of opportunity when the same criteria are applied to pupils irrespective of the fact that they come to PE differently predisposed and positioned to relate to the curriculum on offer. As Talbot (1990) maintains, 'to treat them all the same claim is both inoperable in practice and unequal in its effects' (p. 103). In emphasizing this point, Evans (1989) notes:

> if the starting line is uniform (if all pupils have access to the same PE curriculum) the arrival of the competitors in various states of fitness (social attributes, physical abilities, strengths, competencies, etc....) points to a prior race which has already been run in quite unequal circumstances. (p. 85)

This means that the same treatment in some contexts could be deemed educationally undesirable and unsound. However, it is important to differentiate between 'equal' as the same treatment across pupils of similar abilities, aptitudes, sex, race, etc., and 'equal' as the same treatment across, for instance, the full ability range. The first would represent good educational practice, the second the reverse. 'The same', however, could in educational terms desirably mean uniformity for all pupils with regard to a common core of curricular experience. The notion of equality of experience, represented in a common curriculum, is one favoured by those concerned with equal opportunities. However, as Arnot (1989) points out, this is 'a necessary, but not a *sufficient condition* to break down educational inequalities' (p. 7; my italics).

What might this mean for PE? At worst, curricular provision and practice could be based on an assimilationist model where the norm used is male, and where girls— according to Hargreaves (1990)—would find themselves 'co-opted into a male sphere of activity' (p. 302). Here the notion of equality is reflected in the need for girls to 'catch up', 'shape up' and 'measure up' to male standards. At best, it could mean that all pupils, both girls and boys, are offered a common curriculum of aesthetic, creative, competitive, cooperative and adventure activities which are the core of the same compulsory PE of all pupils, and where opportunity exists for all pupils to experience some measure of satisfaction, achievement and enjoyment. A convenient interpretation of equality is sometimes that of 'equal as equivalent rather than the same' (Vertinsky, 1983, p. 231). However, for girls and women this notion can be somewhat problematic due to the generally low position and prestige accorded to girls' and women's sports, activities and performance in the sporting status hierarchy. As Williams (1989) comments, 'netball is not equivalent to football, neither is rounders equivalent to cricket' (p. 150).

Equality and common humanity

Finally, the ideal of equality can be interpreted within the context of a set of beliefs that hold that *all* persons *are* equal or, if not, then all persons *should* be equal. What makes them equal for Williams (1962) is their 'common humanity' (p. 110), which entitles them to equality of respect and non-discrimination on the basis of their gender, class, race, ability, etc. More positively, such an ideal pivots round the importance of an equal consideration of pupils' needs and interests, with efforts needing to be made to value their experiences and to respect the way in which they may differently make sense of their world. The practical problem, of course, lies in how, within the curriculum practice of teachers, can it be achieved? Furthermore, such a conception of equality can serve to deflect attention away from the structures in society that permit and legitimize status, prestige, hierarchy, and—conversely—contempt and condescension.

THE PHYSICAL EDUCATION CURRICULUM AND TEACHING FOR EQUALITY

During the educational debate on equality and opportunity the subject area of PE came under the microscope because of the way in which it was organized and presented to pupils in schools. For example, Her Majesty's Inspectorate (HMI), reporting on curricular differences in schools in 1976, found that in junior schools separation for traditional games was common and that in most middle and secondary schools such a policy was also the norm. Despite the apparent trend towards mixed-sex grouping that characterized much of the organizational change in the teaching of PE to emerge from the 1980s, Scraton (1986) and Carrington and Leaman (1986) both reported that single-sex teaching remained the dominant organizational form. While there are exceptions, particularly in the case of mixed-sex grouping for options with the more senior pupils, for most of the time the boundaries between the activities defined as appropriate for girls and boys remain sharply drawn. In relation to this, Hargreaves (1986) reports a difference in activity emphasis for girls and boys in that the time spent in PE is distributed differently among the available activities, with girls spending proportionally more curriculum time than boys on the aesthetic and creative activities like gymnastics and dance and less time on major team games. Talbot (1986) also points to the differential provision when she comments that 'in many schools girls' PE is increasingly either an emulation of boys' PE (warts and all) or self conscious declaration of femininity through the adoption of activities like jazz dance, modern rhythmic gymnastics and synchronised swimming, all barred to boys' (p. 122). Such differences in curricular provision may have profound effects at both the overt and covert level in terms of the messages given to pupils with regard to gender-appropriate behaviour and attitudes. On the one hand, equality of access is not possible and both girls and boys may, therefore, have restricted opportunities to develop their potential in the games and aesthetic areas respectively. Alternatively, the separate and different experiences and opportunities made available may reinforce the ideologies, stereotypes and myths associated with femininity, masculinity, physical ability and capacity (see Scraton, 1986). In this sense, in PE the roots of inequality for girls and boys are embedded in history, tradition, and the socially constructed expectations, myths and ideologies that frame conventional and traditional curriculum organization, content, pedagogy, and assessment.

Whilst an historical perspective is beyond the scope of this chapter, and has been covered elsewhere,[7] it is crucial to understand the origins of the contemporary context of PE. In short, Hargreaves (1990) argues that the early model of sex role-stereotyping in PE accommodated to 'traditional biological assumptions' which were then reflected in the notion of 'feminine appropriate sports' and 'masculine appropriate sports' (p. 291). Equally, for teachers of PE their professional socialization reinforced these biological assumptions initiating them, via separate institutions, into different activities thereby promoting within the subject two quite different and qualitatively discrete subcultures. The legacies of such practice are still with us and provide a powerful influence upon the possibilities for the development of equality in PE. As Scraton (1986) suggests, if our teaching and efforts to teach for equality are not to remain 'underpinned by a tradition and ethos informed by sexist ideologies'(p. 88) then we cannot afford to ignore this historical legacy and must attempt to challenge it wherever possible.

INTENTION INTO PRACTICE: STRATEGIES FOR EQUALITY IN PHYSICAL EDUCATION

As Weiner (1985) reminds us: 'Expanding equal opportunities is not just a question of juggling resources or re-arranging option choices ... to liberalise access to an inadequate system might be acceptable in the short term but for more permanent change a major restructuring of all social institutions, including schools is needed' (p. 10). Differences in *how* such ideals may be implemented have led to different approaches towards achieving equality within PE. These different strategies, broadly speaking, often reflect an orientation or allegiance to one of the following stances.

The first of these, and within PE the dominant and 'common sense' strategy of the 1980s, has been an equal opportunities approach based on providing greater access for all pupils—both girls and boys—to physical activities where traditionally an activities gender-label has defined its participants. As mentioned earlier, curricular and extra-curricular initiatives, such as mixed-sex grouping, can be firmly located within this framework.

A second strategy has been defined by Hargreaves (1990) as that of 'separatism' which is similar in some respects to Scraton's (1986) notion of 'girl-centred' PE. These approaches stem from the belief that conventional gender relations and ideologies inhibit girls and women from maximizing their potential in PE and sports. As a consequence, advocates of this position argue for a girl-centred PE with separate access to masculinized sports in order to combat the well-established differences in socialization and to give girls and women the space, time, and opportunity to develop their physical potential. In practice this approach would manifest itself in a single-sex programme but with a changed content, thus widening the boundaries of acceptable female sporting activity and participation while reinforcing their experiences *as women*.

While it might appear that a separatist approach is incompatible with the inclusion of mixed-sex grouping and participation, a third approach is available that is under-pinned by the desire to move away from the dominant competitive sporting ethos. In this alternative model, according to Willis (1982),

> sport could be presented as a form of activity which emphasises human similarity and not dissimilarity, a form of activity which is not competitive and measured, a form of activity which expresses values which are indeed unmeasurable, a form of activity which is concerned with individual well-being and satisfaction rather than with comparison. In such a view of sport, differences between the sexes would be unimportant, unnoticed.
>
> (p. 143)

This conceptualization of sport and physical activity reflects more than just mixed participation in neutral or non-gendered activities or a greater balance between competitive and cooperative activities (cf. Williams, 1989). Rather, it represents a commitment to the idea of shared and cooperative activities where differences do not inhibit the pleasure and satisfaction to be derived from involvement. In this respect, Health-Related Fitness (HRF) as an integrated and integral element of the PE curriculum potentially offers great opportunities for the realization of this particular approach.

STRATEGIES FOR CHANGE: ORGANIZATION, CONTENT, PEDAGOGY, AND ASSESSMENT

When looking at effective strategies for change it is vital to view the PE curriculum in terms of its organization, content, pedagogy and assessment since an understanding of their interrelationship is essential if real, as opposed to superficial, change is to occur. For example, recent innovations within the PE curriculum such as HRF, the Games for Understanding approach, and mixed-sex grouping, that have emerged in response to a variety of political, curricular and pedagogical motivations, reflect significant changes in curricular organization and content. According to Evans and Clarke (1988) these initiatives function in many respects to 'refocus the emphasis in PE teaching' (p. 130). However, while a changed content or organization would seem to suggest that a 'new' or different curriculum has been introduced, Evans and Clarke highlight the limits of just changes of organization and curricular content.

Despite the not insignificant and substantial paradigmatic changes in content and organisation which had been effected by these teachers, there was very little pedagogical change
of a kind which could challenge or change the authority relationships of the classroom or
confront or alter the typical gendered attitudes and behaviours of children or indeed of
the teachers.   (p. 138)

Thus the changes that occurred existed only at a surface level and did not permeate to
a deep structural and ideological level, resulting in the phenomenon of innovation
without change.[8]

Organization

Equal access to the formal PE curriculum and extra-curricular activities, plus equal
opportunity for all pupils, depends heavily on how the curriculum is organized. In
particular, careful consideration must be given to the grouping of pupils. The key
principle governing how pupils are grouped for PE must be to ensure that all pupils
have the same opportunities to fulfil their potential with no pupils being excluded.

The belief that equality is impossible until boys and girls are taught together is a
prominent and currently fashionable notion, one that has tended to dominate thinking
on grouping issues. When introduced as part of a commitment to equality the strategy
of mixed-sex PE marks an important step forwards in the profession's thinking about
the teaching of PE, but in practice it appears from research[9] that such organizational
changes are often based on naïve assumptions and are consequently limited, and
possibly damaging, in their intended impact and outcome. The assumption that
mixed-sex grouping automatically equates with equality of opportunity is one that
currently prevails. However, this position is limited in its understanding of how
gender is conceptualized by teachers, pupils, and the wider society (see Talbot, 1990).
Organizational change *per se* does little to challenge the entrenched and hierarchical
sporting framework within which males and females operate. In seeing the 'problem'
as one of gaining access and having solved that by 'mixing and stirring', little further
attention is then paid to challenging the structure of physical activities for girls and
boys or the pedagogy required to counter the traditional and stereotyped expectation
of themselves and others or to support the organizational changes. The net effect can
be a bitter cocktail, one that can actually announce and reinforce the differences
rather than drawing attention to the similarities between girls and boys.

Within the PE profession there seems no consensus regarding how PE should or
could best be organized to facilitate equal opportunities for girls and boys. Equally,
opinion varies as to the effect on pupils and their learning of the process of mixed-sex
grouping. Research (see Turvey and Laws, 1988; Evans, 1989), more particularly in
the games area, tends to suggest that the process of mixed-sex grouping is not always a
positive experience for either girls or boys. The observed patterns of interaction
between pupils, and between pupils and teachers, demonstrate that there is not always
equal opportunity to learn or play. For example, Griffin (1989) reports that a 'masculine elitist competitive norm of participation pervades classes so that less competitive
and less skilled participants, girls and boys, are shunted to the side as more aggressive
students are allowed to dominate class games' (p. 227). Although this image raises
questions about the grouping of pupils within the mixed setting it is a scenario

reported by others. Bain (1990) suggests that patterns of interaction are heavily influenced by gender, with boy–girl interaction being characterized by verbal or physical hassling by boys with the latter controlling the behaviour of girls (also see Gilroy *et al.*, 1985; Mahoney, 1985). Furthermore, boys in mixed settings tend to dominate active participation as illustrated by Evans (1989). 'Only one girl, whose confidence and ability outshone that of all other boys and girls present, was in a position to contribute significantly to the lesson activity' (p. 85). Similarly, observations of pupil–teacher interaction in mixed settings reveal that gender may be a determining variable for gaining attention. Boys appear to receive more attention than girls (Turvey and Laws, 1988) which in effect reduces, and limits, the contact and interaction that the teacher has with girls.

Therefore, while the process of mixed-sex grouping may offer a common activity, the consequences for pupils of disparity and inequality in terms of experiences, teacher–pupil interaction, activity participation, and performance opportunities support the notion that girls do indeed 'lose out' and that mixed-sex groupings may be a negative and battering experience. These findings and observations raise a number of important issues for PE teachers, along with those involved in initial teacher education and those who provide in-service courses. These include:

1 Teachers and students need information and knowledge about the nature and impact of gender differences before they can attempt to effect strategies to overcome them.
2 Where offered, a common curriculum must be supported by other organizational and pedagogical forms and strategies to be effective.
3 Teachers need support to acquire the pedagogical skills and competencies to allow them to reorganize not only the forms of knowledge presented to pupils, but to allow a far more flexible structure and approach to grouping within lessons.

It would appear that some approaches to mixed-sex PE teaching may make equality of opportunity more of a reality than others and we should be wary of attempts to reduce the issue to just one of integration or segregation. Such an approach is in danger of throwing the baby out with the bathwater. Therefore, in essence, what is important is that we look more carefully at *when* we mix pupils, in terms of age, school phase, experience etc. We need to consider *what* activities and elements of activities within individual lessons are most appropriate for mixed-sex work. We need to think *how* we utilize grouping strategies either to bring pupils together or to work separately. On this issue we know from Scraton that 'mixed games produce problems of levels of participation and confidence' (cited in Turvey and Laws, 1988, p. 254) and that this is likely to be even more so for strongly gendered activities. Evans (1989), however, takes this issue a step further and identifies that within individual lessons in the more 'weakly framed' and styled phases (i.e. game situations), boys tend to dominate, control, and organize the activity. It may be, therefore, that in these particular situations the most effective way to achieve equality is to adopt a more sensitive and flexible grouping arrangement whereby pupils work apart. This refinement implies more than just the 'mix and stir' approach discussed and found wanting. Rather it introduces the different, but related, concept of co-educational PE on to the agenda.[10]

Segregation and separatism

As a strategy this does not have to compromise the principle of equality of opportunity, particularly when based on educational principles underpinned by the ultimate aim of integrating pupils. The decision to teach girls football in a separate group from the boys could be educationally justified by giving girls the confidence, experience, space and time to develop their potential, bearing in mind their previously limited experience of the game, and therefore, their comparative disadvantage *vis-à-vis* boys. The same could be argued for boys and dance.

Positive discrimination, according to Hargreaves (1990), may be yet another interpretation of separate provision where essentially the girl-focused organization would pivot round girls' experiences and the raising of the status of these. Provision of a 'closed space' represents the process by which girls can develop the confidence and motivation to participate and enjoy physical activity. The major weakness in the separatist model is that it tends to reaffirm gender stereotypes, perpetuate myths, and is underpinned by the view that only females can bring about a positive female atmosphere and ethos. Consequently, separatism and exclusionist strategies do not lie easily with the educational principles of integration and cooperation where pupils respect and value differences in order to share their learning.

Content

In attempting to provide equality in PE many of the issues relating to the appropriateness of curricular content, particularly in relation to heavily gendered activities and pupil grouping, have been raised. However, if we are to move forward towards genuine co-educational PE then it is important that in our selection of PE knowledge and pedagogy, we do not transmit specifically male (or for that matter female) definitions of what constitutes PE knowledge. In practice this may require teachers to reselect and repackage traditional forms of knowledge. For example, in the early years of secondary schooling, or before, a principles of games course taught in mixed groups could cover the basic principles of invasive, striking, and net games through the medium of 'neutral' activities such as hockey, softball, and tennis respectively. Furthermore, as Daley (1990) argues, there would be a need to offer a balanced diet in terms of competitive/cooperative elements, individual/team activities and technical/creative experiences. In the provision and blocking of option choices PE teachers need to be aware of and sensitized to the hidden and subtle pressures that may operate to channel pupils towards selecting the activity traditionally offered to their sex. Resources and facilities permitting, option programmes should offer a wide and diverse range of activities to create the opportunities for pupils to experience success and enjoyment. Thought should also be given to when options should be offered in relation to the whole PE curriculum. Traditionally, school PE programmes have offered mixed options towards the end of the pupils' compulsory schooling career when, according to Carrington and Williams (1988), gender differences in attitudes to sport are already well established. Finally, regular and thorough evaluation of the curriculum is also required to ensure that it meets the needs of the pupils and to monitor the relationship between intent and practice with a view to establishing where, if at all, any breakdown occurs.

Pedagogy

Teachers' pedagogy and behaviour is often mediated by the social structure of schools, personal philosophy, and the impact of professional socialization. In view of this, Bain (1990) suggests that their behaviour is often an 'expression of tacit beliefs' (p. 36), and, somewhat significantly, Pratt (1985) has reported that a large percentage of PE teachers are unsympathetic to the notion of equality of opportunity in education. Such findings may help to account for Bain's (1990) assertion that 'there is little indication that the underlying conceptualisations of gender or sport are changing in physical education programmes' (p. 35). As such, the critical questions with regard to the provision of equality in PE include: What is it that pupils learn through the ritual and processes of PE? What are the messages they are receiving through both the formal and hidden curriculum? How can teachers, through their pedagogy, support organizational change to make equality of opportunity more of a reality than it so far is?

Turvey and Laws (1988) have illustrated how teachers themselves can ultimately affect and influence not only the perceptions of the pupils as to their lesson, but also their levels of participation. Teachers who continually direct their attention to the boys for demonstrations and answers unconsciously transmit messages to the pupils about their abilities. There are a number of issues here that can have a bearing on teachers' practice. First, in the more practical sense of pupil–teacher interaction, teachers perhaps need to raise their awareness of their own behaviour and examine this in terms of the role models that they present and encourage pupils to aspire to. Are girls and boys asked to demonstrate equally both in terms of the number of occasions and in the tasks required of them? Do display areas (notice-boards) and forums (assemblies) portray equally, and positively reflect, the image of girls' and boys' achievement in sport and physical activity in general? Or, do they implicitly convey something about hierarchy: that girls' and women's sporting achievements tend to be less valued than those of men and boys?

The second issue to emerge is that of teachers' commitment to the principle of equality of opportunity and their desire and ability to reflect critically on their conception of gender and the impact of this on their own practice. This is an important point because if we wish to encourage and promote greater equality within and outside the school, then teachers need to be in a position to equip pupils to think critically and be aware of hidden agendas. For Bain (1990), emancipatory pedagogy requires that pupils be full and active participants in 'critical discourse in which assertions about knowledge and values are viewed as problematic' (p. 36). For the PE teacher this requires a commitment to this area coupled with the knowledge and confidence to tackle some of the social issues and assumptions related to PE and sport.

Teachers of all subjects need to have a variety of different teaching styles within their armoury and PE teachers are no different in this respect. It is most unlikely that policies relating to equality of opportunity can be effective if teaching is undertaken via the medium of one particular style. Reference has already been made to the fact that some styles and approaches do appear to be more conducive than others to rendering the possibility of equal opportunities a more likely outcome in PE lessons. The point here, however, is that teachers need to be in a position to engage alternative styles in the appropriate context and to recognize the need to do so. Whilst some activities may be best approached through group work, discovery, and problem solving—in which pupils are encouraged to learn from one another and share in this process—in others, greater benefit may be derived from, and call for, a more teacher-directed approach where the teacher is the major resource.

Whilst the ability to utilize the spectrum of teaching styles is important, teacher–pupil verbal communication and interaction is a crucial element in a teacher's pedagogy. Sexism is often unconsciously conveyed through language. Phrases and cliches such as the following: 'don't be a wimp . . . I'll send you to play with the girls', or boys remonstrated with for 'behaving like a load of girls', and requests for 'strong boys to move the goalposts' or 'girls to fold the bibs and boys to carry the equipment', often provide an insight into the assumptions and attitudes that are taken for granted regarding the division of labour and certain conceptions of masculine and feminine physical capacity. Teachers need to be very conscious of their use of language and how they respond to girls and boys for it is easy to deride a pupil's achievement or perpetuate stereotypical conceptions of gender-appropriate behaviour and capacity. Similarly, teachers' responses to tasks set in PE—for example in gymnastics—should avoid rewarding boys only for strength and girls for poise, grace, and flexibility. Equally, tasks involving themes or topics, for instance in the area of dance 'machines' or 'war', should be appropriate, accessible, and broad enough to be within the experience of all pupils. When pupils can relate to a task and judge it as being appropriate they will feel secure and are more likely to work with confidence. What they consider alien and inappropriate they will be more likely to avoid and may, therefore, have limited choice and underachieve. Clearly, in mixed-sex grouping, overly masculine or feminine content should, therefore, be avoided.

Consistency, as a principle, would represent good pedagogical practice and this may manifest itself in a number of different areas. In departmental terms, a consistent approach to the ideal of equality of opportunity is vital. Similarly, consistency in terms of both sexes receiving the same time allowance for PE each week, consistency in terms of expectations regarding kit, safety, and non-participation pre- and post-lesson rituals such as lining up and showering, etc. Consistency in terms of girls and boys sharing the facilities equally during curricular and extra-curricular periods, and receiving equal resourcing.

While each PE department will need to find the best possible arrangement and solution for their own circumstances, in schools where departments are officially separate or operate separately unofficially, there will most likely be a need for compromise if the principle of equality through consistency is to succeed. This, a negotiated strategy, should be driven by the need to accommodate pupils' needs more sensitively. As an example, in mixed-sex grouping kit requirements may need to be relaxed within the framework of safety and appropriateness to allow pupils to wear tracksuits.

Assessment

Many of the issues relating to task setting, content, and language, etc., have already been considered. However, as Murphy (1989) argues, assessment is often underpinned by the assumption that the results can be interpreted in terms of what was intended to be assessed. Such a view ignores the fact that differences in pupils' performance may be related to variables such as experience and, in the case of PE, physiological and anatomical factors such as size and strength. While studies tend to suggest that the differences within the sexes are greater than those between them, it raises a number of implications for the assessment of pupils in mixed-sex grouping. Where sex differences are significant to performance, an inflexible and insensitive approach could result in what Evans (1989) has described as the 'invidious ranking of males against females according to standards which, for physiological or anatomical reasons many of the latter are unable to attain' (p. 87). In such a situation there is a clear need for the assessment of performance to be differentiated in order to promote equality.

Many forms of assessment in PE are based on subjective observations of pupils' performance and participation. These subjective judgements of pupils' capacity are often deeply affected and mediated by stereotypical expectations of gender-appropriate behaviours. Additionally, with the more recent and widespread inclusion of examinations and theoretical elements as a form of assessment in PE, there is a need for PE teachers to address the issues of presentation and style of worksheets and assigments in their planning for equality. In particular the language used and any illustrations should promote positive images of girls and boys in sport and physical activity. Questions should provide differentiation in order to cater for groups of different abilities and experience.

COMMENT

For many schools, although the notion of equality and opportunity is not a new one, the implementation of such an ideal and all that it entails means that in reality the success of equal opportunities initiatives are often contingent on the drive and energy of individual teachers. Unfortunately, in many cases, intention does not manifest itself in practice. This is not to decry the work of individual teachers, but rather to illustrate that what is needed is a collective response to equal opportunities and, in my view, teachers have a professional responsibility to persevere in this respect. Comfort may be found in the knowledge that change of any sort is never easy; often uncomfortable, unsettling and threatening (see Sparkes, Chapter 2 this volume). Indeed, it would be dishonest and non-productive to suggest otherwise. Real change necessitates the learning of new skills in relation to the areas of pupil–teacher interaction, organization and assessment. In view of this, we must see change as a gradual and long-term process.

Finally, the task of effecting equality of opportunity in schools needs to be built on a foundation where:

1   Commitment and support from the LEA, school, department, and individuals within is total. In PE departments any changes need to involve *all* members because initiatives are more likely to receive support if teachers are encouraged to contribute and develop a sense of ownership towards changes.
2   There is support from an equal opportunities policy that is communicated to all staff and where, ideally, the PE department is represented on any committees.

Policies, plans and actions need to be part of a coordinated approach and not just isolated 'pocket' developments.
3 The effects of policy and practice are carefully monitored, evaluated, and incorporated into any subsequent planning and practice.
4 There is support in the form of inservice provision.

Opportunities and support teaching should be available for teachers to acquire the professional and managerial skills that will facilitate a well-grounded approach to teaching for equality.

Additionally, recognizing that change is a developmental process in raising awareness, developing understanding, and in planning strategies and approaches, PE teachers need *time* and *space* to accommodate to these changes. Furthermore, in deciding the best way forward, teachers may need to identify *priority issues* and areas and then to focus on these rather than trying to tackle all the issues at once. Addressing issues of equality will not be easy. However, as PE moves into the 1990s, it is essential that equality as an educational concern remains a central issue and is viewed as a challenge rather than just another problem area. Education has the power to promote social justice, but to this end it must enlist and have the active support of all teachers, parents, governors, and those in the wider community. Equal opportunities in the formal and hidden curriculum are not a luxury, but are synonymous with good educational practice and provision. This is the professional challenge and responsibility of all concerned with education as we move towards the twenty-first century.

NOTES

1 For example, the Girls into Science and Technology Project (Kelly *et al.*, 1984), the Swann Report (DES, 1985), and the Warnock Report (DES, 1978) all reflect the raised consciousness and broadening concept of inequality and educational disadvantage.
2 Evidence of this is also provided by Clarricoates (1980), Delamont (1980), Stanworth (1981), Spender (1982), Kelly *et al.* (1984), Gilroy *et al.* (1985), Turvey and Laws (1988).
3 See the celebrated Theresa Bennett case in 1978 reported in Vertinsky (1983, p. 243); also see Pannick (1983, p. 11).
4 Title IX refers to the 1972 United States federal law designed to make gender discrimination illegal in education.
5 See for example the writings and voices of right-wing groups as reflected in 'Black Papers' 1, 2, and 3 edited by Cox and Dyson.
6 See Evans and Clarke (1988) and Evans (1990) for a more detailed discussion.
7 For a socio-historical analysis of the development of PE and sport for girls and women see Fletcher (1984), Scraton (1986), McCrone (1988), and Kirk (1990).
8 See Chapter 1 by Sparkes in this volume for a more detailed discussion of the phenomenon of innovation without change.
9 Evans *et al.* (1987), Carrington and Leaman (1986), Turvey and Laws (1988).
10 See Evans (1989, p. 86) for a further discussion and conceptual clarification.

REFERENCES

Arnot, M. (1989) Crisis or challenge: equal opportunities and the National Curriculum. *NUT Review* **3**, autumn, 7–13.

Bain, L. (1990) A critical analysis of the hidden curriculum in physical education. In D. Kirk and R. Tinning (eds), *Physical Education, Curriculum and Culture: Critical Issues in the Contemporary Crisis*, pp. 23–42. London: Falmer Press.

Benn, C. (1979) Elites versus equals: the political background of educational reform. In D. Rubenstein (ed.), *Education and Equality*, pp. 191–206. Harmondsworth: Penguin.

Byrne, E. (1985) Equality or equity: a European overview? In M. Arnot (ed.), *Race and Gender Equal Opportunities Policies in Education*, pp. 97–112. Oxford: Pergamon Press.

Carr, L. (1989) Equal opportunities—policy and legislation after ERA. *NUT Review* **3**, autumn, 19–23.

Carrington, B. and Leaman, O. (1986) Equal opportunities and physical education. In J. Evans (ed.), *Physical Education, Sport and Schooling*, pp. 265–79. London: Falmer Press.

Carrington, B. and Williams, T. (1988) Patriarchy and ethnicity: the link between school physical education and community leisure activities. In J. Evans (ed.), *Teachers, Teaching and Control in Physical Education*, pp. 83–96. London: Falmer Press.

Clarricoates, K. (1980) The Importance of being Ernest . . . Tom . . . Jane. The perception and characterisation of gender conformity and gender deviation in primary schools. In R. Deem (ed.), *Schooling for Women's Work*, pp. 26–41. London: Routledge & Kegan Paul.

Cox, C. and Dyson, A. (eds) (1969) *Black Paper One: The Fight for Education*. London: The Critical Quarterly Society.

Cox, C. and Dyson, A. (eds) (1969) *Black Paper Two: The Crisis in Education*. London: The Critical Quarterly Society.

Cox, C. and Dyson, A. (eds) (1970) *Black Paper Three: Goodbye Mr Short*. London: The Critical Quarterly Society.

Daley, D. (1990) *Multicultural Issues in Physical Education*. Cambridgeshire County Council.

Delamont, S.(1980) *Sex Roles and the School*. London: Methuen.

DES (1975) *Curricular Differences for Boys and Girls: Education Survey, 21*. London: HMSO.

DES (1978) *Special Educational Needs* (Warnock Report). London: HMSO.

DES (1981) *The School Curriculum*. London: HMSO.

DES (1985) *Education for All* (Swann Report). London: HMSO.

EOC (1989) *Formal Investigation Report: Initial Teacher Training in England and Wales*. June, EOC.

Evans, J. (1987) Teaching for equality in physical education? The limits of the new PE. Paper presented to the Ethnography and Inequality Conference, St Hilda's College, Oxford 1987.

Evans, J. (1989) Swinging from the crossbar: equality and opportunity in the physical education curriculum. *British Journal of Physical Education* **20**, 84–7.

Evans, J. (1990) Defining a subject: the rise and rise of the new PE? *British Journal of Sociology of Education* **11**, 155–69.

Evans, J. and Clarke, G. (1988) Changing the face of physical education. In J. Evans (ed.), *Teachers, Teaching and Control in Physical Education*, pp. 125–43. London: Falmer Press.

Evans, J., Lopez, S., Duncan, M., and Evans, M. (1987) Some thoughts on the political and pedagogical implications of mixed sex grouping in the physical education curriculum. *British Educational Research Journal* **13**, 59–71.

Fletcher, S. (1984) *Women First*. London: Athlone Press.

Flintoff, A. (1990) Physical education, equal opportunities and the National Curriculum: crisis or challenge. *Physical Education Review* **13**, 85–100.

Gilroy, S., Graydon, J., and Webb, S. (1985) Mixed physical education in the lower secondary school—an evaluation. Paper presented to 28th ICHPER Conference, England. *Conference proceedings*, pp. 185–90.

Goddard-Spear, M. (1984) Sex bias in science teachers' ratings of work and pupils' characteristics. *European Journal of Science Education* **6**, 369–77.

Griffin, P. (1989) Gender as a socialising agent in physical education. In T. Templin and P, Schempp (eds), *Socialization into Physical Education: Learning to Teach*, pp. 219–33. Indianapolis: Benchmark Press.

Hargreaves, J. (1986) *Sport, Power and Culture*, pp. 161–81. Cambridge: Polity Press.

Hargreaves, J. (1990) Gender on the sports agenda. *International Review for Sociology of Sport* **2**, 287–305.

Kelly, A., Whyte, J., and Smail, B. (1984). *Girls into Science and Technology* (GIST). University of Manchester.

Kirk, D. (1990) Defining the subject: gymnastics and gender in British physical education. In D. Kirk and R. Tinning (eds), *Physical Education, Curriculum and Culture: Critical Issues in the Contemporary Crisis*, pp. 43–66. London: Falmer Press.

Lees, S. and Scott, M. (1990) Equal opportunities: rhetoric or action. *Gender and Education* **2**, 333–43.

McCrone, K. (1988) *Sport and the Physical Emancipation of English Women, 1870–1914*. London: Routledge.

Mahoney, P. (1985) *Schools For The Boys? Co-education Reassessed*. Hutchinson.

Murphy, P. (1989) Assessment and gender. *NUT Review* **3**, autumn, 37–41.

Pannick, D. (1983) *Sex Discrimination in Sport*. EOC.

Pratt, J. (1985) The attitude of teachers. In J. Whyte *et al.*, *Girl Friendly Schooling*, pp. 24–43. London: Methuen.

Scraton, S. (1986) Images of femininity and the teaching of girls' physical education. In J. Evans (ed.), *Physical Education, Sport and Schooling*, pp. 71–94. London: Falmer Press.

Smail, B. (1984) *Girl Friendly Science: Avoiding Sex Bias In The Curriculum*. York: Longmans/School Council.

Sparkes, A. (1990a) The changing nature of teachers' work: reflecting on governor power in different historical periods. *Physical Education Review* **13**, 39–47.

Sparkes, A. (1990b) The emerging relationship between physical education teachers and school governors: a sociological analysis. *Physical Education Review* **13**, 128–37.

Spender, D. (1982) *Invisible Women: The Schooling Scandal*. London: Writers and Readers Publishing Co-operative.

Stanworth, M. (1981) *Gender and Schooling: A Study of Sex Divisions in the Classroom*. London: WRRCP.

Talbot, M. (1986) Gender and physical education. *British Journal of Physical Education* **17**, 120–22.

Talbot, M. (1990) Equal opportunities and physical education. In N. Armstrong (ed.), *New Directions in Physical Education* 1, pp. 101–20. Champaign, IL: Human Kinetics.

Thomas, S. (1989) Making sense of the public image of the 'new' physical education. In C. Raymond (ed.), *Physical Education Today*, Perspectives 41, pp. 4–13. School of Education, University of Exeter.

Tinning, R. (ed.) (1990) *Ideology and Physical Education: Opening Pandora's Box*. Geelong: Deakin University Press.

Turvey, J. and Laws, C. (1988) Are girls losing out? The effects of mixed sex grouping on girls' performance in physical education. *British Journal of Physical Education* **19**, 253–5.

Vertinsky, P. (1983) The evolving policy of equal curricular opportunity in England: a case study of the implementation of sex equality in physical education. *British Journal of Educational Studies* **3**, 229–51.

Walker, J. (1988) The way men act: dominant and subordinate male cultures in an inner city school. *British Journal of Sociology of Education* **9**, 3–18.

Weiner, G. (ed.) (1985) *Just a Bunch of Girls*. Milton Keynes, Open University.

Williams, A. (ed.) (1989) *Issues in Physical Education for the Primary Years*, pp. 145–59. Lewes: Falmer Press.

Williams, B. (1962) The idea of equality. In P. Laslett and W. Runciman (eds), *Philosophy, Politics and Society* (second series), pp. 110–31. Oxford: Blackwell.

Willis, P. (1982) Women in sport in ideology. In J. Hargreaves (ed.) *Sport, Culture and Ideology*, pp. 117–35. London: Routledge & Kegan Paul.

Chapter 5

Mainstreaming Physical Education

Geoffrey Meek

On the playing fields of England can be found two scenarios. They are both physical education (PE) lessons, but this is where the similarity ends. Lesson A is a 'games' lesson where the PE teacher has an all-boys group and the activity is rugby. The boys, directed by the teacher, are learning to tackle. The element of tackling they are attempting requires them to kneel and the occasional complaint about dirty knees is countered by the time-honoured mention of showers and character building. One boy is heard to say that he wishes he was Robert. Up to that point everyone had forgotten about Robert and everyone looks over to where Robert is sitting and watching. Robert is idly throwing a rugby ball from hand to hand and is sitting in a wheelchair. Robert is not taking part because rugby is the activity on the games curriculum for this half-term. Rugby has always been a part of Robert's school curriculum and so Robert has to sit out. Robert is excluded because the curriculum has not been adapted to meet Robert's needs.

Lesson B is an outside PE lesson. A mixed group have been set the task of finding as many ways of getting free to receive a pass in an invasion game with netball as the activity. Jane, Kevin, Sally, and Peter are working in a group of four. Peter is trying to get free from Kevin while Jane passes the ball to Peter and Sally receives it from him. Kevin seems to be able to cover every pass when suddenly Peter gets free and Jane bounce-passes the ball into Peter's path, Peter catches it and passes it on to Sally. Although Kevin is annoyed at letting the pass by him, Peter is quick to point out that Kevin was always going to intercept the ball if it goes in the air, 'I'm sitting down, remember?'. Peter has been so successfully mainstreamed that Kevin had forgotten about Peter's lack of height due to his wheelchair!

Two differing lessons, but only one will be the PE lesson of the future, only one can expect to effectively reach the requirements of the Education Acts of 1981 and 1988, and only one comes close to achieving the expectations of the National Curriculum Council (1989) who indicated that 'All pupils share the right to a broad and balanced curriculum' (p. 1). The extent to which all pupils share this right in the same setting is the principle behind mainstreaming. The extent to which physical educators can create the conditions so that all pupils can exercise this right is the focus of this chapter. A paradigm is presented which addresses and identifies the conditions needed to facilitate mainstreaming successfully. The concept of a paradigm for mainstreaming decision-making is not new (Broadhead, 1982, 1985); however, the proposed paradigm that I will focus on identifies those factors that facilitate the implementation, maintenance, and augmentation of mainstreaming. The final section of the chapter stresses that for the facilitator paradigm to be fully effective mainstreaming of PE should be for every child, and consequently that the scenario of Lesson A should become a thing of the past rather than an integral part of a contemporary PE curriculum.

The Education Act (1981) redefined the provision of education to special populations and introduced the concept of special educational need for individual children. A child with a special educational need has a learning difficulty that requires a special educational provision to be made. This definition incorporates the view that a learning difficulty is based on significant individual differences from the majority of children of a similar age or that the child may have a disability which either prevents or hinders the utilization of educational facilities of a kind generally provided in schools. The arrangement by educational authorities of additional or otherwise different educational provision made generally for children of a similar age defines special educational provision and should be in ordinary schools as far as is reasonably practicable (Humberside Policy Document, 1988).

Mainstreaming is part of a process or continuum of integration. Integration involves social, educational, or recreational provision whereby individuals participate and enjoy experiences similar to their non-disabled peers and in the least restrictive, yet appropriate, environment. Groves (1985) highlighted the notion of the least restrictive, yet appropriate, environment through six levels of integration from complete mainstreaming (level 1) to level 6 where the child is in a residential special school. The intervening levels involve decreasing time allocations of special programme support. Currently, not all individual pupils with special educational needs are or can be completely mainstreamed, as the Lesson A scenario implies. Indeed, although Robert's PE teacher may argue that Robert is mainstreamed—certainly he is in a mainstreamed group—he is not receiving mainstreamed teaching. Such a dichotomy is a major failing of lessons that are traditionally based, such as Lesson A, since much of what Lesson A characterizes is an elitist, subject/sport-centred activity and, as such, cannot meet the child's special educational needs and certainly cannot accommodate the shared rights of every pupil to a broad and balanced curriculum.

Accommodating the shared rights of every pupil to a broad and balanced curriculum is the basis upon which a facilitator paradigm or model is developed in the next section. The model presented addresses issues related to the implementation, maintenance, and augmentation of mainstreaming of PE programmes.

A FACILITATOR MODEL FOR MAINSTREAMING PE

Before identifying the facilitators a number of precursors to success must be highlighted:

1   Every facilitator can, by being rejected or by not being effectively introduced, act as a barrier to success.

2   Every facilitator must be taken into account when implementing a mainstreamed individual.

3   Facilitators can be assigned to primary, secondary (Watkinson and Bentz, 1985) and tertiary (Meek, 1986) roles. Primary facilitators are those which can directly influence a student's initial placement or the implementation of mainstreaming in physical education. Secondary facilitators directly influence the progress of the student once mainstreamed—maintaining mainstreaming! And tertiary facilitators are those that can have an indirect influence upon mainstreaming through either primary or secondary facilitators.

Table 5.1. *The facilitator model for mainstreaming PE.*

Primary	Secondary	Tertiary
Individual personality of the mainstreamed child	Attitudes of teachers	Professional preparation
The nature of the disability	Teacher perception of success with mainstreamed students	Level of administrative support
PE facilities	Classroom organization and practice	Community and post-school involvement
The law	Specific physical activities within the curriculum	
Parental involvement		
Preparation of disabled student to enter mainstreamed environments	Communication between educators	
	Age and year levels of schooling	
Teaching models and presentation strategies	Teacher–student interactions	
Flexibility of the school to allow adaptive instruction	The non-disabled child	
	Relative competences of the disabled and non-disabled	
	Extent of support personnel in PE	
	Type and size of school	

The purpose of assigning primary, secondary, and tertiary roles is to focus the physical educator upon issues and decisions that need to be made at various stages of the mainstreaming process.

Primary facilitators for mainstreaming PE

Individual personality of the mainstreamed child

All too often the centre of attention is not the child *per se*, but the disability. Without doubt the nature of the disability is important, but of more importance is the child's personality, since this will ultimately determine whether relationships to peers and teachers provide a successful basis for mainstreaming.

The nature of the disability

Swann (1985) identified sensory disability categories as being successfully mainstreamed, whilst moderate and severe learning disabled and children with behaviour problems remain segregated. Winzer (1984), in a Canadian study, saw 'the disabled child as most favoured, the mentally retarded the least favoured' (p. 23). Even allowing for different cultural contexts such findings suggest that whatever form the disability takes the fact remains that the nature of the disability influences the extent to which mainstreaming occurs. Therefore, the nature of the disability is a key issue that needs to be considered. However, this issue should not be viewed in isolation and needs to be considered in relation to other personal characteristics of the individual, such as personality, interests, motivations and, most importantly, abilities.

The PE facilities and equipment

Are the gymnasium, its equipment, the playing fields and hard areas capable of being used by the mainstreamed child? The physical educator, via capitation, the ordering and/or modifying of equipment and awareness of accessibility into the physical education environment, has a major role to play with regard to this issue. Watkinson and Bentz (1985) studying mainstreaming of the physically disabled identified indoor barriers as: stairs/steps with no ramp; multistoreyed schools with no elevator; and no wheelchair access to locker or changing rooms and gymnasiums. Outdoor barriers were identified as: soft surfaces, curbs or steps to play areas; and no hard open surfaces. By providing a ramp for wheelchair access, for example, these barriers can be overcome. Dismantling each barrier, however, must be related to the separate needs of individuals in the school and unfortunately, in a climate of scarce resources, the tendency has been for schools and local education authorities to give the upgrading of buildings and equipment a low priority. It remains that if mainstreaming is to be supported resources need to be made available.

The law

Enactments and legal precedent dictate many decisions that will be made regarding mainstreaming. However, enactments such as the Education for All Handicapped Children Act (1975) and the Education Acts of 1981 and 1988 have processes and clauses by which teachers, parents, and governors can influence and shape the extent of mainstreaming. In the UK there is an increasing likelihood that the shape of mainstreaming will be determined by litigation especially with parental choice of schools and parental consultation and rights of appeal over 'in-house' and formal professional assessment and consultations. The legal challenge for mainstreaming is likely to centre on the determination of the efficient use of resources by schools and the ability of the school to meet the child's special educational needs. At present, litigation is not as widespread in Britain as in America where successful mainstreaming of mildly disabled students has led parents of severely disabled students to challenge and win the legal right for their children to be mainstreamed (Lehr and Haubrich, 1986), but it remains likely that the American experience may well cross the Atlantic. Therefore, the law, as a primary facilitator, will become more important in the implementation of mainstreaming.

Parental involvement

The extent to which parents become involved in the placement process is a primary facilitator and takes the form of litigation or representation to the local authority, but parental involvement goes beyond legal aspects related to mainstreaming. Parents play a major role in assisting the pastoral system of any school and the physical educator should develop these links with special reference to PE, especially for a child being mainstreamed.

No other subject has such an opting-out system as the excuse note or request and parents of a disabled child may decide to use or abuse this system for their own child due to their own memories of PE or because of the overt physical nature of the subject. PE is a subject where physical differences and skill levels are on public display. Failing to catch a ball can be noticed by the whole class, whereas not being able to read or write correctly is generally more concealable, thus parents may decide to over-protect their child from the potentially adverse situations found in PE. The negative aspect of parental involvement that opting out entails requires physical educators to be prepared to sell PE through the benefits that it can bring—this may be only possible in a Lesson B-style scenario—and also to be prepared to harness parents as very knowledgeable support teachers for their child, since this allows the parents first-hand experience of the curriculum and makes parent involvement a very positive facilitator to mainstreaming.

Preparation of disabled students to enter mainstreamed environments

Upgrading—i.e. to minimize the differences between disabled and non-disabled persons before mainstreaming occurs—of fitness and skill levels of all disabled students would considerably alleviate any problems of integrating children into a new environment. In the Cross-Canada Survey (Watkinson and Bentz, 1985) 60 per cent of the physical educators did not think that upgrading was a necessary precursor to mainstreaming, which immediately raises questions as to the awareness of physical educators of what is attempted in other educational and special educational environments.

Teaching models and presentation strategies

What is taught and how it is presented are part of a fundamental debate in physical education generally and mainstreaming further heightens the importance of the decisions made with regard to pedagogy. However, the possibility remains that the effects of a bad programme can be outweighed by the combined positive effects of all the other facilitators of the model, but this should not distract or lessen the need to implement effective teaching strategies. Gillet (1982) indicates 'the mainstreaming model chosen means assessing and then meeting the very special needs of the exceptional children' (p. 12). Meeting the needs of all children, including exceptional children, will require greater emphasis on varied teaching styles and methodology (Mosston, 1981).

Closely linked to teaching styles are presentation strategies. Jowsy (1990) provides four differing presentation strategies that can allow for a challenging and balanced mainstream programme in PE. The four strategies are: adapted lessons where everyone is working on the same adapted activity; parallel lessons where different activities are performed in the same environment; alternative lessons where different activities are provided for a small group, including non-disabled children as well; and lessons at alternative facilities, such as sports centres or neighbouring special schools.

With the acceptance of such teaching style and presentation developments the PE curriculum will become accessible and diverse enough to accommodate a mainstreamed child without major last minute alterations to existing structures and activities. If this is achieved every individual regardless of ability should be able to feel unrestricted and comfortable in physical education.

Flexibility of the school to allow adaptive instruction

This facilitator focuses attention on the parental right of choice of schools. Schools and physical education departments, by what is officially included or even excluded from the curriculum, will influence parent's choice of schools. Similarly the school's past track record with mainstreamed children will also influence parental choice.

Secondary facilitators for mainstreaming PE

Attitudes of teachers

Teachers' attitudes, according to Winzer (1984), 'may be a far more important dimension in ultimately determining success of mainstreaming than curricula or administrative strategies' (p. 23). This view may have some validity judged on the plethora of literature concerned with teachers' attitudes (Horne, 1983; Zigmond *et al.*, 1985; McEvoy *et al.*, 1984; Hoover and Cessna, 1984), and yet teachers' attitudes remain a complex issue to the extent that Macmillan *et al.* (1974) claim 'the research to date does not reflect sufficient appreciation for the complexity of the dynamics of how the attitudes operate' (p. 260). This complexity is due to a number of studies assuming that attitudes predict behaviour (Ajzen and Fishbein, 1980); however, a review of the attitude–behaviour relationship literature indicates that the situation is not as clear-cut (Meek, 1987). Despite an overemphasis on the attitude–behaviour assumption there is no doubt that teachers' attitudes play a major role in the equation determining mainstreaming success, but not to the extent of Winzer's claim.

Teacher perception of success with mainstreamed students

Larrivee and Cook (1979), in analysing a number of school-based variables, found that teachers' perception of degree of success with mainstream students was an influential determinant of effective mainstreaming. Teachers' perceptions are due, according to Larrivee and Cook, to information levels about disabled individuals, the specific skill acquisition and knowledge base of disabled individuals, and previous contact and experience with exceptional children. The factors influencing teachers' perceptions are essential elements to assist teachers gain success in any mainstream environment and must be found in both pre- and in-service teacher training.

Classroom organization and practice

The extent to which mainstreamed students participate in PE is as much an indication of classroom organization and practice as it is of curriculum content and development. In the Cross-Canada survey (Watkinson and Bentz, 1985) it was found from a total of 336 respondents that only 19 per cent of respondents with mainstreamed students in their classes had these children participate in all activities; 67 per cent organized their lessons in such a way that mainstreamed students participated in some activities; 9.2 per cent of teachers reported that special physical education classes were introduced; 8.6 per cent of respondents had children attend but not participate; and 1.25 per cent of teachers reported that physically disabled children did not attend at all. What is interesting to note are the differences in what physical educators considered as mainstreaming within their classes, since these discrepancies undermine the mainstreaming process. Obviously the nature of the physical activity being taught plays a part, however, Watkinson and Bentz's (1985) results suggest that not even the presence of a physically disabled child can interrupt what Sparkes (1986) termed 'the separate world of the classroom' (p. 167), where the teacher still controls what happens in the gymnasium or out on the field. Therefore, classroom organization and practice are likely to delay and impede any initiated changes for mainstreaming due to teacher autonomy.

Specific physical activities within the curriculum

Watkinson and Bentz (1985) analysed the extent to which the activities offered in the curriculum allowed full participation by physically handicapped children. Dividing responses into five categories (participates fully, participates in a special active role, participates in a special non-active role, participates as an observer, does not participate) they found that only aquatics, floor hockey (a gym-based derivative of ice hockey), dance, fitness, tenpin bowling, and children's games (unspecified) had full participation reported by 30 per cent of PE teachers. Conversely archery, curling, golf, ice hockey, skating, skiing, tennis, weight-lifting, and wrestling all had no participation at all reported by 40 per cent of PE teachers. Although the term physical disability can include a host of disabilities and ranges of movement problems, concern must be expressed as to the extent to which mainstreaming is attempted and achieved. This concern can be further highlighted by responses for aquatics where 48 per cent of PE teachers had full participation and 25 per cent had no participation at all. Therefore, certain physical activities will have considerably more 'mainstreaming potential' than others and it may well be that each physical activity's 'mainstreaming potential' may determine the choice of activities for the curriculum.

Communication between educators

Mainstreaming is a whole school issue (Thomas and Jackson, 1986) and so the ability of physical educators to effectively use information gained from other curriculum areas to aid their teaching is as important as the information that can flow from PE to other areas. This two-way flow of information is very often no more than a trickle in many schools. Two developments can increase the flow and quality of information. First, physical educators must be prepared to complete all aspects of assessment processes, including statements of need for special needs children. This will require a working knowledge of testing and prescriptive devices, such as the Test of Motor Impairment (Stott *et al.*, 1984). And second, many schools also require each department to have a special educational needs liaison teacher, who has such responsibilities as acquiring additional knowledge of special needs, being prepared to advise colleagues about children with special needs and curriculum arrangements, and participating in curriculum developments with other liaison teachers. If such arrangements are in place the flow and quality of information within schools will be greatly improved and can only enhance mainstreaming.

Age and year levels of schooling

With obvious differences between primary and secondary PE there may well be important variations in mainstreaming success related to year levels. The continuity that is expected from the National Curriculum will help alleviate problems that manifest themselves in this area. However, with the proportion of primary and secondary children being mainstreamed increasing between 1982 and 1986 (Swann, 1988), and with primary age levels being more successfully mainstreamed in PE (Watkinson and Bentz, 1985), secondary-based physical educators will need to improve the relative lack of success in secondary schools—especially as the proportion of disabled children in mainstream settings is predicted to increase. Certainly movement between schools and between junior and senior grades in secondary schools will always disturb effective tutor-based relationships that are important to the success of mainstreaming, but physical educators must not assume that successful mainstreaming is easy to achieve or that age and year level factors can be overlooked.

Teacher–student interactions

Gillet's (1982) concern for the dependence of mainstream programmes on the personalities involved is the essence of this facilitator. Clashes of personality and contrasting expectations between teacher and student will always be a source of tension in schools regardless of ability. Therefore, in such a sensitive undertaking as mainstreaming, positively maintained teacher–student interactions must be a high priority. For example, Peter's teacher (Lesson B) will have discussed with Peter his capabilities, motivations, and aspirations as well as any potential problems that may be encountered in certain activities and these discussions will form the basis of a positive relationship.

The non-disabled child

The ability of the non-disabled to accept and work with the mainstreamed child is a crucial factor in the complete picture of mainstreaming. If this facilitator becomes a barrier then the whole process could be put under pressure. Unfortunately, negative attitudes towards differentness pervade society as a whole and result in an intolerance of individual differences. These differences can often be exaggerated in overt physical environments and the preparation of the non-disabled child is an important consideration for the physical educator. Therefore, the non-disabled child will require preparation for mainstreaming such as empathy exercises, consciousness raising, and even reverse mainstreaming where non-disabled children visit and attend special schools.

Relative competences of the disabled and non-disabled

Age-related skill competences must be taken into consideration when mainstreaming. In physical environments mental and skill equivalences between disabled and non-disabled can often be considerably offset by physical size, presence, and unawareness of relative strength. This problem is accentuated in that inclusion of older handicapped children into a mainstreamed class may be detrimental to the non-disabled already present. Therefore, matching relative competences is not as viable in physical environments as it would be in other areas of the curriculum, although Down's Syndrome children, who are generally smaller than their similarly aged non-disabled peers, may prove the exception in matching physical competences (Henderson, 1985).

Extent of support personnel in PE

In physical education, where support personnel are not common or are seen as a low priority, the problem is either how the special education teacher can be incorporated into the PE programme (Thomas and Jackson, 1986), or what other options are available. King (1990) highlights a number of ways of working support situations including: class teacher and support personnel circulating around a mixed-ability group; joint planning, preparation, and teaching; a 'double-act' routine; 'targeting' of particular pupils; and mirror-teaching to half groups. Support teaching certainly influences teacher autonomy and raises a number of organizational problems. However, the attainment targets of the National Curriculum make the provision of support personnel a greater concern, since any lack of progress by a child will be very noticeable and will be very difficult to justify to parents, especially if the curriculum is not applicable and/or additional support is not available.

Type and size of school

These secondary facilitators have received very little attention in the research litera-ture. However, Larrivee and Cook (1979) studied both facilitators related to teachers' attitudes towards mainstreaming and found that neither had any effect on attitudes. It would seem in terms of influencing mainstreaming that the assumption can be made that these institutional variables will have an effect on the extent of success. As with many other facilitators, however, the extent of their influence may be difficult to quantify; for example, in secondary grades interpersonal relationships between physi-cal educators and children will be harder to develop in larger schools—but how much harder?

Tertiary facilitators for mainstreaming PE

Professional preparation

This tertiary teacher facilitator divides into preservice and in-service training.

In preservice situations new course developments along with the Council for the Accreditation of Teacher Education (CATE, 1989) requirements will play a major role in preparing students, but there remain a number of difficult issues. First, as students progress through their training there is a natural four-year delay before new initiatives such as the CATE requirements become effective. Second, schools often utilize an implicit experience ladder, posts of responsibility, and the widely held belief that in the first years of teaching newly qualified teachers do not need or gain extra responsibility—which means new teachers may take even longer to exert an impact on mainstreaming programmes. Furthermore, change initiated from below, especially by new staff, is often resented and seen as threatening. Teachers have traditionally seen probationers as a method of gleaning new ideas to aid current teaching, but not as potential curriculum development initiators.

In-service teacher education raises other complex issues related to the implemen-tation of mainstreaming. In-service is often seen as ineffective for the following reasons: some see it as a day off work, others resent forced attendance and very often placement is based on a first-come-first-served basis which can discriminate against those that could best utilize the information; and very often the process of feedback either dilutes or distorts the information thus rendering it ineffective. All these factors will militate against in-service as an effective method of providing teachers with the knowledge and confidence to implement and maintain mainstreaming programmes. Certainly localized school budgets and individuality of school planning for in-service are improving the situation. However, at the present time the prioritizing of in-service commitments in physical education will probably see mainstreaming as a lower prior-ity than National Curriculum or other curriculum developments.

Level of administrative support

Administrators, including headteachers and senior management, can have a drastic influence on teachers' effectiveness in implementing new initiatives such as mainstreaming. The level at which a decision is made, the speed of implementation required (Virgilio, 1984), and the degree to which decisions are made by administrators will impact upon the existing curriculum which in turn will influence many primary and secondary barriers (Thomas and Jackson, 1986; Savage, 1980).

Community and post-school involvement

The extent to which a mainstreamed child can be involved in community-organized programmes is a tertiary facilitator in that reinforcement and continuation of mainstreaming in after-school and holiday-time activity will considerably improve the effectiveness of school-based programmes. However, mainstreamed physical activity settings are often noticeably absent in post-school settings and this may necessitate an alteration in the aims of extra-curricular activities based at school. For example, rather than running elitist school-team based clubs, which often duplicate activities found in the local community, it would be much more appropriate to provide extra-curricular activities for individuals with special educational needs or activities in which everyone can take part.

MAINSTREAMING PE FOR ALL

The facilitator model provides physical educators with identifiable aspects of the mainstream equation that must be achieved, influenced, or taken into consideration for success to be a possibility. The underlying emphasis of the facilitator model is that challenges to the 'traditional' provision of PE are inevitable if mainstreaming is to be successful. With these challenges to traditional thinking in mind it is much more appropriate to consider mainstreaming as a process for every child regardless of ability, that is, mainstreaming rests upon the assumption that physical education is for *all* children. Therefore the question remains how can mainstreaming for *all* be achieved? Auxter (1981), in analysing equal educational opportunity for the disabled in physical education, identified a subtle yet fundamental question which must influence curriculum decisions towards mainstreaming PE for all. Is the intention of physical educational programmes to provide equal opportunity for PE or to provide equal opportunity through PE?

Equal opportunity *for* PE creates the opportunity to access PE programmes or more simply the individual conforms to the activity. This is the most likely and the most limiting PE provision for, as Auxter (1981) states, 'the mere provision of physical education opportunities has little value for handicapped persons unless meaningful leisure skills and quality of life can be developed' (p. 12). Indeed such an argument can be presented for all children with the overriding emphasis being that success of mainstreaming in education and in society must be far more culturally important and valued than the maintenance of certain physical activities or sports to which the mainstreamed must conform. Therefore, equal opportunity for PE does little to provide a curriculum to which all children may have access.

In contrast, equal opportunity *through* PE, according to Auxter (1981), 'places the focus on the benefits of PE for developing functional skills that provide for health, safety and leisure welfare of the handicapped person' (p. 12). Adopting such a stance means that PE becomes a subject that lives up to its name and is not simply a pseudonym for sports activities. For Murdoch (1990) PE, through equal opportunity, allows 'access to the knowledge, understanding, skills and attitudes necessary to promote the optimisation of capabilities central to participation in . . . physical activities' (p. 224). In such a context, PE becomes not an end itself but both a means to an end and a valuable curriculum experience.

Sugden (1990) supports this view. In highlighting the improvements in our understanding regarding movement skill development Sugden (1990) states, 'the stress should now be on acknowledging the individuality of each child, providing a curriculum that is developmentally appropriate, and analysing schools to ensure maximum access to this curriculum' (p. 249). This presents a strong challenge to traditional PE programmes. For example, if we are to acknowledge the individuality of each child and can achieve equal opportunity through PE then many physical educators may have to alter or augment their objectives. This would include the risk of losing aspects of their beloved, traditional, and culturally valued sports skills in a trade-off to accommodate mainstreaming for all, and such a shift in orientation is likely to be threatening. A common response in such conditions might be 'why should the PE curriculum be altered so dramatically to accommodate the mainstreamed?'. Or 'why should the rest suffer loss of culturally valued sports?'. In response the case needs to be made that as educators we should place emphasis on achieving developmentally appropriate knowledge, understanding, functional skills, attitudes and provision for the health and leisure welfare of every child in PE and then look at which physical activities can best meet these aims. Equal opportunity through PE necessitates aims before activities, an order which has been traditionally reversed.

Perspectives of physical educators

Alterations to the curriculum to accommodate mainstreaming for all could be seen as extremely egalitarian and may strike fear into the hearts of many traditionalists. All this serves to prove is that the nature of one's physical education background and reasoning for entering the profession may have implications as to the success of mainstreaming, and indeed, many other curriculum initiatives. Becker *et al.* (1961) state that a perspective is 'a coordinated set of ideas and actions a person uses in dealing with some problematic situation' (p. 34). If this is so, then two polarized perspectives seem to pervade the current views of physical educators towards their subject. These are, according to Sparkes (1986), the 'sporting perspective' and the 'idealist perspective'. The sporting perspective 'is subject-centred, concerned with the development of physical skills and maintaining "standards" within a meritocratic system where the focus of attention is on the elite performer and more able pupils in order to produce successful school teams' (p. 160). Furthermore, there is considerable motivation to perpetuate such views and they pervade the PE curriculum (with PE and Games being dichotomized); also physical educators who hold these views often encourage leisure and participation habits that they themselves follow.

Diametrically opposite, suggests Sparkes (1986), is the idealist perspective which is 'child-centred, egalitarian and concerned with personal and social development via individual self-paced activities, such as educational gymnastics and swimming' (p. 160).

Mainstreaming physical education for all children forms part of this idealist perspective.

My own personal observation of schools in Canada and England leads me to suggest that most physical educators fall into the traditional or sporting perspective and that idealists or egalitarians are in the minority. The former would be less inclined to implement mainstreaming while the latter would be more likely to mainstream for all. To produce schools full of egalitarian-orientated physical educators may seem the wish of an idealist, but if the option is highly competitive, sexist and elitist individuals who fail to adequately educate every child in their charge, then there is little option but to make this wish a reality. Such a situation will not occur overnight, especially since the sporting perspective is not confined to physical educators. For example, Golby and Brigley (1989) suggest that many school governors hold such traditional views and in contrast the egalitarian perspective may seem to be a life-threatening type. Although child-centred, egalitarian physical educators are in the minority at present, the future of the subject within a National Curriculum, where PE may become marginalized at post-14, will only be acceptable based on the idealist perspective. This may be hard to accept for many holding a sporting perspective, but the mere fact that curriculum marginalization causes consternation and unease shows the shallow ideological basis upon which the sporting perspective is based.

Mainstreaming extra-curricular activities for all

Low post-school participation figures raise questions as to how effective the curriculum (especially extra-curricular aspects) is at promoting post-school participation. Many schools run elitist extra-curricular activities in the mistaken belief that post-school participation will be enhanced or even that the community is not capable of providing such activities as effectively. The current situation is far from ideal and requires a reanalysis of how extra-curricular activities (even assuming teachers' leisure time is their own) can achieve mainstreaming for all. In relation to this Smith (1986) provides an all-encompassing model for physical activity participation. The model is divided into a Participation Opportunity/Organizational Infrastructure and Personal Developmental Processes.

The Participation Opportunity/Organizational Infrastructure contains unstructured participation where individuals or groups are actively involved under conditions that they select, create and control themselves, such as skipping or throwing a ball around at break or lunchtime. Structured participation is more organized yet essentially non-competitive in nature, such as a pick-up game of soccer in the playground. Recreational competition involves activities that are both structured and competitive. Developmental competition involves elements of coaching, conditioning and selection, as in house or intramural competitions. School teams are examples of high-intensity competition, and county and national selection describe high performance.

Generally in PE one or two organizational infrastructures predominate extra-curricular practice (most commonly low and high-intensity competition). However, mainstreaming extra-curricular activities for all requires a greater emphasis on the other areas of Smith's opportunity infrastructure such as unstructured and structured participation, since this will create a demand for these areas that the community will eventually supply. Community supply for such areas requires the ability of the PE

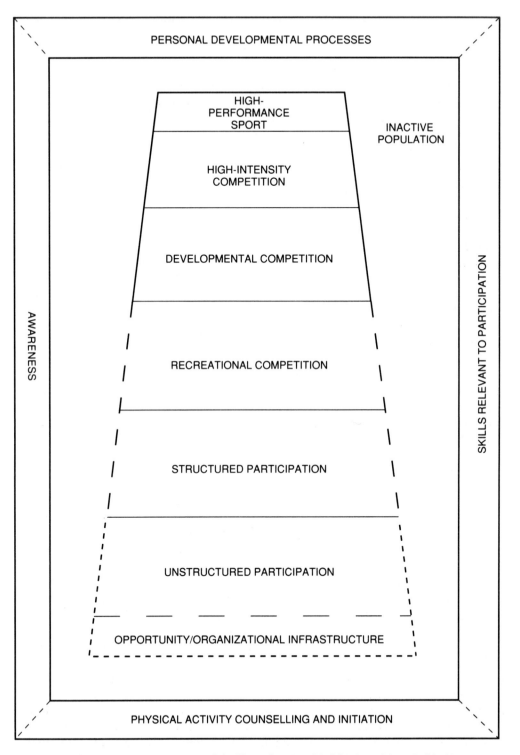

Figure 5.1 *A diagrammatic representation of the Physical Activity Model* (adapted from Smith, 1986).

departments to extend the links between school and community (Meek and Meehan, 1990), thus providing greater opportunities for post-school participation for all children. Ultimately, this process must be initiated by schools through an imaginative and varied extra-curricular programme.

The Personal Developmental Processes of Smith's (1986) models are areas where physical educators need to show greater commitment and understanding to initiate links between curriculum, extra-curricular, and community-based activities to achieve mainstreaming for all.

The Awareness component of Smith's model requires that everyone understands and appreciates the importance of physical activity as an integral part of their lives. An awareness of the importance of physical activity must be translated into action or involvement by every individual. This requires a more diverse and applicable process initiated at school whereby children can be introduced and directed towards activities in the community that are available and can be continued after school (Meek and Meehan, 1990); it also requires that children should receive leisure counselling from physical educators that, according to Smith (1986), 'matches an individual's personal resources and interests to the demands and values of various physical activities' (p. 6). The final personal development process that Smith (1986) proposes (Basic Skill Acquisition) has been altered to 'Skills Relevant to Participation', which includes social, cooperative, leadership, planning, and reviewing skills and more appropriately achieves the aims of physical education that are being proposed to mainstream for all. At present the application of Smith's (1986) model is not widespread in curriculum and extra-curricular contexts and certainly threatens teachers' own leisure-time. But if physical educators are serious about the provision of their subject to all children regardless of ability then the implications of the Smith model need addressing and may result in fundamental changes in how physical education is provided, especially in extra-curricular activities.

COMMENT

Within a whole-school approach, if physical educators are serious about mainstreaming their subject then traditional provision must be challenged, as this is the antithesis of mainstreaming, as Lesson A implies. A facilitator model was proposed that destroys the illusion that physical educators can escape from implementing mainstreaming programmes due to a lack of knowledge or to unsuitable facilities or curriculum. Implicit in the model is the assumption that mainstreaming is not an easy option and the model details the complexities involved. The model's purpose is to assist and organize our thinking regarding mainstreaming and to increase the likelihood that mainstreaming can become not only viable, but also successful.

The proposed facilitator model is only part of the profession's response to mainstreaming. In this chapter it was argued that the concept of mainstreaming should be enlarged to include not only individuals who are disabled, but *all* children. Mainstreaming for all requires a greater acceptance of the egalitarian aims of the idealist perspective; however, this is only part of the answer. Physical educators need to adopt the concepts and challenges of equal opportunity through PE (Auxter, 1981) and those implicit in Smith's (1986) participation model, thus providing PE with the ability to become a valuable curriculum experience free from fear of its future. These challenges and viable curriculum alternatives place mainstreaming not at one end of a continuum of integration, but within a truly comprehensive provision of education for all. Indeed, if physical educators become idealist—capable of providing equal opportunity through PE and also capable of providing the complete participation model—then the facilitator model becomes superfluous and this must be the biggest challenge of all.

Finally, what scenarios will be played out on the playing fields of the future? As mentioned before, Lesson A is a thing of the past. Rugby has become an activity in the extra-curricular and community spheres because it cannot satisfy the requirements of the idealist perspective, equal opportunity, and has a low 'mainstreaming potential'. Lesson B is still taking place and others have been implemented. Additional curriculum developments may include more diverse support teaching, individualized PE programmes, and GCSE projects in PE involving analysing activity patterns in extra-curricular areas. Extra-curricular activities of the future may involve coaches and leaders running after-school community-orientated clubs (and includes physical educators getting paid for their extra commitment!); community activity fayres where clubs and organizations can attract pupils to their activities; facilities such as tennis courts and tennis equipment being booked out and used by pupils, not for profit but to cope with demands made upon them; and equipment used (and returned!) at breaks and lunch-times. The final scenario is the prediction that PE provision will be total and all-encompassing because the physical educator of the future has mainstreamed for *all*.

REFERENCES

Ajzen, I. and Fishbein, M. (1980) *Understanding Attitudes and Predicting Social Behaviour.* Englewood Cliffs, NJ: Prentice-Hall.

Auxter, D. (1981) Equal opportunity for the handicapped through physical education. *Physical Educator* **38**(1), 8–14.

Becker, H., Geer, B., Hughes, E., and Strauss, A. (1961) *Boys in White*. Chicago, IL: University of Chicago Press.

Broadhead, G. D. (1982) A paradigm for physical education for handicapped children in the least restrictive environment. *The Physical Educator* **39**(1), 3–12.

Broadhead, G. D. (1985) Placement of mildly handicapped children in mainstream physical education. *Adapted Physical Activity Quarterly* **2**, 307–13.

Council for the Accreditation of Teacher Education (1989) *Initial Teacher Training: Approval of Courses*. Department of Education and Science. Circular No. 24/89. Great Britain: HMSO.

Education for All Handicapped Children Act (1975) Congress of the United States of America (Public Law 94–142).

Education Act (1981) Department of Education and Science. Chapter 60. Great Britain: HMSO.

Education Act (1988) *Education Reform Act 1988: The School Curriculum and Assessment*. Department of Education and Science. Great Britain: HMSO.

Gillet, P. (1982) Models for mainstreaming. *Journal of Special Educators* **19**(1), 1–12.

Golby, M. and Brigley, S. (1989) *Parents as School Governors*. Tiverton, Devon: Fairway Publications.

Groves, L. (1985) With whom shall children with special needs be physically educated? *British Journal of Physical Education* **16**(1), 38–9.

Henderson, S. E. (1985) Motor skill development. In D. Lane and B. Stratford (eds), *Current Approaches to Down's Syndrome*, pp. 187–213. London: Cassell.

Hoover, J. J. and Cessna, K. (1984) Preservice teachers' attitudes toward mainstreaming prior to student training. *Journal of Teacher Education* **35**(4), 49–51.

Horne, M. D. (1983) Attitudes of elementary classroom teachers toward mainstreaming.*The Exceptional Child* **30**(1), 93–8.

Humberside Policy Document (1988) *Mainstream Approaches to Meeting Special Educational Needs: Policy and Guidelines for Schools and Colleges*. Beverley: Humberside County Council Education Department.

Jowsy, S. (1990) Left on the sidelines. *Special Children* **38**, 16–17.

King, V. (1990) Support teaching. *Special Children* **33**, 1–4.

Larrivee, B. and Cook, L. (1979) Mainstreaming: a study of the variables affecting teacher attitude. *Journal of Special Education* **13**(3), 315–24.

Lehr, D. and Haubrich, P. (1986) Legal precedents for students with severe handicaps. *Exceptional Children* **52**(4), 358–65.

McEvoy, M. A., Nordquist, V. M., and Cunningham, J. L. (1984) Regular- and special-education teachers' judgements about mentally retarded children in an integrated setting. *American Journal of Mental Deficiency* **89**(2), 167–73.

Macmillan, D. L., Jones, R. L., and Aloia, G. F. (1974) The mentally retarded label: a theoretical analysis and review of research. *American Journal of Mental Deficiency* **79**(3), 241–61.

Meek, G. A. (1986) A barrier-approach model to mainstreaming success. Unpublished manuscript. University of Alberta.

Meek, G. A. (1987) Attitudes towards physical activity of physically awkward children. M.Sc. thesis, University of Alberta.

Meek, G. A. and Meehan, P. A. (1990) The community resource guide: from supermarket to shopping mall. *British Journal of Physical Education* **21**(4), 412–14.

Mosston, M. (1981) *Teaching Physical Education* (2nd edn). Toronto: Charles E. Merrill.

Murdoch, E. (1990) Physical education in the National Curriculum: interim working group progress report. *British Journal of Physical Education* **21**(1), 223–4.

National Curriculum Council (1989) *A Curriculum for All 2: Special Educational Needs in the National Curriculum*. York: National Curriculum Council.

Savage, C. A. (1980) Breaking down the barriers to mainstreaming: a perspective for administrators. *Journal for Special Education* **17**(1), 71–77.

Smith, M. F. R. (1986) Strategies for change in adapted physical activity. Paper presented at The Jasper Talks: Strategies for Change in Adapted Physical Activity in Canada. Canadian Association for Health, Physical Education and Recreation. Jasper, Alberta.

Sparkes, A. C. (1986) The micropolitics of innovation in the physical education curriculum. In J. Evans (ed.), *Teachers, Teaching and Control in Physical Education*, pp. 157–77. London: Falmer Press.

Stott, D. H., Moyes, F. A. and Henderson, S. E. (1984) *Test of Motor Impairment: Henderson Revision*. Ontario: Brook Educational Publishing Ltd.

Sugden, D. A. (1990) Developmental physical education for all. *British Journal of Physical Education* **21**(1). 247–49.

Swann, W. (1985) Is integration of children with special needs happening?: an analysis of recent statistics of pupils in special schools. *Oxford Review of Education* **11**(1), 3–17.

Swann, W. (1988) Trends in special school placement to 1986: measuring, assessing and explaining segregation. *Oxford Review of Education* **14**(2), 139–61.

Thomas, G. and Jackson, B. (1986) The whole-school approach to integration. *British Journal of Special Education* **13**(1), 25–8.

Virgilio, S. J. (1984) A paradigm for curriculum innovation. *Journal of Teaching Physical Education* **4**, 57–63.

Watkinson, E. J. and Bentz, L. (1985) *Cross-Canada Survey on Mainstreaming Students with Physical Disabilities into Physical Education in Elementary and Secondary Schools*. Report to The Canadian Association for Health, Physical Education and Recreation. Ottawa, Ontario.

Winzer, M. (1984) Mainstreaming the handicapped child: attitudes of teachers and non-teachers. *Canadian Journal for Exceptional Children* **1**(1), 23–6.

Zigmond, N., Levin, E., and Laurie, T. E. (1985) Managing the mainstreamed: an analysis of teacher attitudes and student performance in mainstream high school programs. *Journal of Learning Disabilities* **18**(9), 535–41.

Chapter 6

Motivating Achievement in Physical Education: A Psychology of Success and Failure[1]

Stuart Biddle

INTRODUCTION

All teachers want children in their classes to 'achieve' and to have a sense of 'achievement'. The introduction of the National Curriculum, it is often claimed, is to 'raise standards'—presumably another term for helping children achieve. Part of this process will involve defined targets and assessment procedures. Similarly, much of the physical education programme in British schools is based on activities involving competition, and achievement is often judged by sporting excellence. It is not intended to debate this but merely to highlight the issue that physical education is an 'achievement' context of some potency, and this is likely to increase within the National Curriculum. Coupled with this is that physical education often provides a very visible arena in which to succeed—and fail!

The purpose of this chapter, therefore, is to provide a psychological perspective on motivation and achievement in physical education. Since this is a potentially vast field I will focus on the psychology of success and failure, often drawing on research in sport contexts. In particular I will highlight the way people make sense of success and failure—the 'attributions' people give in achievement contexts. More detailed reviews of attributions in sport and physical activity can be found in Biddle (1984, in press) and Rejeski and Brawley (1983).

Attributions are the reasons and causes people give for behaviours and outcomes. They are often the answers to the question 'why?'—why did I lose that game of squash?'; 'why did I get such a high mark on that test?'. Of course, in education attributions are often made in response to an achievement or assessment context, although not exclusively so.

Achievement attributions will be reviewed, and in particular research conducted in competitive sport settings will be covered since this is often the most readily available and potent achievement context in physical education. The chapter will then consider individual difference factors that might affect the type of attributions made. Finally, consideration will be given to the consequences of making attributions, the reactions of some people to failure, and how an analysis of attributions for failure may assist physical educators in helping students recover from negative experiences.

ACHIEVEMENT ATTRIBUTIONS

Although research on attributions started in the 1940s, it was Weiner's work on attributional responses to academic success and failure in the classroom that made educators aware of this social psychological perspective (Weiner, 1979; Weiner *et al.*, 1972). This has now been developed further and is documented in Weiner (1985b, 1986).

ATTRIBUTION ANTECEDENTS AND ATTRIBUTIONS IN SPORT

Much of the sport psychology research on attribution theory (AT) has focused on the variables that precede the making of attributions—such as individual differences or expectations—and the nature of the attributions themselves.

Attribution elements and dimensions

The approach adopted by Weiner *et al.* (1972) was used in early research on AT in sport. They identified four main attributions ('attribution elements') used in achievement contexts. These were ability, effort, difficulty of the task, and luck. Roberts and Pascuzzi (1979), however, have suggested that a great deal more varied attributions are used in sport and it is widely accepted that attributions beyond ability, effort, task difficulty, and luck will be used in sports competition and related settings (the weather, officials, or the opponent are examples).

Weiner *et al.* (1972) also categorized the four main elements into dimensions. Their original model is shown in Figure 6.1 whereby attributions are classified along the dimensions of 'locus of causality' (originally 'locus of control'), and 'stability'. Attributions associated with the individual are 'internal' (ability and effort) whereas those outside of the individual are 'external' (task and luck). Attributions related to enduring features are labelled 'stable' (ability and task), whereas factors thought to be more variable are labelled 'unstable' (effort and luck).

Weiner (1979) later added a third dimension, that of 'controllability'. This was to distinguish between elements that are internal but not under a great deal of personal control, such as 'natural ability', and internal factors that are more controllable, such as personal effort. The consequences of attributions in terms of their dimensional placement will be discussed later. Weiner's three-dimensional model is shown in Figure 6.2. The modification to Weiner's earlier model proposed for sport settings by Roberts and Pascuzzi (1979) is shown in Figure 6.3.

Attributions in sport

Given that attributions are responses to specific events, it is not surprising to find that the nature of the event itself will affect the attributions reported. Nevertheless, it has been found that certain trends exist in the types of attributions given in sport, although most analyses have been made at the level of dimensions rather than

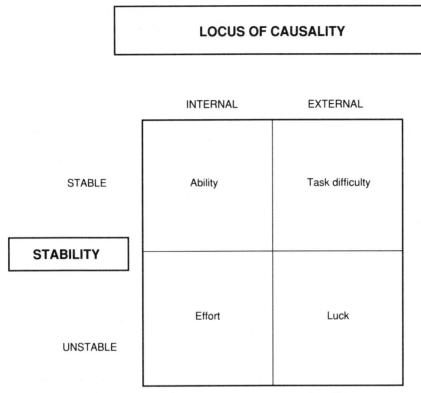

Figure 6.1 *A model of achievement attributions* (proposed by Weiner *et al.*, 1972).

elements. Similarly, there is very little research in physical education contexts other than in competitive sport.

Support has been found for the 'self-serving bias' (SSB) in sport AT research. The SSB suggests that people operate strategies that try to protect or enhance their self-esteem. This means that people may make a conscious decision to distort their attributions, such as making external attributions for failure so as to protect self-esteem. Alternatively, people may actually perceive themselves as being more responsible for successful or positive outcomes than unsuccessful ones. The conscious distortion is likely to be the result of motivational influences and is more likely to occur in situations of importance. A review by Miller and Ross (1975) found that self-enhancing attributions were common under success conditions, but that self-protecting attributions in failure were not so common. The nature and origins of the SSB have been the topic of some debate in psychology, but Brawley (1984) has suggested that the SSB is a function of memory. In a study of tennis, he found evidence for players more frequently and easily remembering their own inputs to team (doubles) efforts.

Much of the work in sport psychology has investigated the differences in attributions made by winners and losers. McAuley and Gross (1983) found that winners of table tennis matches made attributions that were significantly higher on ratings of internal, unstable, and controllable than attributions made by losers. Mark *et al.* (1984) found that squash tournament winners gave more stable attributions than losers, and also slightly stronger controllable attributions. A follow-up study showed

LOCUS OF CAUSALITY			
INTERNAL		**EXTERNAL**	
STABLE	UNSTABLE	STABLE	UNSTABLE

CONTROLLABILITY	STABLE	UNSTABLE	STABLE	UNSTABLE
CONTROLLABLE	Stable effort	Unstable effort	Other's stable effort	Other's unstable effort
UNCONTROLLABLE	Ability	Mood	Task ease	Luck

Figure 6.2 *Modified model of achievement attributions* (proposed by Weiner, 1979).

that winners made more stable and controllable attributions than losers (Mark *et al.*, 1984, study 2). Overall, the research suggests that winners are likely to report strong internal, and possibly controllable, attributions, but that the prediction of attributions in terms of stability is less clear.

In addition to investigating attributions for outcome by comparing winners and losers, sport psychologists have also looked at attributions in relation to perceived success and failure. Although winning and losing is an important aspect of sport to investigate, attributions are also likely to be related to other criteria such as perceptions of personal performance. For example, winners may be dissatisfied with their overall play, and alternatively losers may be satisfied with their play.

Spink and Roberts (1980) elicited attributions for winning and losing from players after racketball matches. Then, based on their assessment of satisfaction with their performance, subjects were classified as follows: satisfied winner ('clear win'), dissatisfied loser ('clear loss'), dissatisfied winner ('ambiguous win'), and satisfied loser ('ambiguous loss').

The results showed that winners made more internal attributions than losers, in accordance with the SSB. However, clear outcome players were shown to have higher internal attributions than those with ambiguous outcomes. Clear outcomes yielded attributions to ability and effort, while ambiguous outcomes were related to attributions of task difficulty. This study alerted sport psychologists to the issue of differentiating outcome from performance when studying attributions.

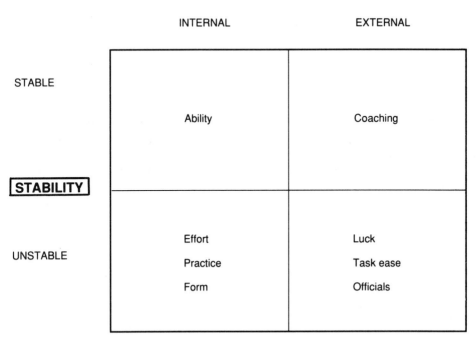

Figure 6.3 *Sport attribution model* (adapted from Roberts and Pascuzzi, 1979).

The studies discussed so far have focused on attributions given for individual performance or outcomes. Many sport situations involve a group outcome and performance, and some studies have addressed this issue. Bukowski and Moore (1980) asked 11- and 12-year-old boys to evaluate the importance of various factors as possible causes of team success and failure in sport. They found that luck and task difficulty were *not* perceived to be important attributions, and that team success was perceived to be related to internal attributions and failure to external attributions.

Spontaneous causal thinking: do we really make attributions in sport?

The initial studies in sport attribution research relied almost exclusively on having subjects rate attribution statements supplied by the experimenters. Although these results have been reasonably consistent, they raise the fundamental question of whether people actually engage in such thought after sports events. Few studies have analysed naturally occurring discourse in sport from an attributional perspective. Open-ended questionnaires have been used, but these still force subjects into thoughts that might not have otherwise been evident.

The study of naturally occurring attributions, particularly in achievement situations, is not extensive. Weiner (1985a) located seventeen published studies which investigated 'spontaneous' attributional thought, and found clear support for the proposition that attributions do occur as a part of everyday life. However, attributions were found to be more likely when (a) a goal was not attained or (b) when an event was unexpected. Assuming participants in sport have some commitment to winning and playing well, it is likely that those who lose, especially unexpectedly, and/or are dissatisfied with their performance, will engage in more attributional thought than others.

Johnson and Biddle (1988) investigated the attributional response of students who experienced 'failure' on a balance board task. Subjects were given feedback that they had failed but were then asked to try again and to perform as many trials as they wished. This was used as a measure of 'persistence'. During these extra trials subjects were asked to give their thoughts and feelings. These were recorded and later coded. The subjects were split into two groups of 'persisters' and 'non-persisters' on the basis of the median score. Free-response attributions were then analysed. Non-persisters made proportionately more negative self-statements and attributions than persisters, while the persistent subjects made more strategy-related statements.

Application

Attribution theory research in sport suggests that children, after competition, are likely to attribute success to internal and controllable factors more so than losers, but that success and failure will not necessarily be seen as synonymous with winning and losing. Similarly, it appears that attributions are made in everyday contexts and that children in physical education will more likely seek a reason for their behaviour after an unexpected outcome or when a goal has not been reached. Further implications of this are discussed later.

ATTRIBUTIONS AND INDIVIDUAL DIFFERENCES

The focus so far has been on the types of attributions made by winners or losers, or those satisfied or dissatisfied with their performance in sport contexts. In addition, other individual difference factors such as gender, age, and culture may be important antecedents of attributions.

Gender differences

It is often reported that attributions following sports competition will differ as a function of gender. Specifically, reviews of research have suggested that males have higher perceptions of competence and more positive expectations in achievement settings than females, and therefore tend to attribute success to stable and internal factors. Similarly, females, it has been suggested, have low expectations of success and therefore attribute success to luck or other unstable and external causes, and failure to internal stable factors such as lack of ability. However, this attributional 'modesty' on the part of women is far from clear (Blucker and Hershberger, 1983).

Lenney (1977) has argued that the assumption that girls and women lack self-confidence in achievement contexts, while true in some situations, ignores some important and fundamental issues associated with the situational context. She says that women's self-confidence will be dependent on the nature of the task (particularly whether the task is 'sex-typed' or not), the availability of clear and unambiguous performance feedback, and the nature of social comparisons being made. In other words, situational cues will be important and since these are likely to affect the attributions made for performance, it questions the assumption that gender differences will exist in sport achievement contexts (Corbin, 1984).

In a similar analysis, Maehr and Nicholls (1980) have argued that spurious results have been arrived at when defining the cognitions of women in terms of male perspectives. They say that 'the situations and tasks used in the study of achievement behaviour reflect a masculine definition of achievement more than a feminine definition' (p. 245). Maehr and Nicholls say that males and females hold different achievement goals and therefore define achievement in different ways. This could have important implications for the way we view 'success' and 'achievement' in physical education. As they comment:

> in those situations where it has been studied, achievement behaviour has been most often conceived and interpreted in a fashion that is consistent with what we have termed the ability-oriented form of achievement motivation. This turns out to be reasonably appropriate for males but it fits poorly for females. Female achievement behaviour is better described as a combination of ability-oriented motivation and social-approval motivation.
>
> (p. 245)

To date, the evidence on gender differences in attributions is not strong, at least in the sport domain. Although early research suggested that the attributional modesty of women was consistent (see McHugh *et al.*, 1978), subsequent research has reported that males and females are quite similar in the types of attributions they make in most cases (e.g. Biddle and Hill, 1988), although small gender differences have been reported on some attribution variables (e.g. Tenenbaum and Furst, 1985).

Weiner (1986) has suggested that attributional differences of males and females may be the result of different expectations of success. However, the lack of gender differences reported in sport AT studies suggests that expectancies are similar for the two groups in sport situations. This could be the result of sport being predominantly competition *within*, rather than between, gender groups, which may not be the case in other achievement contexts. Similarly, the studies of attributions in sport invariably investigate males and females who have already made the decision to participate, therefore the gender differences may not be so marked as for other groups. In short, the assumption that males and females attribute success and failure in different ways in sport has not been supported with confidence. However, it may be different within physical education where the element of choice is reduced compared with leisure-time sport involvement, and where more classes are mixed-gender than previously. This is an area ripe for interesting research.

Age differences

In a review of attribution theory in sport, Rejeski and Brawley (1983) stated that:

> one glaring omission in the sport attribution research is the absence of developmental studies ... most research focuses on a limited age range with little concern for

population representativeness. The assumption that similar attributional patterns for achievement outcomes will result across age-groups is erroneous.   (p. 94)

This criticism is a valid one and has been echoed by others (Weiss *et al.*, 1990), yet it is surprising that AT research in sport has not adopted a developmental framework since AT and the study of children have both been popular topics in sport psychology for a number of years.

An influential developmental perspective in achievement psychology is that of Nicholls (1984), which has subsequently been discussed in the context of children's sport (Duda, 1987). Specifically, Nicholls and his colleagues suggest that children develop a differentiated set of beliefs concerning achievement (Nicholls and Miller, 1984). Children aged approximately 5–7 years appear not to be able to differentiate effort, ability, and outcome. Their responses indicate that children think people who try hard are successful and those who are successful must have tried hard. Perceptions of ability around the age of 5 or 6 years stem from success or failure at a task (i.e. mastery orientation), whereas slightly older children (6–7 years) might start adopting more of a normative perspective by seeing whether others can or cannot do the task. In other words, they will think that tasks that few people can do are 'hard' and success at hard tasks equates to high ability. Children aged 7–9 years tend to think in terms of effort as the cause of outcomes, and then later (9–10 years) ability and effort start to be differentiated as potential causes of outcomes. It is not until the ages of about 10 or 11 that this differentiation appears to be complete and children can then see that ability is 'capacity' and that this will limit the effect of effort on the outcome of a task (Duda, 1987; Nicholls and Miller, 1984).

Given these developmental 'stages', it suggests that research into attributions with children must adopt a perspective that accounts for different perceptions of ability, effort, and perceived causes of outcomes.

Bird and Williams (1980) investigated the attributions given by four age groups of boys and girls: 7–9, 10–12, 13–15, and 16–18 years. These children were asked to evaluate three stories each having three different cues. These cues were the athlete's gender, sport outcome (success/failure), and type of sport (basketball, tennis, floor exercise/balance beam). The four gender/outcome situations were presented for each sport and the children had to assess the extent to which the outcomes were the result of ability, effort, task difficulty, or luck. The results showed that children aged 7–9 years explained the sport outcomes for both males and females primarily in terms of effort and luck. Between 10 and 15 years, attributions were similar for the outcomes of males and females. Children aged 10–12 perceived a relationship between effort and outcome as well as luck and outcome, whereas the 13–15 group perceived a relationship only between effort and outcome. These were independent of the gender of the performer. However, sex-role stereotypes emerged quite strongly in the 16–18-year-old group. In particular, male performance was attributed to effort whereas female performance was more related to luck.

Cultural differences

Aspects of culture, race, and ethnicity in sport psychology have often been ignored. Duda and Allison (1990) analysed 199 papers published in the *Journal of Sport and*

Exercise Psychology between 1979 and 1987 and found that over 96 per cent did not report the racial or ethnic composition of their subjects. Duda and Allison (1990) argue for a greater recognition of cultural factors in sport psychology and for more use of cross-cultural methodologies. Given the increasing importance of multicultural education in the UK, further consideration ought to be given to attributions, perceptions of achievement, and culture.

The study of attributions, it has been argued, has been dominated by a 'Western' perspective (Bond, 1983). Given the epistemological foundations of the study of attributions, and the importance of processing information from the surrounding social environment, to ignore cultural and cross-cultural issues in attributions would be a mistake.

To this end, a number of attribution researchers have addressed this issue in several different contexts, including general achievement motivation (Duda and Allison, 1989) and sport (Duda, 1986; Whitehead, 1986).

Cultural differences have been shown by Duda (1986) even for groups of different cultural backgrounds residing in the same country. She investigated the perceptions of success and failure held by white, black, and Hispanic adolescents attending high school in Los Angeles. Using an open-ended format, Duda asked the subjects to think of a time when they felt successful in their favourite sport activity. They then had to respond to the questions 'what was "success" in this instance? That is, how did you know that you were successful?' (Duda, 1986, p. 217). The same format was used for the recall and rating of a unsuccessful experience.

Duda found that four major criteria formed the foundation of these subjects' perceptions of success. The four categories identified were task mastery (demonstration of skill, self-improvement), social comparison (competition against others: winning/losing), social recognition or approval (recognition or approval of performance by others), and group solidarity (affiliation and friendships). Results from this study showed that perceptions of success and failure in sport differed as a function of both gender and cultural background. In particular, white males tended to value social comparison (competitive) goals. Hispanics favoured mastery goals, whereas blacks differed as a function of gender—girls being more orientated towards social comparison, boys towards mastery.

In summary, sport attribution studies have all but ignored cultural and cross-cultural issues. Most attribution theorists agree that much of the research into achievement attributions, using perspectives such as Weiner's, is culturally biased and further work is required which expands into different cultural groups. Teachers of physical education may wish to find out how different cultural groups define achievement and how they react to success and failure.

Differences in achievement motivation and goal orientation

As already stated, much of the attribution research in sport has been based on Weiner's achievement attribution model developed in the 1970s. This was based on research conducted primarily in classroom contexts. As a result, one of the factors thought to affect achievement attributions is 'achievement motivation'. The traditional way of defining achievement motivation (AM) is to use the approach of

Atkinson and McClelland (see McClelland *et al.*, 1953; Atkinson, 1977). Specifically, Atkinson (1977) states:

> achievement motivation has been referred to as the need for achievement ... It is an important determinant of aspiration, effort and persistence when an individual expects that performance will be evaluated in relation to some standard of excellence. Such behaviour is generally called achievement oriented.   (p. 25)

From AM theory it is predicted that challenging situations will arouse expectations of success and failure and that resultant achievement behaviours will be determined by the personality dispositions of the need to achieve and the need to avoid failure. AM theory also predicts that individuals high in AM will choose tasks of intermediate difficulty, thus providing a challenge, whereas those low in AM will tend to select tasks that are difficult (to protect self-esteem when failing) or very easy tasks (where success is likely). It has been suggested that those individuals high in AM will persist longer and generally try harder on achievement tasks than people low in AM.

Given the importance of AM in sport contexts, AM constructs would appear to be important for the study of attributions. For example, Roberts (1978) found children high in AM tended to attribute sport success to ability and sport failure to low effort. Children low in AM attributed their success in sport to luck and ease of the task and failure to a lack of ability. Such differences in AM, therefore, may be important predictors of attributions and motivation for children in physical education.

This 'traditional' approach to AM, however, has now been modified and extended. For example, Maehr and Nicholls (1980) state that 'achievement motivation should be defined in terms of its purpose or meaning for people rather than in terms of overt behaviour or the characteristics of situations in which the behaviour occurs' (p. 227). That is to say that we need to find out the *meaning* of achievement for different people and we should not assume that achievement is universally defined in the same way.

Success and failure are subjective appraisals of desirable personal qualities and hence will be defined in different ways by various people. Again, to quote from Maehr and Nicholls (1980), the analysis of achievement behaviour is the analysis of how people infer presence or absence of desirable qualities in themselves and the effects of such inferences on behaviour' (p. 236). They go on to define three types of AM, rather than the one that has been traditional, these being ability orientation, task orientation, and social approval orientation previously discussed in the section on culture but also reviewed briefly here.

The ability orientation refers to behaviour characterized by a striving to maintain a favourable perception of one's ability. Children who endorse this orientation will want to maximize their chances of attributing success to high ability and will therefore judge their success in terms of beating other people—a social comparison perspective on achievement. The second achievement goal identified by Maehr and Nicholls (1980) is that of task orientation, sometimes referred to as the mastery oriented achievement goal. This is where children will judge their success in terms of the quality of their work; they wish to solve problems for their own sake rather than demonstrate high ability. Some researchers have used this ability/mastery distinction to infer differential attributional thinking after achievement tasks. For example, Dweck and Leggett (1988) suggest that children hold at least two different goals for academic achievement: performance goals (where they are concerned with performing better than others and gaining favourable judgements of their ability), and learning goals (where they are concerned with task mastery and increasing personal competence). Dweck and Leggett propose that children who are primarily orientated towards performance goals, but have a low perception of their ability, will develop 'helpless' behaviour patterns by avoiding challenge and giving up easily and hence will display poor persistence. Attributions for failure will be to low ability which, as discussed in the section on learned helplessness later, can be particularly damaging. Those who are orientated towards performance goals but have a high perception of their ability will seek challenges and have high persistence. Similarly, children with learning goals, regardless of perceived ability, will adopt a mastery behaviour pattern, use effort and strategy attributions, and will seek challenging situations that enhance learning. Hence, the goals will determine the type of attributions used and the behavioural consequences of success and failure. More will be said on this later in the sections on behavioural reactions to failure and attribution retraining.

The third achievement goal identified by Maehr and Nicholls (1980) is that of social approval. This is associated with virtuous intentions and personal commitment, and to gain approval from significant others. Roberts (1984) argues that this focuses the individual on attributions to effort and is more appropriate for young children in sport when they are trying to please the teacher, coach or their parents. For example, a child may aim to be accepted socially and is therefore quite happy being part of the sports team even though he/she may only be a substitute and not obtain much playing time.

It is likely that the achievement goals held by an individual will influence attributions for success and failure, and this has been shown in sport settings (see Duda, 1989). This approach appears to hold more potential than traditional approaches to AM which have emphasized a unidimensional trait perspective.

Application

This section has dealt with factors that might influence the type of attributions made for success and failure. Physical educators ought to be aware of these differences so that they can respond more appropriately to the different ways children may react to achievement contexts in physical education. So far, the research evidence points to meaningful differences in attributional thinking, at least under some circumstances, emanating from the variables of gender, age, culture, and achievement orientation.

CONSEQUENCES OF ATTRIBUTIONS

So far the chapter has covered the types of attributions made in sport achievement contexts and some of the likely factors affecting the making of such attributions. The next important issue to address is that of the consequences of making attributions. Does it matter what type of attribution is made in terms of motivation, feelings, expectations, and behaviour?

Expectations and attributions

Developing confidence is associated with having positive thoughts about the future, and attribution research has shown that the stability dimension in Weiner's model (Figures 6.1 and 6.2) is related to expectations about the future. For example, stating that 'my good performance today was due to my ability' is saying that 'I have good ability for this task' and 'this ability will remain with me for some time to come'. Confidence in repeating a good performance, therefore, should be enhanced when a stable attribution (ability) has been made. Conversely, attributing success or failure to an unstable factor such as effort does not yield much information for the future in terms of expectancies since effort is unstable and could therefore change from one situation to the next. In short, attributions that are stable will give clearer indications for expectancies than unstable attributions.

Teachers should avoid making attributions for the failure of a child to stable factors such as ability, and similarly children themselves should avoid such attributional statements. This is because stable attributions for failure predict low confidence and an expectation that failure will recur in similar situations in the future.

Emotional reactions to success and failure

Attributions can also be associated with the emotional reactions that accompany success and failure in sport or physical education. Weiner *et al.* (1978, 1979) have argued that there are at least two types of emotion generated from achievement situations. First, the outcome (success/failure) will produce positive or negative emotion that is dependent on the outcome itself not on the attributions for the outcome. This has been called 'outcome-dependent' emotion and might include more general emotions such as pleasure and dissatisfaction.

Weiner has also stated that emotion will also be produced as a result of the way people appraise the outcome. In other words, attributions will be influential—hence he refers to 'attribution-dependent' emotion (Weiner, 1986; Weiner *et al.*, 1978, 1979). This is similar to Vallerand's analysis of emotion in sport where he proposes that an immediate ('intuitive') appraisal of the outcome is made and this generates emotion, as does a 'reflective' appraisal of the outcome. The reflective appraisal will involve attributional thinking and so is more akin to attribution-dependent emotion (see Vallerand, 1983, 1984, 1987).

The initial research on attributions and emotions suggested that it was the locus of causality dimension that was important. Internal attributions were thought to intensify emotion (after both success and failure), and external attributions to reduce emotional feeling. Although this often is the case, it does not go far enough. For example, Biddle and Hill (1988) also found that emotions that were related to self-esteem (such as pride) were more likely to be felt after internal attributions for success were made *and* when it was considered important to win.

In addition to the locus of causality dimension, Weiner (1986) has suggested that emotions related to time (such as hope) are related to the stability dimension. Similarly, social emotions such as guilt and pity are related to the controllability dimension. However, although these relationships have been proposed, they have not always been demonstrated clearly in research. Robinson and Howe (1989), for example, studied over 700 Canadian boys and girls aged 13–14 years. They found that attributions did not predict emotion as clearly as Weiner had proposed. Indeed the main predictor of emotion was how well one perceived oneself to have played (perceived performance) rather than attributions for the performance. This is supported by Biddle (1989) and Vallerand (1987). Also, Robinson and Howe (1989) found that although the three attributional dimensions of locus, stability, and controllability did predict emotion, they did so in variable ways under success and failure.

Behavioural reactions to failure

Attributions have also been used as a way of understanding how people behave after failure. In the 1960s a number of experiments with animals identified a behaviour pattern termed 'learned helplessness' (LH). This was a negative or apathetic response to a situation after repeated failure. Dweck (1980) has defined LH as 'the perception of independence between one's responses and the occurrence of aversive outcomes ... that is, the belief that what you do will not affect the course of negative events, that you have no control over negative events' (p. 2). Research has also identified LH in humans, although the exact nature of LH remains the subject of much debate.

Rather than see LH as independence between response and outcome, Abramson *et al.* (1978) have suggested that LH is a negative emotional, cognitive, and behavioural response to failure *mediated by attributions*. In particular, LH is thought to be more likely to occur when attributions for failure are: (a) internal, thereby increasing feelings of self-blame and negative emotion; (b) stable, hence no change in the future is seen to be possible; and (c) global, whereby failure is generalized to situations beyond the one in which failure occurred. This is likely to depress self-esteem.

Individuals with ego-orientated (competitive) goals in sport, as already suggested, tend to focus on ability attributions. Attributing lack of success to low ability, however, will more likely lead to feelings of LH than other attributions. This is because such an attribution is internal, stable, and possibly 'global', although this will depend on the individual's perceptions.

Very little research has been conducted on LH in sport or physical education. In 1980, Dweck suggested that the evidence on LH in children in classroom settings could provide useful parallels for sport. For example, she suggested that children react to failure in at least two distinct ways. 'Mastery oriented' children are characterized by:

- perceptions of control;
- thoughts that imply that success can be repeated and that failure can be changed;
- thoughts that are positive and orientated towards the future;
- the seeking out of solutions to problems;
- confidence in their own ability.

Conversely, 'learned helpless' children are characterized by:

- thoughts that their response will not produce the desired outcome;
- thoughts that imply failure is inevitable;
- lack of confidence in their own ability.

The helpless response, therefore, is related to attributions. However, more recent formulations, such as that by Dweck and Leggett (1988), attempt to identify how certain attributional styles are developed. For example, they suggest that whether children view intelligence as fixed or changeable will lead to different thoughts about success and failure in classroom settings. Such an analysis is required in physical education. Are the children who opt out of physical education those who believe that success in physical activity is not possible for them and that their attributions are such that they predict a helpless orientation? (see Robinson, 1990).

In their perceptive review, Dweck and Leggett (1988) suggest that different children will pursue different goals in academic achievement and that these goals may predict attributions and subsequent adaptive or maladaptive behaviour patterns following failure. As Dweck and Leggett suggest, 'helpless children might be pursuing *performance* goals, in which they seek to establish the adequacy of their ability and avoid giving evidence of its inadequacy' (p. 259). They go on to say:

> mastery-oriented individuals . . . might be pursuing *learning* goals. They may tend to view achievement situations as opportunities to increase their competence and may pursue, in these situations, the goal of acquiring new skills or extending their mastery. Thus, in challenging achievement situations, helpless children might be pursuing the performance goal of *proving* their ability, whereas the mastery-oriented children might be pursuing the learning goal of *improving* their ability.   (p. 259)

Such interesting notions require testing in physical achievement domains. Let us also hope that the National Curriculum does not force children to adopt an overtly performance-orientated goal at the expense of mastery goal orientations. Certainly this kind of analysis has implications for the way physical educators view their programmes. For example, overtly product-orientated forms of assessment in physical education within the National Curriculum (NC) could force children into more of a performance goal orientation. This would be damaging for motivation for those lacking confidence. However, this is somewhat speculative at present and one should await feedback and research once the NC is in place for physical education. Nevertheless, evidence from classroom settings does provide a warning against this approach.

Attribution re-training

Once attributions were found to play an important role in children's reactions to and recovery from failure, it was logical to expect people to attempt to make changes in attributions in an effort to change subsequent behaviour. This 'therapeutic' approach to attributions has become popular and is used widely in clinical psychology (Brewin, 1988). Similarly, attribution change or attribution 're-training' programmes have been developed (Forsterling, 1988).

One of the first studies to investigate this area was conducted by Dweck (1975) with 8- to 13-year-old children. She sought to determine whether 'altering attributions for failure would enable learned helpless children to deal more effectively with failure' (p. 674). Dweck studied twelve children who had shown strong reactions to failure on problem-solving tasks and gave them one of two 'treatments'. One group received 'success only' and the other 'attribution re-training'. This group was shown how to take responsibility for failure, such as by attributing it to lack of effort, so that future attempts may be viewed more positively. The results showed that the success-only group continued to show negative reactions after failure whereas the attribution re-training group maintained or improved their performance. Two possible attribution re-training sequences are show in Figure 6.4.

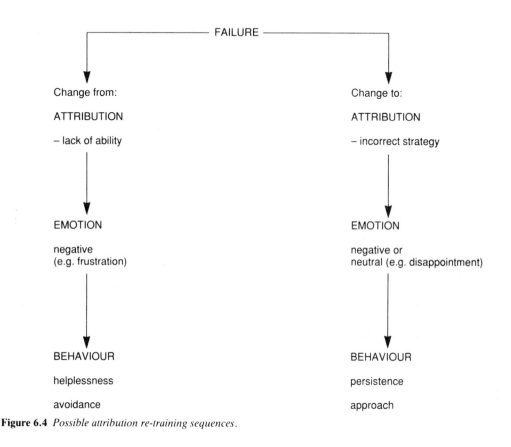

Figure 6.4 *Possible attribution re-training sequences.*

Application

This section has considered the consequences that may follow particular types of attributions. These include changes in expectancies, emotions, and behaviour. As far as the physical educator is concerned, listening to the attributions made by children in physical activity contexts may provide useful information pertaining to how the child feels, what he or she expects, or future behaviour. Attributions are more positive after successful experiences if the child attributes this success to internal and stable factors, yet after failure the child should avoid attributions that are internal and stable and instead seek reasons that are more personally controllable. This will likely lead to higher levels of confidence, more positive emotion, and more persistent behaviour in the face of obstacles.

CONCLUSION

This chapter has outlined one perspective from social psychology—attribution theory—that may shed light on issues of motivation within the achievement context of physical education. Much remains to be known, but since a great deal of the research into achievement attributions has been conducted in classroom settings, the conceptual leap to physical activity environments may not be too great. In conclusion, therefore, physical educators might find this approach useful for the development of interpersonal skills in teaching, and how children get to grips with success and failure in achievement contexts. The following broad guidelines are offered in conclusion.

1   Children will make attributions for success and failure in physical education and these are likely to impact on expectations, emotions, and behaviour.
2   The types of attributions made may differ for children of different ages, gender and cultural background, as well as by the type of achievement orientation that they have. Knowing this kind of information may be helpful for teachers in dealing with the ways that some children may view achievement contexts in physical education.
3   Maladaptive responses to failure in physical education may be related to the attributions made, although this will not necessarily be true in all cases. Where attributions are thought to be influential, teachers may wish to discuss the types of attributions made by the child and, where appropriate, encourage the child to reattribute the events to more positive factors which emphasize a greater likelihood of success in the future.

NOTE

1   Parts of this chapter are based on a more extensive review of attributions in sport (Biddle, in press).

REFERENCES

Abramson, L. Y., Seligman, M. E. P. and Teasdale, J. D. (1978) Learned helplessness in humans: critique and reformulation. *Journal of Abnormal Psychology* **87**, 49–74.
Atkinson, J. W. (1977) Motivation for achievement. In T. Blass (ed.), *Personality Variables in Social Behaviour*, pp. 25–108. Hillsdale, NJ: Erlbaum.
Biddle, S. J. H. (1984) Attribution theory in sport and recreation: origins, developments and future directions. *Physical Education Review* **7**, 145–59.
Biddle, S. J. H. (1989) Attributions for outcome and performance in sports competition and their relationships with emotional reactions. *Proceedings of the 7th World Congress in Sport Psychology*. Singapore: Singapore Sports Council.

Biddle, S. J. H. (in press) Attributions. In R. N. Singer, M. Murphey and L. K. Tennant (eds), *Handbook on Research in Sport Psychology*. New York: Macmillan.

Biddle, S. J. H. and Hill, A. B. (1988) Causal attributions and emotional reactions to outcome in a sporting contest. *Personality and Individual Differences* **9**, 213–23.

Bird, A. M. and Williams, J. M. (1980) A developmental attributional analysis of sex role stereotypes for sport performance. *Developmental Psychology* **16**, 319–22.

Blucker, J. A. and Hershberger, E. (1983) Causal attribution theory and the female athlete: what conclusions can we draw? *Journal of Sport Psychology* **5**, 353–60.

Bond, M. H. (1983) A proposal for cross-cultural studies of attribution. In M. Hewstone (ed.), *Attribution Theory: Social and Functional Extensions*, pp. 144–57. Oxford: Blackwell.

Brawley, L. R. (1984) Unintentional egocentric biases in attributions. *Journal of Sport Psychology* **6**, 264–78.

Brewin, C. R. (1988) Editorial: Developments in an attributional approach to clinical psychology. *British Journal of Clinical Psychology* **27**, 1–3.

Bukowski, W. M. and Moore, D. (1980) Winners' and losers' attributions for success and failure in a series of athletic events. *Journal of Sport Psychology* **2**, 195–210.

Corbin, C. B. (1984) Self-confidence of females in sports and physical activity. *Clinics in Sports Medicine* **3**, 895–908.

Duda, J. (1986) Perceptions of sport success and failure among white, black and Hispanic adolescents. In J. Watkins, T. Reilly and L. Burwitz (eds), *Sports Science*, pp. 214–22. London: E. & F. N. Spon.

Duda, J. (1987) Toward a developmental theory of children's motivation in sport. *Journal of Sport Psychology* **9**, 130–45.

Duda, J. (1989) Goal perspectives and behaviour in sport and exercise settings. In C. Ames and M. Maehr (eds), *Advances in Motivation and Achievement: Motivation Enhancing Environments* 6, pp. 81–115. Greenwich, CT: JAI Press.

Duda, J. and Allison, M. T. (1989) The attributional theory of achievement motivation: cross-cultural considerations. *International Journal of Intercultural Relations* **13**, 37–55.

Duda, J. and Allison, M. T. (1990) Cross-cultural analysis in exercise and sport psychology: a void in the field. *Journal of Sport and Exercise Psychology* **12**, 114–31.

Dweck, C. S. (1975) The role of expectations and attributions in the alleviation of learned helplessness. *Journal of Personality and Social Psychology* **31**, 674–85.

Dweck, C. S. (1980) Learned helplessness in sport. In C. Nadeau, W. Halliwell, K. Newell and G. Roberts (eds), *Psychology of Motor Behaviour and Sport—1979*, pp. 1–11. Champaign, IL: Human Kinetics.

Dweck, C. S. and Leggett, E. L. (1988) A social-cognitive approach to motivation and personality. *Psychological Review* **95**, 256–73.

Forsterling, F. (1988) *Attribution Theory in Clinical Psychology*. Chichester: John Wiley.

Johnson, L. and Biddle, S. J. H. (1988) Persistence after failure: an exploratory look at 'learned helplessness' in motor performance. *British Journal of Physical Education Research Supplement* **5**, 7–10.

Lenney, E. (1977) Women's self-confidence in achievement settings. *Psychological Bulletin* **84**, 1–13.

McAuley, E. and Gross, J. B. (1983) Perceptions of causality in sport: an application of the causal dimension scale. *Journal of Sport Psychology* **5**, 72–6.

McClelland, D. C., Atkinson, J. W., Clark, R. A., and Lowell, E. L. (1953) *The Achievement Motive*. New York: Appleton-Century-Crofts.

McHugh, M. C., Duquin, M. E., and Frieze, I. H. (1978) Beliefs about success and failure: attribution and the female athlete. In C. Oglesby (ed.), *Women and Sport: From Myth to Reality*, pp. 173–91. Philadelphia: Lea & Febiger.

Maehr, M. L. and Nicholls, J. G. (1980) Culture and achievement motivation: a second look. In N. Warren (ed.), *Studies in Cross-Cultural Psychology II*, pp. 221–67. London: Academic Press.

Mark, M. M., Mutrie, N., Brooks, D. R., and Harris, D. V. (1984) Causal attributions of winners and losers in individual competitive sports: toward a reformulation of the self-serving bias. *Journal of Sport Psychology* **6**, 184–96.

Miller, D. T. and Ross, M. (1975). Self-serving biases in the attribution of causality: fact or fiction? *Psychological Bulletin* **82**, 213–25.

Nicholls, J. G. (1984) Achievement motivation: conceptions of ability, subjective experience, task choice, and performance. *Psychological Review* **91**, 328–46.

Nicholls, J. G. and Miller, A. T. (1984) Development and its discontents: the differentiation of the concept of ability. In J. G. Nicholls (ed.), *Advances in Motivation and Achievement* 3, pp. 185–218. London: JAI Press.

Rejeski, W. J. and Brawley, L. R. (1983) Attribution theory in sport: current status and new perspectives. *Journal of Sport Psychology* **5**, 77–99.

Roberts, G. C. (1978) Children's assignment of responsibility for winning and losing. In F. L. Smoll and R. E. Smith (eds), *Psychological Perspectives in Youth Sports*, pp. 145–71. Washington, DC: Hemisphere.

Roberts, G. C. (1984) Toward a new theory of motivation in sport: the role of perceived ability. In J. Silva and R. S. Weinberg (eds), *Psychological Foundations of Sport*, pp. 214–28. Champaign, IL: Human Kinetics.

Roberts, G. C. and Pascuzzi, D. L. (1979) Causal attributions in sport: some theoretical implications. *Journal of Sport Psychology* **1**, 203–11.

Robinson, D. W. (1990) An attributional analysis of student demoralization in physical education settings. *Quest* **42**, 27–39.

Robinson, D. W. and Howe, B. L. (1989) Appraisal variable/affect relationships in youth sport: a test of Weiner's attributional model. *Journal of Sport and Exercise Psychology* **11**, 431–43.

Spink, K. S. and Roberts, G. C. (1980) Ambiguity of outcome and causal attributions. *Journal of Sport Psychology* **2**, 237–44.

Tenenbaum, G. and Furst, D. (1985) The relationship between sport achievement responsibility, attribution and related situational variables. *International Journal of Sport Psychology* **16**, 254–69.

Vallerand, R. J. (1983) On emotion in sport: theoretical and social psychological perspectives. *Journal of Sport Psychology* **5**, 197–215.

Vallerand, R. J. (1984) Emotion in sport: definitional, historical and social psychological perspectives. In W. F. Straub and J. M. Williams (eds), *Cognitive Sport Psychology*, pp. 65–78. Lansing, NY: Sport Science Associates.

Vallerand, R. J. (1987) Antecedents of self-related effects in sport: preliminary evidence on the intuitive-reflective appraisal model. *Journal of Sport Psychology* **9**, 161–82.

Weiner, B. (1979) A theory of motivation for some classroom experiences. *Journal of Educational Psychology* **71**, 3–25.

Weiner, B. (1985a) 'Spontaneous' causal thinking. *Psychological Bulletin* **97**, 74–84.

Weiner, B. (1985b) An attributional theory of achievement motivation and emotion. *Psychological Review* **92**, 548–73.

Weiner, B. (1986) *An Attributional Theory of Motivation and Emotion*. New York: Springer-Verlag.

Weiner, B., Frieze, I. H., Kukla, A., Reed, L., Rest, S., and Rosenbaum, R. M. (1972) Perceiving the causes of success and failure. In E. E. Jones, D. E. Kanouse, H. H. Kelley, R. E. Nisbett, S. Valins, and B. Weiner (eds), *Attribution: Perceiving the Causes of Behaviour*, pp. 95–120. Morristown, NJ: General Learning Press.

Weiner, B., Russell, D., and Lerman, D. (1978) Affective consequences of causal ascriptions. In J. H. Harvey, W. Ickes, and R. F. Kidd (eds), *New Directions in Attribution Research* 2, pp. 59–90. Hillsdale, NJ: Erlbaum.

Weiner, B., Russell, D., and Lerman, D. (1979) The cognition–emotion process in achievement-related contexts. *Journal of Personality and Social Psychology* **37**, 1211–226.

Weiss, M. R. McAuley, E., Ebbeck, V., and Wiese, D. M. (1990) Self-esteem and causal attributions for children's physical and social competence in sport. *Journal of Sport and Exercise Psychology* **12**, 21–36.

Whitehead, J. (1986) A cross-national comparison of attributions underlying achievement orientations in adolescent sport. In J. Watkins, T. Reilly, and L. Burwitz (eds), *Sports Science*, pp. 297–302. London: E. & F. N. Spon.

Chapter 7

Assessment Developments and Challenges in Physical Education[1]

Peter Drewett

INTRODUCTION

Assessment in some form pervades our everyday life and has traditionally played a central role in the process of education. In recent years it has become a key issue and the source of increasingly heated debate. This debate has taken place in response to various sets of demands, varying from professional interests inside schools to other political, economic, and social forces that exist beyond the school gates.

Prior to the early 1970s, assessment in schools was largely confined to an elaborate public examination system, as reflected by the School Certificate and Higher School Certificate of 1917, the General Certificate of Education of 1951, and the Certificate of Secondary Education of 1965. The Ruskin College speech of 1976, given by the then Prime Minister Jim Callaghan, called into question the effectiveness of educational provision. He called for greater government interest in the issues of accountability and standards of learning and teaching in schools. As such, the 1980s have been described by Hargreaves (1989) as an 'era of assessment-led curriculum reform' (p. 41). Much of the government investment has centred on the summative aspects of assessment, with examination reform and testing having the highest priority.

Broadfoot (1986) has attributed this steady growth of government interest in assessment policies to the following main themes. First, she suggests that government attempts to control the school curriculum were failing and assessment offered a vehicle for redirection. Second, there was increasing cost-consciousness and overt concern with the need for increased accountability. Third, there was a reaction to 'the pressure to respond to industry's demands for a more skilled and vocationally prepared work force' (p. 206).

At the same time, according to Murphy and Torrance (1988), educationalists have also been reflecting on the excessive control which the examination system has traditionally exercised over the secondary school curriculum. In particular, the determining role of assessment with regard to teaching methods, the relationship of assessment to learning, and the uncertain validity and reliability of results generated by examinations, have been critiqued and debated. This has highlighted the increasingly common opinion that the public examination system, as it stands, represents a narrow and unambitious approach to the problem of measuring educational achievements.

In support, the conclusions of the European Community Brighton Conference (held in May, 1988), which discussed assessment of pupil achievement, motivation and success, demonstrated the widespread commitment by educators to finding more constructive approaches to assessing pupil achievement. A number of negative aspects of current assessment contexts and traditions, which largely refer to examinations, were highlighted. These were: (a) a preponderance of norm-referenced assumptions (see glossary of terms on pp. 119–20); (b) an overemphasis on the summative purpose of assessment; (c) the restriction of assessment to lower order cognitive elements of academic curricular content; (d) the perception and treatment of pupils as passive recipients of assessment; and (e) the manner in which the aggregation of pupils' achievements across the curriculum masks specific achievements and difficulties. The participants at the Brighton Conference also identified some new directions for the assessment of pupil achievement. Many examples focused upon child-centred, person-orientated aspects of profiling processes and included more emphasis on formative feedback and the assessment of more aspects of achievement (for example, physical, practical, and affective). Also discussed were better specification of learning targets, more individualized pacing of learning, involving the pupil as partner in assessment, and forms of certification which ensure progression to worthwhile training after compulsory schooling.

Central government initiatives implemented through the Education Reform Act of 1988 and reflected in the adoption of the National Curriculum have added a further dimension to the assessment debate. The requirement of national standardized tests at ages 7, 11, 14, and 16 calls for extensive formal summative assessment. The 1990s, therefore, begin with the potential complexities that arise when this intervention is set alongside a general educational trend calling for greater involvement of the child in more formative approaches to assessment.

The first purpose of this chapter, in the context of these general educational trends, is to address the evolution of approaches to assessment in physical education. This will prepare the ground for a discussion of some of the major assessment issues and problems which remain to be resolved as we face the demands of the National Curriculum and the challenges of the 1990s.

ELEMENTS OF ASSESSMENT IN EDUCATION

Before engaging in a specific analysis of assessment in physical education it may be useful to provide a brief overview of what are generally considered to be the main purposes and functions of educational assessment. According to Broadfoot (1987) the purposes of assessment in education can be categorized into three major themes. These are assessment for curriculum, assessment for communication, and assessment for accountability. The elements involved in these themes are featured in Figure 7.1. Assessment within the curriculum has a diagnostic function for the improvement of learning. This involves factors such as the provision of information for monitoring student progress as well as feedback for evaluating curriculum effectiveness and initiating its modification. Curriculum assessment also functions to supply information which may act as a source of mastery and motivation for both student and teacher. In relation to communication, assessment has a certification function, which credits pupils with varying degrees of achievements. The communication theme also has a selection element which, for example, enables future employers and further or higher education establishments to choose appropriate pupils. Assessment for accountability refers to whether a school is satisfying its own, the government's, and society's expectations of schooling.

The curriculum theme, to a greater extent, has tended to be associated with a formative emphasis in assessment, especially where information is used for recording and reporting progress. On the other hand, assessment for communication has traditionally adopted a summative approach, which has been closely linked with the formal examination system.

Broadfoot (1987) has identified a 'nightmare of conflicting pressures on schools and teachers in which curriculum concerns battle for a place alongside the communication imperatives to which schools are subject' (p. 9). The purposes and priorities of assessment differ according to interest groups such as pupils, teachers, parents, governors, and employers. This presents continual constraints on curricular policy and time allocation. For example, the characteristics of the selection function of assessment favoured by employers may be educationally at odds with the diagnostic purposes of assessment used by teachers. Furthermore, even though assessment functions may not conceptually conflict, time and resource constraints may not allow dual or multiple assessment mechanisms to exist side by side.

However, within the context of the recent assessment debate discussed earlier, it would appear that the formative and summative elements of assessment associated with the curriculum and communication themes are becoming increasingly interwoven. In recent years, for example, there has been a reappraisal of the involvement of pupils in the learning and assessment process within the certification element of assessment (see Figure 7.1). Continuous assessment methods in early CSE initiatives have been followed by a similar approach in the more recent Technical and Vocational Education Initiative (TVEI) programmes, giving impetus to the curriculum aspect of assessment. In many schools, pupils are actively involved in experiential learning, active tutorial work, active learning, supported self-study, resource-based learning, individualized learning, negotiated learning, and reciprocal teaching. Such developments have given rise to a number of in-course assessment techniques, such as graded tests, negotiated assessments, student self-assessment, and peer assessment where pupils are required to collaborate in the assessment process either with each other or with teachers, or to contribute by themselves.

However, tensions still remain between the formative aspects of assessment which are used as a means of encouraging learning, and the summative aspects which are examination and product orientated and primarily used for selection and certification purposes. To reduce this friction, Broadfoot (1987) believes that a summative assessment procedure should be utilized that 'recognises not only the skills and knowledge measured in written examinations but also the practical skills, social attributes and personal qualities which represent the wider aims of education' (p. 9). The motivation for those involved in the emergence of profiling as a vehicle for assessment has been to successfully identify a procedure which incorporates all the elements described here.

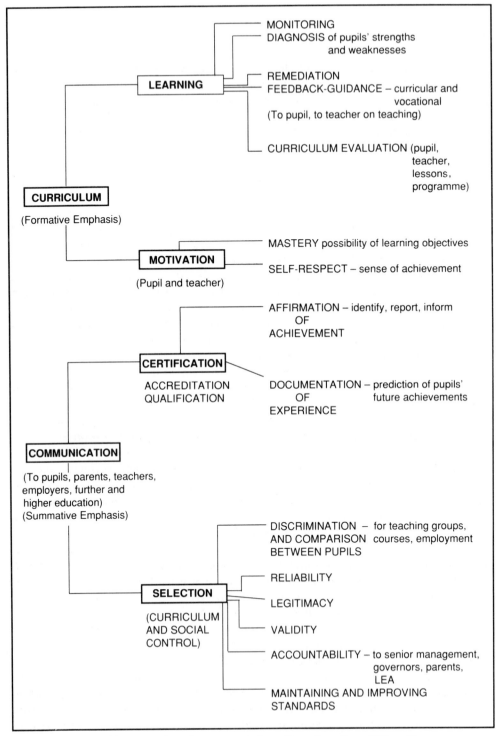

Figure 7.1 *Aspects and functions of pupil assessment* (adapted from Broadfoot, 1987, p. 7).

Profiling and the records of achievement which often accompany it will be discussed in more detail later in this chapter.

DEVELOPMENTS IN ASSESSMENT IN PHYSICAL EDUCATION

The purposes of assessment have also been discussed within the context of physical education (Booton, 1986; Carroll, 1986, 1990; Skelthorne, 1986). Reeves (1986) has described the following reasons:

1   To demonstrate that we value the pupil's work by formally assessing it.
2   To enable pupils to receive information about themselves.
3   To give information to others who may require it, such as parents or prospective employers.
4   To evaluate teaching effectiveness.

However, in practice, at least until the last twenty years, assessment in physical education has taken a relatively informal stance. Much of the day-to-day assessment of pupils in physical education has been restricted to an informal routine of verbal comment given by teachers and pupils, which might refer to performance, attitude, effort, or cooperation. Qualitative assessment has dominated, where physical educators use their professional experience to make subjective observations of children's physical performance. Teachers have relied on this type of information to select teams and individuals for school sport representation and as the basis for end-of-term or yearly reports.

More recently, quantitative assessment, in the form of standardized tests of physical performance, has been increasingly used. These have often been packaged by sport-governing bodies as award schemes for specific sports and activities. Examples have included the British Amateur Gymnastics Association Awards, the Amateur Swimming Association Awards, and the Amateur Athletics Association Five Star Scheme. Commercial sponsorship has also grasped the opportunity to provide proficiency schemes, for example, in basketball (Seven-Up) and football (Coca-Cola). Along the same performance lines, the health-related fitness movement has stimulated increased interest in the use of fitness test batteries and schemes in schools throughout the 1980s.

In summary, assessment in physical education in the main can best be described as having been low key and primarily kept in-house for purposes of selection, recording and reporting, and motivating students. This state of affairs has perhaps evolved because the curriculum has had the luxury of remaining untethered for so many years to the constraints of public examination systems.

THE EMERGENCE OF ACCREDITATION

The changing nature of the 14–19 curriculum in schools during the last decade has witnessed the emergence, on an increasingly large scale, of a whole range of accredited courses relating to physical education and sport. These have been designed to satisfy vocational demands, and provide both sports coaching and academic qualifications.

Table 7.1 indicates the array of accredited PE related courses, which are either currently offered or in the process of being established and validated. As a result, physical educators have been forced to reappraise their role in assessment and the issues concerned with the measurement of pupil achievement and attainment.

Table 7.1. *The developing range of accredited courses relating to PE and sport.*

1 GCSE (General Certificate of Secondary Education)—Dance
                                                  —Physical education
2 A level—Physical education
            Sport studies
            Dance
3 CFS (Certificate of Further Studies)—Sport studies
   (Developed by Associated Examination Board)
4 Records of Achievement—Summative document
                  (Profiling—Formative process)
5 Governing body award schemes—examples:
   (a) CCPR (Central Council for Physical Recreation) Community Sports Leaders Award
   (b) Basic expedition training award
   (c) ASA (Amateur Swimming Association) Preliminary Teaching Award
6 Vocational awards—Recreation and leisure industry
                  (Sports centres, sports coaching, management)
   (a) CPVE (Certificate of Pre-Vocational Education)—Health studies
                                                   —Sports studies
                                                   —Leisure studies
   (b) TVEI (Technical and Vocational Education Initiative)—Modular courses: First aid, Diet, Sports
        leadership are examples
   (c) BTEC (Business and Technician Education Council)
           Leisure studies—BTEC First, National and Higher National Certificate/Diploma courses
   (d) CGLI (City and Guilds of London Institute)
           Certificate in recreation and leisure studies (481)

For the first time on a large scale, accreditation courses have introduced examinations as an integral part of the assessment procedures of many PE programmes. The 1970s saw the emergence of CSE Physical Education courses, and more recently, GCE, GCSE, and A-level courses have extended physical education's bid for academic involvement. In 1985, 13,109 pupils were examined in CSE PE, and in 1989 32,700 were entered for GCSE PE examinations thus indicating the increased interest. Presently, several examination boards offer GCSE Physical Education (see Appendix, pp. 120–1).

These courses have exposed the emergence of a major assessment dilemma in PE: a conflict of interest between theoretical and practical performance. For the first time, a significant component of academic or cognitive-based content has been included in the programme. Depending on the examination board, for instance, a theory component founded in aspects of anatomy, physiology, psychology, and sociology has been incorporated into the syllabus. Additionally, knowledge which is specific to the laws, rules, tactics, and techniques of sports and activities has also been required. Subsequent assessment has involved paper-and-pencil examinations typical of the more traditionally academic subjects. This academic content has been set against a continued drive by many physical educators to feature and reward the demonstration of quality physical performances. The result is that for many courses, pupils are required to exhibit expertise in a range of sports and physical activities which usually include team games, racket sports, and individual activities such as gymnastics, swimming, and track and field. The relative weights given to theory and practical elements of these courses have been heavily debated, the outcome being a compromise of 50 per cent of marks usually assigned to each. The need to provide standardized and comparative forms of assessment of physical performance and skill has also highlighted the tremendous difficulties in achieving objectivity and validity. For a more complete discussion on the structure and nature of examinations in physical education see Carroll (1990).

PROFILING AND RECORDS OF ACHIEVEMENT

In response to the general trend in education to seek out assessment instruments and systems which are capable of fulfilling both summative and formative functions, there has been a growth in interest and application of profiles and records of achievement in physical education (Booton, 1986; Drewett and Sparkes, 1989; Skelthorne, 1986; Skinsley, 1988). Records of achievement and profiling have quite a long history which needs to be considered in order to fully appreciate their development in physical education. As early as 1911, the Consultative Committee on Education noted that examination results alone could never give an accurate picture of the qualities, achievements, and attributes of a pupil. Much later, the Newsom Report (1963) stated:

> some form of leaver's certificate which combined assessment with a record of the pupil's school career would be valued by parents, future employers and colleges of further education, and should, we believe, be available to all pupils who complete a full second-ary course.   (p. 80)

The raising of the school leaving age to 16, in 1973, and the resultant concern about motivation of so-called 'less able' fourth and fifth year pupils, highlighted the need to broaden the profile of a student's achievements beyond a straight list of examination results. A further turning point in the development of profiles came with the Further Education Unit's publication of *A Basis for Choice* in 1979, which recommended that profile methods of recording student assessment should be developed in further education to assist the process of vocational selection. The Department of Education and Science (DES) published *Records of Achievement: A Statement of Policy* in July 1984, which set the objective of establishing records of achievement for all school leavers in England and Wales by 1990, giving the innovation further support and credibility. Currently, the Report of the Records of Achievement National Steering Committee (DES, 1989) and the Pilot Records of Achievement in Schools Evaluation Report (Broadfoot *et al.*, 1988) offer insights into the successes and difficulties experienced by the pilot schemes which were set up in 1984 and outline national guidelines for the introduction of records of achievement.

Records of achievement have the following main purposes:

1   To provide recognition of a wider range of experience and achievement than that measured by traditional public examinations.
2   To increase pupils' motivation and personal development.
3   To provide feedback on the effectiveness of the curriculum, teaching, and organization.

4   To provide a summative document or record which is valued and recognized by employers and institutions of further and higher education.

For the sake of clarification, *a profile* is not, in itself, a method of assessment, it is a document which can record assessments of students across a wide range of abilities, including skills, attitudes, personal achievements, personal qualities, and subject attainments (both within the classroom and outside of school). It frequently involves the student in its formation and therefore fulfils a formative as well as a summative function (Hitchcock, 1986). The process of *profiling* refers to reviewing, reflecting on learning, and target setting for student and teacher. The diagnostic function of profiling is operational when pupils are encouraged to ask themselves: 'What have I achieved?', 'What have I not achieved?', 'What are my strengths and weaknesses?', 'Where am I going?', 'How do I get there?' Conversely, a *profile* or *record of achievement* is a summary document which is based on information gathered during the profiling process.

For a number of physical educators the emergence of the profiling movement has created the opportunity to review their curriculum, teaching methods, reporting systems, and assessment methods. For instance, teachers have valued the progressive build up of information which accompanies profiling, allowing for the preparation of more meaningful student reports. According to Hitchcock (1986), 'The most exciting effect of successful profiling is that it prompts teachers to look afresh at what they are teaching and how they are teaching' (p. 99). Perhaps due to the autonomy afforded a subject area which is free from the strait-jacket constraints of examination boards and syllabuses, some physical educators have been more inclined and able to experiment with new ways of assessing their pupils in this way. Furthermore, this freedom has sometimes resulted in a number of schools developing PE subject profiling systems which have been adopted as examples of good practice by other subject areas, thus enhancing the status of PE in those schools (Carroll, 1990; Drewett and Sparkes, 1989).

REMAINING CHALLENGES AND ISSUES

According to Carroll (1986), the emergence of recognized accreditation courses and the examination systems which have tended to dominate their assessment mode, has been enthusiastically welcomed by many physical educators. In particular, examined courses have been seen as a route to achieving higher academic status for physical education, which in turn has procured resources and greater curricular time allocation. However, the development of these schemes has not progressed without some criticism. Some observers have, for example, commented on the benefits of physical education remaining a non-examined area and have viewed the search for status as unnecessary and divisive. In short, there are a range of advantages and disadvantages, summarized in Tables 7.2 and 7.3, which still require considerable debate and discussion in the future.

As opposed to the development of examination courses in physical education which have been underwritten by largely extrinsic motives, profiling has evolved primarily to create a more productive partnership between pupil and teacher in the learning

Table 7.2. *Advantages of examinations in PE.*

1   *TIME* not lost and maybe increased timetable space.
        More likely to secure scarce resources.
2   *EQUAL CREDIT* for pupils in their strong subject.
3   *STATUS* of the subject could be improved. Also political move to establish and safeguard the place of
    PE in the school curriculum.
4   *SATISFACTION* of pupils might be increased.
5   *EMPLOYERS* could be given more guidance.
6   *STRUCTURE AND DIRECTION* could be given to the PE curriculum. A stimulus for programme
    development in PE. Involves teachers in curriculum-making process which in turn may promote their
    professional development. Shift in teacher's role from recreationalist to educationalist. (See Carroll,
    1986.)
7   *STANDARDS* might improve and more motivation will be given to 'academic' pupils.
8   *A FOUNDATION* will be provided for future study in college and university. Argue for specialist
    trained teachers and career structure similar to other subjects.
9   PE is one of the few subjects in which examinations are not generally available. Creates an
    opportunity to introduce knowledge 'about' physical activity as a legitimate and necessary ingredient
    of the subject. (See Kirk, 1988.)

Table 7.3. *Disadvantages of examinations in PE.*

1   *RESTRICTION* of scope: physical educators required to submit to some form of external and
    centralized control of their work.
2   *PLAY* element could be lost. Knowing 'about' physical activity may gain precedence over active
    engagement in physical activities, e.g. A-level PE 30 per cent practical component, 70 per cent
    theoretical.
3   Too many examinations already in schools: PE has a *SOCIALIZING* role.
4   It is not an examinable area. It is done *'for its own sake'*. The intrinsic nature is not accessible.
    'Physical education's non-academic character is the very source of its importance in the provision of a
    balanced education for all' (Hargreaves, 1982, p. 6).
5   *ADMINISTRATIVE* problems are too great. Increase in workload for physical educators. Other areas
    of the PE curriculum might suffer because time and resources are allocated elsewhere.
6   It might take up *teaching time* in testing. Also teaching to the test can lead to rote learning amongst
    pupils, didactic teaching methods, and content-dominated course.
7   Examinations might create and *advertise failure* in a subject where all children can gain success.
    Standards might be predominantly external. For pupils, passing the examination becomes all
    important, not necessarily the worth of the subject. The measurement and quantification of
    performance could lead, and thus distort, knowledge in the curriculum. PE could become 'just another
    subject'. (See Kirk, 1988.)
8   Sufficient reward and motivation is already available by tutor, house or school team representation,
    and proficiency tests and awards.
9   Possibility of *deskilling* PE teachers if they are not given appropriate in-service provision and the
    opportunities to educate themselves to teach new programmes.

process. Summative end-of-term PE profiles are increasingly including space for both teachers' and pupils' free responses, resulting in a negotiated final statement between both parties which covers a wide variety of achievements, qualities, skills and attainments, both within and outside school. Although time consuming for the PE teacher, this approach is intended to promote positive teacher–pupil relationships and to humanize the whole assessment process. Many termly PE profiles also include a section for parental and guardian comment in attempts to promote a productive three-way dialogue between parents, teachers, and pupils. Furthermore, profiling and records of achievement may offer a more comprehensive mode of assessment for certain accredited courses in physical education.

Although profiling and records of achievement are indicating considerable promise, there remain several problems to be resolved. Hargreaves (1986) expresses concern that teachers will use the profiling process for the purposes of selection, surveillance and retaining their hierarchical role, rather than for promoting pupil independence, self-realization, motivation, and mutual respectful and responsible partnership between pupil and teacher. In this case, it is possible that profiles will merely replicate the selection and social control functions that have been associated by some with traditional examinations. Hitchcock (1986) has also warned that 'it would be naive to imagine that the introduction of profiling into a school will not be accompanied by difficulties' (p. 149). The DES (1989) document and the Records of Achievement Report (Broadfoot *et al.*, 1988) described the occurrence of some of these difficulties. These refer to issues of confidentiality, ownership, privacy, hierarchy, pupil empowerment, class, gender, and assessment in the affective domain.

Physical educators have also reported related problems and tensions. At one level, there has been the exposure of a clash of ideologies and attitudes between department members concerning the purposes of physical education and assessment. Some colleagues have also felt threatened by the implicit pupil empowerment involved with profiling and the need to adopt new management and teaching styles to enable successful profiling to operate. At a more practical level, the initial demands for time, resources, and the need for in-service provision accompanying any innovation have been perceived as an obstacle to development (Drewett, 1991; Skelthorne, 1986).

A unique profiling problem for physical educators revolves around pupil safety in their lessons. Even when PE teachers utilize the whole spectrum of teaching styles with their pupils, the potentially dangerous nature of the pupils' tasks in the gym, on the playing field, or in the swimming pool, makes it difficult for the teacher to engage in prolonged and meaningful dialogue with individuals. In contrast, a mathematics teacher or form tutor can safely set work for the class before confidentially discussing a child's progress in a quiet part of the classroom while the work is being done.

There have been moves to overcome some of the problems of profiling. Skinsley (1988), in response to the difficulties experienced by PE teachers in finding time to negotiate with pupils, has developed a computer-assisted profiling system designed to speed up the process. The pressures of time and the unique environment in which PE teachers work have also forced them to develop profiling tools which are quick and easy to administer.

According to Hargreaves (1986):

> The promise of profiling is that of an assessment system which can make a reality of the aims of education which we set ourselves. It offers a vision of education which is characterised by democratic teacher–pupil relations, in which pupils have a sense of self-worth; in which they may voluntarily negotiate their own curriculum path; in which they develop the ability to be self-critical and thus to take responsibility for their own learning, and in which the competition is primarily with themselves and their own previous performance rather than with others. (p. 230)

Recent Department of Education and Science and Department of Employment statements (Jones and Forrester, 1990) on records of achievements would suggest that the process of profiling will become an integral element of future assessment plans. In particular, it could serve to unite the diversity of assessment that currently exists with future initiatives such as the National Curriculum.

In conclusion, a coherent role appears to have emerged in the 1980s for examinations and accreditations in physical education. More recently, largely through the efforts of teachers at grass roots level, the value of profiling and recording systems has achieved extensive recognition. There remain, however, many issues at the conceptual, ethical, and practical level still to be resolved before an integrated assessment package emerges which serves the multiple demands of contemporary education.

This chapter has chosen to address the assessment issue at the systems and organizational level. It would not serve the reader to ignore a major assumption on which assessment systems, such as those described here, have been allowed to develop. The question still remains regarding our capability to produce reliable and valid information which can fuel assessment systems. The diversity of objectives in physical education has created a minefield of measurement problems in the subject area. The assessment of static and fluid physical skills alongside lower-order knowledge and higher-order evaluative and analytic skills is proving difficult. Additionally, the increasing statement of lifetime objectives in physical education has raised the complex issue of the assessment of lasting affective change reflected in attitudes and self-perceptions. A failure to address and resolve these issues of measurement validity will result in assessment packages which are meaningless.

GLOSSARY OF TERMS

Student profile — is a document recording experiences, achievement and progress following valid forms of assessment. It is a type of report. In practice it is often an innovation in that it refers to/reveals non-subject performances over a wide focus of cognitive and affective behaviour—the student is made more visible.

A record — is evidence on which outsiders can make judgements.

A report — is judgement which outsiders can take as evidence.

Profiling — is a process of interaction between pupil and tutor to present various evidence to a third party. The interaction is intended to have a motivating effect on the pupil.

Criterion-referenced assessment — is designed to show what individual learning objectives the student has mastered, without comparison with any other student. A student's performance is measured against explicit criteria; the student either achieves or does not achieve the criteria.

Norm-referenced assessment — is designed to be used to make comparisons among individuals. The mark/grade awarded to a student is dependent not only on the quality of the student's own performance, but also on the quality of the performances of other students.

Ipsative assessment (sometimes called ideographic) — is that which compares the student's performance with his/her previous performance, but makes no attempt to compare the student with others.

Formative assessment — is assessment that informs student development. It takes place during the course of teaching and can be used by teachers in discussion with students to motivate students, to offer remedial support and to alter the nature of the course of study.

Summative assessment — is assessment that measures the student's final achievement. It takes place at the end of the course.

Graded assessment — is a form of staged assessment that implies progression. The assessment is in the form of a series of graded tests at progressive levels of difficulty designed to be taken at a time when the student has a high probability of passing the test.

Moderation — is the procedure by which the results of assessments from a number of assessors responsible for the assessment of their own candidates are aligned with an agreed, accepted, standard.

Modes of assessment — are the different methods by which a student can be assessed. The main modes of assessment are: written tests, oral activities prepared or spontaneous, classroom-based course work, aural tests, projects and practicals. Some of these methods are more suitable for continuous and/or informal assessment and some more suited to structured and/or formal organization of assessments.

Accreditation — This is the process whereby a body, possibly established specifically for the purpose, grants its imprimatur to other agencies to undertake activities on its behalf. This tends to involve the licensing of an institution to operate an education scheme and provide certification. The granting of a licence can be subject to rigorous conditions and involve inspection, and over the whole process hangs the power to revoke that licence.

Negotiation — A process of discussion between pupil and teacher, either to draw out and nourish a view of significant experience and achievement in the past or to plan some future action, course, or curriculum. A process whereby the aims, objectives, goals and content of a training programme are agreed jointly by tutor/trainee/student.

Negotiation presupposes open relationships between students and staff, where discussion of issues can come to mutually agreed acceptable conclusions without undue pressure or prejudice by one party or the other, and where due allowance is made for inexperience, lack of maturity, or inarticulateness.

Reliability — This refers to the consistency or accuracy of an examination component. A component is completely reliable if it would yield the same results when repeated by the same candidate under the same conditions.

Validation — The process whereby approval is given to arrangements for the development of courses of study and their related assessment in accordance with an agreed set of rules and regulations. In a very elementary form it may mean the signature by someone (usually an adult) that a statement by a pupil is true.

Validity — The extent to which an assessment does that which it was designed to do. Since assessments are designed to do a wide variety of different things their validity can be assessed in a number of different ways.

APPENDIX

1 *GCSE*

SOUTHERN EXAMINING
ASSOCIATION
c/o South East Regional Examinations
Board,
Beloe House,
2/10 Mount Ephraim Road,
Royal Tunbridge Wells
Kent TN1 1EU.
Tel: Tunbridge Wells (0892) 35311
Physical education—GCSE
Dance—GCSE (syllabuses £1.00 each)

MIDLAND EXAMINING GROUP
c/o West Midlands Examinations Board,
Norfolk House,
Smallbrook Queensway,
Birmingham B5 4NJ.
Tel: 021 631 2151
The theory and practice of physical
education—GCSE
Dance—GCSE (syllabuses £0.60 each)

WELSH JOINT EDUCATION
COMMITTEE
245 Western Avenue,
Cardiff CF5 2YX.
Tel: Cardiff (0222) 561231
Physical education—GCSE
(syllabus £0.75; specimen papers:
Paper 1 Dance or Gymnastics,
Papers 2 and 3 compulsory—£0.20 each)

SCOTTISH EXAMINATION BOARD
Ironmills Road,
Dalkeith,
Midlothian EH22 1LE.
Tel: 031 663 6601
Physical education—Standard grade
examination at Foundation, General, and
Credit Levels

NORTHERN EXAMINING
ASSOCIATION
c/o Joint Matriculation Board,
Manchester M15 6EU.
Tel: 061 273 2565
Physical education—GCSE
Dance—GCSE (syllabuses £0.60 each,
minimum order £1.00)

LONDON AND EAST ANGLIAN
EXAMINING GROUP
'The Lindens'
Lexden Road,
Colchester CO3 3RL.
Tel: Colchester (0206) 549595
Physical education—GCSE
Dance—GCSE (syllabuses £0.75 each)

2 *A LEVEL*
ASSOCIATED EXAMINING BOARD
Stag Hill House,
Guildford,
Surrey GU2 5XJ.
Tel: Guildford (0483) 506506
Sports studies—A level
Physical education—A level

LONDON REGIONAL EXAMINING
BOARD
104 Wandsworth High Street,
London SW18 4LF.
Tel: 081 870 2144
Dance—A level

3 *VOCATIONAL QUALIFICATIONS*
CITY AND GUILDS OF LONDON
INSTITUTE
46 Britannia Street,
London WC1X 9RG.
Tel: 071 278 2468
Certification in recreation and leisure studies
(481)

BUSINESS AND TECHNICIAN
EDUCATION COUNCIL
Central House,
Upper Woburn Place,
London WC1H 0HH.
Tel: 071 388 3288
Leisure studies—BTEC First, National and
Higher National Certificate/Diploma courses

NORTHERN IRELAND SCHOOLS
EXAMINATIONS COUNCIL
Beechill House,
42 Beechill Road,
Belfast BT8 4RS.
Tel: Belfast (0232) 704666
Physical education—GCSE

NOTE

1   Thanks go to Dr Ken Fox for his helpful comments on an earlier draft of this chapter.

REFERENCES

Booton, P. (1986) One form of assessment. *The Bulletin of Physical Education* **22**, 32–42.
Broadfoot, P. (1986) Assessment policy and inequality: the United Kingdom experience. *British Journal of Sociology of Education* **7**, 205–24.
Broadfoot, P. (1987) *Introducing Profiling: A Practical Manual.* London: Macmillan.
Broadfoot, P., James, M., McMeeking, S., Nuttall, D., and Stierer, B. (1988) *Records of Achievement: Report of the National Evaluation of Pilot Schemes.* London: HMSO.

Carroll, R. (1986) Examinations in physical education: an analysis of trends and development. In *Proceedings of the VIII Commonwealth and International Conference on Sport, Physical Education, Dance, Recreation and Health, Trends and Developments in Physical Education*, pp. 233–9. London: E. and F. N. Spon.

Carroll, R. (1990) Examinations and assessment in physical education. In N. Armstrong (ed.), *New Directions in Physical Education* 1, pp. 137–60. Champaign, IL: Human Kinetics.

DES (1984) *Records of Achievement: A Statement of Policy*. London: HMSO.

DES (1989) *Records of Achievement: Report of the Records of Achievement National Steering Committee*. London: HMSO.

Drewett, P. (1991) Profiling as a curriculum innovation in school: a case study from physical education. M.Ed. dissertation. University of Exeter.

Drewett, P. and Sparkes, A. (1989) Adopting profiling: key issues for consideration by department heads. *The British Journal of Physical Education* 20, 19–21.

FEU (1979) *A Basis for Choice*. Further education curriculum and development unit report of a study group on post-16 pre-employment courses. London: HMSO.

Hargreaves, A. (1986) Record breakers? In P. Broadfoot (ed.), *Profiles and Records of Achievement: A Review of Issues and Practice*, pp. 203–27. London: Cassell.

Hargreaves, A. (1989) The crisis of motivation and assessment. In A. Hargreaves and D. Reynolds (eds), *Educational Policies: Controversies and Critiques*, pp. 41–63. London: Falmer Press.

Hargreaves, D. H. (1982) Ten proposals for the future of physical education. *The Bulletin of Physical Education* 13, 5–10.

Hitchcock, G. (1986) Instituting profiling within a school. In P. Broadfoot (ed.), *Profiles and Records of Achievement: A Review of Issues and Practice*, pp. 146–65. London: Cassell.

Jones, A. and Forrester, D. (1990) Joint letter circulated by Department of Education and Science and Department of Employment, *A National Record of Achievement*, December. London: HMSO.

Kirk, D. (1988) *Physical Education and Curriculum Study: A Critical Introduction*. London: Croom Helm.

Murphy, R. and Torrance, H. (1988) *The Changing Face of Educational Assessment*. Milton Keynes: Open University Press.

Newsom, J. (1963) *Half Our Future*. A Report of the Central Advisory Council for Education (England): HMSO.

Reeves, B. (1986) Assessment in physical education. *The Bulletin of Physical Education* 22, 29–31.

Skelthorne, A. (1986) The development of a profiling system. *The Bulletin of Physical Education* 21, 43–7.

Skinsley, M. (1988) Profiling and assessment in school: the management of change. *The British Journal of Physical Education* 19, 101–3.

Chapter 8

Physical Education and its Contribution to Health and Well-Being[1]

Kenneth R. Fox

More than ten years have passed since we first began to see the term health-related fitness extensively used in the British physical education literature. During this period it has been rewarding to see increasing numbers of physical education programmes rise to the challenge that this innovation has presented. At the same time, research evidence supporting the need for increased involvement in physical activity across the lifespan has grown considerably, to the extent that a causal link between ill health and inactivity is now widely accepted by the medical profession (Harris *et al.*, 1989; Powell *et al.*, 1987).

Accompanying this advancement in research has been a steadily increased understanding among physical education professionals regarding the important concepts underlying health-related fitness education. In particular, the emphasis placed on promoting *lifetime* rather than *immediate* fitness gains has been sound. The sensible adoption of an educational rather than comparative or competitive approach to fitness testing appears to be the norm rather than the exception. In many schools, there has been a move away from programmes which are exclusively concerned with sports performance to a rationale based on lifetime sport and exercise involvement, with success measured by children's interest and continued participation in activity.

As the health-related fitness movement has gained momentum it has come under increasing scrutiny and has perhaps deservedly been the subject of criticism from some curricular theorists (see Kirk, 1988; McNamee, 1988; Sparkes, 1989). These critiques have generally fallen into two camps. The first has focused on the dominance of *individualism* which has underpinned the health-related fitness evolution. Throughout, educational objectives have been built around the enablement of youngsters to take on the personal responsibility of adopting a healthy, active lifestyle. Critics have rightfully argued that health has other potent determinants which have been largely ignored. Many are beyond the direct control of the individual, have socio-political implications, and are better tackled from a communal rather than an individual viewpoint. The second theme of criticism arises from the difficulties that the health-related fitness movement has had in adequately defining and conceptualizing the relationships between fitness and exercise, and the more holistic parameters such as health and well-being.

It is undoubtedly true that since the early 1980s the health-related fitness movement has been orientated towards education for individual lifestyle change. A simplistic functional approach to health has been adopted which has been based on a 'get fit, stay fit, and be healthy' message. Health, in this context, has been primarily defined in terms of avoidance of hypokinetic illness (disease partially attributable to lack of activity), particularly with reference to coronary heart disease (CHD). From the early stages therefore, increased fitness through its impact on disease prevention has been seen by many physical educators as their primary route for health promotion.

Although it is premature to claim that we have full understanding of the complex relationships involved in the promotion of health, steadily accumulating research evidence is allowing a more sophisticated picture to emerge. It is the purpose of this chapter to help physical educators face and deal with some of the conceptual confusion that accompanies health promotion. For the sake of simplicity, comments will be restricted to that which is unique to physical education in the curriculum package: the medium of physical activity and exercise. At the same time, an argument will be presented suggesting that the singular fitness-related health promotion track should be replaced by a more holistic health enhancement perspective which is concerned with overall quality of life.

THE COMPLEXITIES OF HEALTH

Efforts to rationally dismantle the construct of health inevitably run into a philosophical minefield. The problem is heightened in the context of education where the teacher is faced with the delivery of a concept which is not easy to objectively define and which is essentially value laden. However, if educators are to adopt a health improvement role, they have no choice but to tackle the definitional issues concerned with health and must seek some agreement as to its constitution and characteristics.

This is not a simple task. Health undoubtedly has multiple biological, social, cultural, and political determinants and several models have been put forward to capture some of the interrelationships between important factors (Baranowski, 1981; Eberst, 1984). Furthermore, health is usually conceptualized as multidimensional in nature, having—among others—physical, emotional, social, and spiritual facets. Attempts to influence singular aspects of the equation, therefore, provide at best only a partial solution. Some authors (for example, Greenberg, 1985) have concentrated on the need to create a balance among the different elements, suggesting that too much attention paid to one aspect, such as physical health, may produce an asymmetrically unhealthy profile. For example, an individual may become obsessive and overdependent on jogging to the extent that it disrupts family life and/or leads to social isolation.

Other authors have focused on a health–illness continuum in attempts to establish the differences between poor health and optimal health. Most of us are familiar with the World Health Organisation's (1947) description of health as a state of complete physical, mental, and social well-being and not merely the absence of disease or infirmity. Taking this approach, it has perhaps been easier to define degrees of lack of health, as symptoms of mental or physical illness are often clinically identifiable. It has been far more difficult to establish a working definition for the good end of the health continuum. This is because, in the absence of serious illness, health becomes phenomenologically determined. In other words, health becomes personalized and is represented by the degree to which a positive state of being is *felt or experienced*.

Terms such as 'wellness' or well-being have been frequently applied to such states. Wellness is an American term used to imply not only a lack of illness but also 'the capacity of the person to fulfil personal goals and perform socially defined role tasks' (Baranowski, 1981, p. 251). It describes the person's state of health in terms of his/her positive adaptation to the functional roles involved in society and is therefore to a large extent culturally determined. Given the functional connotations underlying wellness, it is not surprising that it has been widely adopted as the basis of the widespread corporate health promotion movement in the United States. The concept of wellness has also been criticized by some sociologists who describe it as the 'new vitalism'. They suggest that dangers arise as wellness becomes yet another acquisition or status symbol, in much the same way as slenderness has become a sought-after commodity in women.

Well-being, or subjective well-being as it has been termed by psychologists, is much less prescribed (see Diener, 1984). It represents a relatively stable positive life state which is expressed in terms of happiness, self-satisfaction (an aspect of self-esteem), and life satisfaction, in harmony with reduced negative mood and depression. Once again, there are multiple determinants of well-being, some of which may be physical; but social, economic, and personality factors are equally important. Wealth, virtue and comfort are not seen as essential elements of well-being although they may be common contributors, and their perceived absence may have a greater impact than the degree of their presence. Actual physical health, and to a greater degree *perceived* physical health, appear to be important contributors to subjective well-being. Absence of infirmity and suffering of pain are influential, but also the freedom that good health provides for involvement in social activities is important. Ultimately, however, well-being becomes a quality of life experience which is expressed by the individual as positive feelings or emotion and its basis can be diverse.

A HEALTH AND FITNESS COMPARISON

To date, health promotion in physical education has largely been directed through increased physical activity and fitness improvement, yet the relationships between these two concepts and with health are generally poorly understood. Asking school children or adults, for instance, to express their views by depicting fitness and health as two circles reveals an interesting array of perceptions regarding the relationship between the two. Questions concerning the relative sizes of each circle and the nature and degree of their overlap allow a better understanding of how the semantics of health and fitness are received by different populations. A similar effect can be achieved by asking for the attributes of a fit versus a healthy person. Even among physical educators there is often only a vague notion of the relationship between health and fitness. This sometimes results in a confounding of the two, accompanied by exaggerated and unsubstantiated claims about the benefits of fitness. The issue is made more complex by the fact that physical activity involvement, while being an important contributor to physical fitness, appears to relate in many ways to health, independently of fitness levels.

It is doubtful that total agreement regarding health and fitness definitions and relationships will ever be reached. However, for the sake of those who are faced with the delivery of these concepts, it is important to try to establish a workable model that might encourage some unity in thought and mission. Although its simplicity belies the real complexities involved, I have found that the diagram depicted in Figure 8.1 has encouraged some meaningful dialogue. Health, fitness, and physical activity provide three separate but related continua.

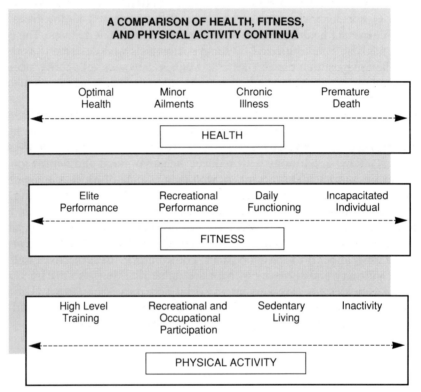

Figure 8.1 *A comparison of health, fitness, and physical activity continua.*

A health continuum

The health continuum featured in Figure 8.1 shows premature death as the extreme case of ill-health. Chronic life-threatening diseases and mental illness are of course associated with this end of the continuum. Well-being or wellness might represent the optimal health state. At this point, agreement as to the exact nature of positive health is not essential for the discussion to progress. However, we can perhaps picture a well-balanced happy and sociable individual who has a particular zest for life and who manages to keep relatively free from serious illness and minor ailments. It is perhaps a state that many of us are striving towards, with few succeeding for significant periods of time. Many others may go through life blindly unaware of the existence of well-being, never experiencing the heightened psychological state and being constantly plagued by problems such as viruses, headaches, and backaches. Conversely of course, it is also possible to feel well while falling victim to the early stages of serious diseases such as cancer or CHD. It is therefore recognized that this continuum is an incomplete expression of the diversities of health, particularly because it fails to adequately describe relationships between the mental and physical aspects of health.

To date, comprehensive measures of health do not exist and so it is not possible to accurately place an individual on a hypothetical health continuum such as that provided in Figure 8.1. Indicators of physical health, such as blood pressure readings and blood lipid profiles, are constantly in use through the medical profession. Psychologists have attempted to devise questionnaire and interview instrumentation capable of measuring aspects of mental health (such as self-esteem, subjective well-being, wellness, life satisfaction) as well as indicators of mental ill-health (such as depression and neuroticism scales). However, with such a diverse and complex concept as health it has not been possible to produce a singular tool for its measurement. Health risk appraisal instruments, which often provide a combination of risk of ill-health with aspects of positive health, appear to come closest at present.

A fitness continuum

Fitness is simply an indicator of physical function and consequently can be regarded as a measure of our ability to move efficiently. It therefore represents a capacity or a product. There are several well-established and accepted dimensions of fitness which contribute to our movement capabilities. Some aspects of fitness have indicated that they are more related to health than others, which is why cardiovascular fitness, muscular strength and endurance, flexibility and body composition have been grouped into the category of health-related fitness. Other aspects of physical performance such as power, coordination, agility, and balance are more skill-related and are not likely to influence health—at least directly. All are important for high-level sports performance and represent elements of functional capacity. This could be expressed as how fast we can run, how much force we can exert, how far we can stretch, or how efficient our bodies are at performing specific physical tasks. At one end of the spectrum, therefore, is the individual who is incapable of efficient movement, represented by perhaps a severely obese person or someone who has had a lengthy confinement to bed. Towards the lower end is the inactive individual whose body has become very limited in functional capacity with poor levels of strength, flexibility, and cardiovascular efficiency, and deteriorating balance and agility. Such people probably represent the societal norm rather than the exception and surprisingly may cope reasonably well with the day's physical demands, usually because they have adopted a lifestyle which is not physically demanding! In the middle ranges we have incremental degrees of fitness associated with involvement in fitness-enhancing recreation, sport, or exercise. At the fittest extreme, we have athletes who are at the highest level of training for performance, such as the Olympic 1500-metre runner or the weight-lifter. Each excels in one aspect of fitness, but perhaps is limited in some others. It could be argued that to truly reach ultimate fitness would require excellence in every dimension.

The measurement of fitness has been the subject of considerable debate over the past five years. As with health, the multidimensional nature of fitness makes it imposs-ible to devise a singular measure for its assessment. This has resulted in the wide-spread use of test batteries. Where health has been of interest, measures of each of the health-related aspects of fitness are included. Where selection for sports performance is the concern, tests which assess the performance requirements of the sports, which are usually a combination of health and skill-related aspects, are used.

A physical activity continuum

Physical activity has been defined in this text as all voluntary skeletal movement. Exercise is viewed as a sub-category of physical activity which is planned, structured, repetitive and purposeful. Physical activity should be regarded as a process or beha-vioural pattern and thus is clearly distinguishable from the products or capacities representing physical fitness. The very restricted activity levels of some institutiona-lized older citizens and people with severe physical handicaps would fall at one end of the continuum. The sedentary lifestyle of the vast majority would also be placed towards this inactive pole. Recreational and occupational activity levels will tend to fall towards the middle of the continuum with the levels of energy expenditure typified by a high-level triathlon training regime representing the most active group.

Several techniques have been developed to assess physical activity. The recent combined use of indirect calorimetry and doubly labelled water techniques have provided the most accurate non-invasive assessments of energy expenditure. How-ever, they are expensive and impractical on a large scale so that heart-rate monitoring, pedometry, motion sensors, and the use of self-report through questionnaires, inter-views and diaries are most commonly used (see Saris, 1986). Given these techniques, it is possible to provide a singular indication of an individual's movement, and thus their position along an activity continuum.

Some may question the need to add an activity continuum to Figure 8.1 because physical activity and exercise represent the precursors of fitness and are automatically encompassed by the fitness continuum. Of course, physical activity, through the principle of training overload, does result in improved functional capacity. Lifting more weight, for example, will improve strength, while walking further each day will increase muscular endurance and perhaps cardiovascular fitness. Similarly, physical practice will improve other aspects of fitness such as coordinaticn and balance. How-ever, although training and practice clearly work, ultimately the capacity to perform physically will be limited by genetic factors which control body size, somatotype, muscle fibre type, and stage of maturation through the lifespan. The ability to achieve excellence in fitness, therefore, is restricted to the minority who are gifted with a suitably equipped body.

At present, there is much less evidence available supporting a direct link between this inherited component of fitness and health than its activity component. The Har-vard alumni study (Paffenbarger *et al.*, 1986), for example, has indicated that natural sports ability, represented by selection for college teams, has no increased protection over sedentary living against subsequent premature mortality. From current evidence, it seems likely that the links between fitness and health are to be derived from the physical activity which leads to fitness rather than inherited physical ability. Furthermore, involvement in regular activity appears to provide additional mental and physical benefits which are independent of fitness improvements. These factors suggest a focus on the assessment of physical activity levels, rather than fitness, may be more fruitful when unravelling the complex relationships with health. This appears to be particularly the case when considering children where fitness is poorly related to physical activity levels (Armstrong *et al.*, 1990). The genetic component appears to dominate fitness scores in children, possibly because lack of activity has not had sufficient time to cause functional deterioration. Certainly, at this point, it is prudent to continue to view fitness and physical activity as separate but related entities when considering health promotion. The remainder of this chapter will focus on physical activity. Where the term fitness is used, comments will refer to the component of fitness which has accumulated as a result of increased activity, rather than genetic factors.

PHYSICAL ACTIVITY AND THE HEALTH CONTINUUM

It is quite clear that fitness is *not* health. Similarly, large amounts of exercise will not ensure good health. Given the usual definitions of fitness as aspects of functional capacity, it is possible to be fit and at the same time be very unhealthy. Several examples come to mind: the steroid-taking champion power-lifter, the athlete who is plagued with recurrent back pain, the sports star who is suicidal because of competitive stress, or the basketball player with a congenital condition such as Marfan's Syndrome. The case of Jim Fixx brings the point home well. Jim was a journalist/born-again distance runner who died of a heart attack in 1984 while training for a marathon. Although he was quite fit, the post-mortem revealed that he had extensive blockage of his coronary arteries, probably as a result of a combination of a very unhealthy lifestyle before taking up running and a family history of heart disease. Fitness may have kept him alive for longer, but it wasn't sufficient.

There are also several examples of situations where too much exercise or concern with fitness can be detrimental to health. This ties in with Greenberg's notion of health asymmetry. Exercise addiction or dependence has been identified whereby the need to participate in daily extended bouts of vigorous exercise is so great that it has caused a health imbalance. Family or social life suffers and psychological problems develop. Often anorexics use excessive amounts of exercise to increase weight loss. They achieve a high level of cardiovascular fitness while at the same time progressively suffering from a very dangerous disease.

Sports performers who are required to train at a very intense level place themselves under higher health risk. They may be more susceptible to the isolation problems of the exercise addict simply because of the long and often unsociable hours required. There is also increasing evidence that high levels of training can actually detract from health by weakening the body's immune system. Athletes at a high level of training, for example, appear to be at increased risk of viral infections (Fitzgerald, 1988). Additionally, we are all aware of the risk with regard to both chronic and acute injury which accompany extreme exercise-induced stresses on the body. It is hardly surprising that cynics take delight in bringing down those of us who live for sport (which includes most physical educators) when a large percentage at any given moment seem to be bandaged, in plaster casts, or supported by crutches! If physical health is a major concern, there seems to be a strong case for avoiding the excessive exercise required for peak fitness or sports performance.

At the other end of the fitness continuum, the question remains in debate as to how healthy one can be with very low levels of fitness and minimal amounts of exercise. Certainly there are many examples of physically handicapped people whose functional capacities are very limited but who still achieve a high level of mental well-being. However, they appear to be at similar risk to everyone else regarding vascular and central organ disease if their bodies are not exercised.

It is also easy to fall foul of the 'Uncle Ernie' syndrome. Everyone seems to know of somebody who has lived to 94, never exercised and smoked 40 cigarettes a day! Of course, the relationship between fitness and health is entirely statistical. The 99.9 per cent of other Uncle Ernies have long since passed with lung cancer, heart disease, or emphysema. Uncle Ernie is the statistical freak.

There are two ways of developing the discussion concerning this statistical relationship. First, we can assess the evidence regarding the degree to which physical activity and associated levels of fitness prevent and alleviate disease and disability: the preventive model. Second, we can discuss their impact on the enhancement of well-being: the health enhancement model. Both are important in health promotion.

PHYSICAL ACTIVITY AND ILLNESS PREVENTION

The prevention approach has characterized the health-related fitness evolution in physical education throughout the world. This has been stimulated by accumulating epidemiological and experimentally based research aimed at establishing (a) the extent of the relationship between inactivity and ill-health, and (b) mechanisms behind this relationship. It has recently become clear that a reasonable degree of fitness which is maintained over long periods of time will greatly improve the chances of avoiding certain physical health problems. Blair *et al.* (1989) concluded from their epidemiological research at the Aerobics Institute in Dallas that 'The results show a strong, graded and consistent inverse relationship between physical fitness and mortality in men and women ... Moderate levels of physical fitness that are attainable by most adults appear to be protective against early mortality' (p. 2401). Similarly, a wealth of convincing epidemiological evidence now exists which has helped to establish that regular physical activity, whether it is in the form of occupational, recreational, or fitness-related exercise is effective in reducing disease and disability risk (see Harris *et al.*, 1989). This relationship primarily operates through the reduction of CHD, and recently the medical profession have recognized that lack of physical activity is a *primary* risk factor which ranks alongside high blood pressure, cholesterol, and smoking in importance. Furthermore, Blair *et al.* (1989), conclude 'the high prevalence of sedentary habits and low physical fitness levels produce high attributable risk estimates and suggest that these characteristics constitute an important public health problem that deserves remedial attention' (p. 2401). Some degree of credit should be given to those physical educators who have reacted to this evidence, especially as Britain now has the highest incidence rate of CHD in the world. This high death and disability rate not only causes suffering to the victims, their families, and friends but indirectly affects health in other ways. It overloads the National Health Service so that other treatments are given lower priority. Additionally, national productivity is reduced, eventually lowering living and health standards.

Although CHD has dominated the fitness/illness debate we must remember that exercise has a contribution to make in the avoidance and alleviation of other physical disabilities. For example, over 12 per cent of British women and 8 per cent of men are classed as obese to the extent that they suffer adverse health and reduced life expectancy (Gregory *et al.*, 1990). Also, the obese suffer psychological problems as they are often the subject of discrimination due to their condition, are consequently less socially active, and are invariably more dissatisfied with themselves. Exercise is now an established aspect of obesity prevention, treatment, and weight-loss maintenance (Segal and Pi-Sunyer, 1989).

Similarly, incidence of low back pain is widespread and has resulted in extensive personal suffering, remaining the leading cause of lost working days. Stretching and strengthening exercises have been established that provide both prophylactic and therapeutic value for reducing the condition. Regular exercise is also emerging as valuable in the management of hypertension, asthma, adult-onset diabetes, and the avoidance of osteoporosis (for summaries of research evidence concerning the impact of exercise on these conditions see Bouchard *et al.*, 1990).

The result of the accumulating evidence is a gradual recognition that exercise has great value in community medicine and public health promotion policy. The Department of Health and Human Services in the United States has included several objectives which refer to exercise and fitness in its plans for the 1990s (Powell *et al.*, 1986). The majority of large American corporations now have well-established exercise policies and facilities. Although there remains much ground to be covered, similar sentiment is reflected in Britain through the strategies of the Sports Council, the British Heart Foundation, the Coronary Prevention Group, Heartbeat Wales, and other organizations. Physical education clearly has an important responsibility via its curriculum to inform the population of these threats and the solutions that regular physical activity offers.

How much activity is required.

The case is clear that there are considerable health risks attached to inactivity. However, there still remains the question of how much exercise or fitness is sufficient for health? Using the medical phraseology often adopted with the preventive model, the question becomes 'what is the required exercise dosage?'. Unfortunately, this remains a largely unanswered question. Following the principle that 100 aspirins are no more effective than two or three in dealing with a headache, it does not necessarily follow that reductions in health risk are linearly tied to increased activity. As indicated earlier, there are potentially detrimental effects attached to high levels of training or over-rapid progression in exercise. Somewhere between the two extremes lies a broad spread of physical activity involvement which can be regarded as health-related. Although health benefits may continue to accrue with increased exercise to a point, it is apparent that the relationship is best described as a curve of diminishing returns. Epidemiological studies reveal that the greatest disease reduction results in comparisons between the sedentary and mildly recreative groups. Similarly, the study of Blair *et al.* (1989) showed that more substantial health benefits were acquired with a move from the lowest to the moderate cardiovascular fitness category. It is now apparent that low-intensity recreational activities such as walking the dog, gardening, and cycling are important contributors to reduced risk, particularly for older and obese populations. It is interesting to note that the American College of Sports Medicine (1990) has recently softened its stance on exercise prescription for fitness, and will shortly put out new guidelines regarding the recommended amounts for health. However, to date, although we have guidelines for improving fitness, we still have no clear directives for the amount of strength or endurance, flexibility, cardio-vascular fitness, or adiposity for health. At best, we can only offer the suggestion that exercise and increased fitness is good for you up to a point, beyond which it becomes risky or unproductive. Given current information, public health initiatives, including physical education, would appear to be most profitably directed at stimulating moder-ate amounts of activity in the large sector of the community who can be classed as sedentary and unfit.

PHYSICAL ACTIVITY AND HEALTH ENHANCEMENT

The disease prevention approach has been well-represented in the rationale which has underpinned the health-related fitness movement. It is becoming increasingly clear, however, that physical activity involvement through participation in sport, recreation, and specific exercise activities has a prominent role to play in the broader context of health enhancement—a role which has received much less attention. This largely involves the potential impact of physical activity on the promotion of mental well-being, wellness, and factors concerning the quality of life. Certainly, a disease preven-tion perspective provides only a partial answer to health promotion. For example, although CHD is the leading cause of death, it can go undetected in an individual for several decades and thereby does not necessarily deter from life quality until symp-toms finally emerge. Ironically, death may be the first indication for some, particularly males, so that the mental impact of the disease is experienced by the victim's family and friends.

The research evidence supporting the mental benefits of exercise involvement is increasing (see Biddle and Mutrie, 1991; Morgan and Goldston, 1987). It has been difficult to identify and isolate the mechanisms involved and it looks as though there are several explanations which may dominate according to the person, the activity, and the degree of involvement. The different forms that physical activity can take—competitive team sports, individual health-related activity (such as lunch-time walking or jogging), outdoor activities (such as canoeing or backpacking), or high risk activi-ties (such as climbing)—mean that each will have a unique package of mental benefits attached. Within each activity these packages appear to differ from person to person. It is not difficult to appreciate, for example, that sky-diving may be invigorating for some while excruciatingly stressful for others.

A more detailed summary of the literature regarding the psychological benefits of exercise is available elsewhere (see Biddle and Fox, 1989). While recognizing that these benefits are essentially interwoven, for the sake of convenience they can be categorized as follows

Acute benefits

Consistently reported by regular exercisers are exercise responses which have been described as the 'feeling good' phenomenon or the 'exercise halo' effect. It may occur during (sometimes known as the exercise high) or after exercise (the healthy exercise glow) and may emanate through a variety of biochemical and physiological mechanisms. The origins of these effects have been difficult to pin down but thermogenesis, endogenous opiates (endorphins), brain wave-pattern modification, mental diversion, or sense of accomplishment and empowerment have been suggested. Commonly, they are associated with a release of muscular tension and anxiety and enhanced mood, and are often accompanied by a post-exercise reduction in blood pressure and improved blood sugar and lipid profile. Some effects such as thermogenesis and reduced muscular tension appear to be more readily induced by vigorous rhythmical aerobic exercise such as jogging. However, it is becoming evident that many of the benefits are also available from exercise of low to moderate intensities. Regardless, the effects seem to be sufficiently powerful to motivate many to return to exercise on a regular basis.

Social benefits

Social and recreational contact are important correlates of well-being (Diener, 1984). Some forms of sport and exercise, through their team and club structure, provide a recreational medium for increased social interaction and the development of friendships. With decreasing work hours, it has often been predicted that sport and leisure pursuits will become increasingly significant in maintaining a balanced and fulfilled lifestyle. Indeed some definitions of mental health have included the notion of a balance between work and play.

Self-esteem benefits

Self-esteem has been widely accepted as an indicator of mental and social adjustment. Physical self-perceptions concerning attractiveness, fitness, physical abilities and achievements, and confidence contribute to self-esteem throughout the lifespan. Fitness activities, sports, and dance provide a particularly powerful arena for these perceptions to develop. Studies in which attempts have been made to estimate the impact of sport and exercise participation on self-esteem have generally supported their effect. This operates through improvements in body image and satisfaction, particularly with fitness-related activities, a sense of accomplishment resulting from increased fitness or developing sport skills or achievement. In the case of activities which are highly valued among peers, success may also lead to elevated social status which has the potential to enhance confidence and self-esteem.

Sensory enhancement

Although less well-established through research, physical activities also provide a medium for enriching quality of life through the variety of sensory experiences that they either offer or to which they allow access. It cannot be denied, for example, that for many a leisurely walk by a picturesque river at lunch-time can be as rewarding in terms of relaxation and well-being as somewhat more arduous effort is to the jogger whose attentional focus is on extreme exertion! Similarly, sports and activities which involve high risk, physical contact, or thrill and excitement such as climbing or white-water canoeing can have a particularly prolonged emotional effect. The sensory rewards of being involved in a pleasingly aesthetic performance provide another example. Given a broad-based description of activity such as this, there appears to be potential for enhancing the well-being of people of all types and ages.

This brief summary shows a wide range of routes through which involvement in physical activity can enhance well-being and consequently improve quality of life. Furthermore, the maintenance of a reasonable amount of fitness and activity throughout the lifespan helps delay the ageing process, adding life to years as well as years to life.

PHYSICAL EDUCATION AND HEALTH PROMOTION

This chapter has attempted to crystallize some of the broader conceptual issues concerned with physical education's role in the promotion of health. To date, the strategy of physical education has been to focus heavily on the physical problems associated with poor fitness levels and inactivity. As described here, the potential for physical education to impact upon the psychosocial aspects of well-being and quality of life has been less adequately explored. There are multiple routes, therefore, through which physical education can make an impact on physical and mental health (see Figure 8.2).

The major impact is seen to be made through involvement of youngsters in physical activity. This provides the unique contribution of physical education to the curriculum, and participation in sport, dance, outdoor pursuits and exercise can directly and independently promote disease-risk reduction and enhance well-being. Physical education provides a rich arena for fun, excitement, accomplishment, and relaxation. The accompanying increases in fitness will add to these benefits. Fitness itself can provide an achievement medium, and if maintained throughout life, can offset the effects of ageing by retention of functional capacities and the encouragement of a richer recreational and social lifestyle. The development of physical skill through movement and sport education will also contribute to a more solid foundation to physical self-worth, and will stimulate further long-term participation.

Physical educators can also directly influence the present and future health of youngsters in several ways other than their immediate involvement in curricular physical activity. The educational process can raise awareness to the factors which influence health and develop expertise and strategies which can bring about changes to enhance health. Currently, this type of work has been directed at empowering

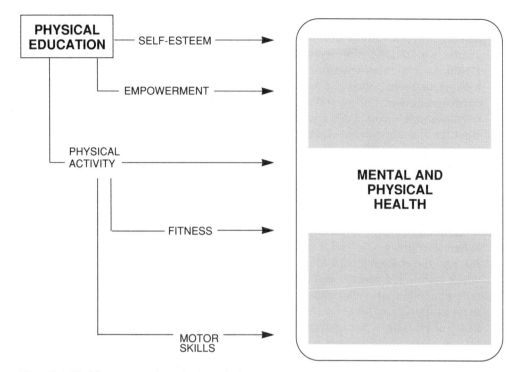

Figure 8.2 *Health promotion through physical education.*

individuals to adopt active and healthy lifestyles. Equally important is the need to raise awareness regarding the media, social, and political influences on health, although curricular materials dealing with this broader picture are still sparse.

In addition to the messages and expertise which teachers pass on, they can improve the sense of worth and well-being of students simply by the quality of the student–teacher relationship. Self-esteem is not only dependent on competence and achievement, but also on the degree of social support an individual experiences. In particular, social support which is not conditional on a person's abilities and characteristics appears to be extremely valuable in producing a stable foundation to self-esteem. To be appreciated as a person rather than a performer provides a firmer foundation for growth. Physical education teachers are in a position to provide this type of support through their relationships with children. Equally, the modelling of healthy attitudes and behaviours by teachers can be influential on the habits of impressionable youngsters.

Successful health promotion in physical education is ultimately dependent on the ability of schools and teachers to adopt teaching styles and deliver programmes which are conducive to the development of health. While there is clearly tremendous potential to have a positive impact on health, the converse is also true. Bad teaching and insensitive or inappropriate content can destroy children's self-esteem and turn them away from physical activity for life. Several basic implications emerge:

1   The least active or physically gifted are at greatest health risk and so warrant

special attention. At present, the design of many physical education programmes, whether intentionally or not, has resulted in rewards and incentives which are only available to an able minority.

2   Health is a lifetime investment and so physical educators should be forward-looking in their policies. Long-term rather than short-term gains must dictate curricular design. The mental and physical benefits attached to physical activity are only available through continued involvement. Programmes must prepare youngsters for the difficulties which continued physical activity involvement poses in adulthood.

3   Different activities appeal to different people and will result in different psychological health benefits. Providing a wide array of activities, which might include competitive sports, dance, outdoor pursuits and fitness activities, will help more youngsters find a compatible pursuit and enhance the chances of continued involvement.

4   Whereas sports and exercise success can produce a sense of competence and self-esteem, the challenge still remains in physical education to produce programmes which encourage success and achievement in children of vastly different physical potential. This can only result from a reward system built on individual improvement in sports and fitness activities, rather than on performance.

5   Physical education has restricted its role to the teaching of children. If the profession really wants to seek an active role in the promotion of public health it is well past the time for the adoption of a lifespan perspective. It has become apparent that the exercise benefits of illness avoidance and maintained physical function increase with age. The physical education profession has been blinkered by its concern for quality provision for school children. We should be taking a more active role in preparing fitness and recreation professionals who are equipped to promote adult exercise in community, corporate, and medical settings.

Finally, the complexities involved in health promotion create many difficult dilemmas and ambiguities for the physical educator. Quite often these are triggered by tensions which emerge between objectives designed to prevent disease on the one hand and those designed to develop mental well-being or achievement on the other. For example, the necessity to alert classes of children to the health problems of obesity may cause further isolation of a child who is already obese. At the same time, our attempt to discourage inactivity and obesity may serve to support society's obsession for slimness which seems to contribute to increasing stress, bulimia, and anorexia in teenage girls and depressed mood in women. A more effective health strategy in this case might be to find ways of critically appraising media pressures or encouraging self-acceptance. Similar decisions have to be made regarding the development of young sporting talent which requires a heavy training schedule and perhaps the deprivation of a more balanced and varied life experience.

Examples such as these raise our awareness of the complexities involved in health promotion. Questions and decisions arise which are difficult to face and answer, underlying the extent of our responsibilities. Ultimately, our ability to achieve in the health, and perhaps the education, field will be determined by our willingness to open our minds and appraise our actions within the broader health perspective. This will allow a more critical appraisal of our teaching styles and our curriculum, and will help drive physical education towards a more effective role in public health promotion.

NOTE

1 Some of the material included in this chapter was first presented at the annual General Meeting of the Physical Education Association of Great Britain and Northern Ireland, held at Bristol University in April 1990 and also has been published in the Conference Report entitled *Fitness, Health and Well-being*. It is reproduced here with permission.

REFERENCES

American College of Sports Medicine (1990) The recommended quantity and quality of exercise for developing and maintaining cardiorespiratory and muscular fitness in healthy adults. *Medicine and Science in Sports and Exercise* **22**, 265–74.

Armstrong, N., Balding, J., Gentle, P., Williams, J., and Kirby, B. (1990) Peak oxygen uptake and physical activity in 11–16 year-olds. *Pediatric Exercise Science* **2**, 349–58.

Baranowski, T. (1981) Toward the definition of concepts of health and disease, wellness and illness. *Health Values* **5**, 246–56.

Biddle, S. J. H. and Fox, K. R. (1989) Exercise and health psychology: emerging relationships. *British Journal of Medical Psychology* **62**, 205–16.

Biddle, S. J. H., and Mutrie, N. (1991) *Psychology of Physical Activity and Exercise: A Health-Related Perspective*. New York: Springer-Verlag.

Blair, S. N., Kohl, H. W., Paffenbarger, R. S., Clark, D. G., Cooper, K. H., and Gibbons, L. W. (1989) Physical fitness and all-cause mortality. *Journal of the American Medical Association* **262**, 2395–2401.

Bouchard, C., Shephard, R. J., Stephens, T., Sutton, J. R., and McPherson, B. D. (eds) (1990) *Exercise, Fitness, and Health*. Champaign, IL: Human Kinetics.

Diener, E. (1984) Subjective well-being. *Psychological Bulletin* **95**, 542–75.

Eberst, R. M. (1984) Defining health: a multidimensional model. *Journal of School Health* **54**, 99–103.

Fitzgerald, L. (1988) Exercise and the immune system. *Immunology Today* **9**, 337–9.

Greenberg, J. S. (1985) Health and wellness: a conceptual differentiation. *Journal of School Health* **55**, 403–6.

Gregory, J., Foster, K., Tyler, H., and Wiseman, M. (1990) *The Dietary and Nutritional Survey of British Adults*. London: HMSO.

Harris, S. S., Casperson, C. J., DeFriese, G. H., and Estes, E. H. (1989) Physical activity counselling for healthy adults as a primary preventive intervention in the clinical setting. *Journal of the American Medical Association* **261**, 3590–8.

Kirk, D. (1988) Health-based physical education: five issues we need to consider. *British Journal of Physical Education* **19**, 122–3.

McNamee, M. (1988) Health-related fitness and physical education. *British Journal of Physical Education* **19**, 83–4.

Morgan, W. P. and Goldston, S. E. (1987) *Exercise and Mental Health*. Washington: Hemisphere Publications.

Paffenbarger, R. S., Hyde, R. T., Wing, A. L., and Hsieh, C. C. (1986) Physical activity, all-cause mortality, and longevity of college alumni. *New England Journal of Medicine* **314**, 605–13.

Powell, K. E., Spain, K. G., Christenson, G. M., and Mollenkamp, M. P. (1986) The status of the 1990 objectives for physical fitness and exercise. *Public Health Reports* **101**, 15–21.

Powell, K. E., Thompson, P. D., Casperson, C. J., and Kendrick, J. S. (1987) Physical activity and the incidence of coronary heart disease. *Annual Review of Public Health* **8**, 253–87.

Saris, W. H. M. (1986) Habitual physical activity in children: methodology and findings in health and disease. *Medicine and Science in Sports and Exercise* **18**, 253–63.

Segal, K. R., and Pi-Sunyer, F. X. (1989) Exercise and obesity. *Medical Clinics of North America* **73**, 217–36.

Sparkes, A. (1989) Health-related fitness: an example of innovation without change. *British Journal of Physical Education* **20**, 60–2.

World Health Organisation (1947) Constitution of the World Health Organisation. *Chronicle of the World Health Organisation* **1**, 1–2.

Chapter 9

Health-Related Physical Activity

Neil Armstrong

The evidence that appropriate physical activity will improve all health-related aspects of physical fitness is overwhelming (Fentem *et al.*, 1988). Regular weight-bearing physical activity is essential for the normal growth and development of the skeleton (Astrand and Rodahl, 1986). It is well documented that regular physical activity has beneficial effects on mental health including improved feelings of well-being, positive mood, decreased anxiety and depression, and elevated levels of self-esteem (Armstrong and Biddle, 1991). Numerous epidemiological surveys have reported an inverse association between adults' level of physical activity and the incidence of degenerative diseases, especially coronary heart disease (CHD) (reanalysed by Powell *et al.*, 1987). Yet, until recently very little was known about British children's level of habitual physical activity and the likelihood of children's physical activity patterns tracking[1] into adult life. This chapter will therefore focus on the research into British children's habitual health-related physical activity and review the data which link children's physical activity patterns with those of adults.

CHILDREN'S HEALTH-RELATED PHYSICAL ACTIVITY

What is the volume (intensity, duration, and frequency) and type of physical activity which is associated with the improvement and /or maintenance of children's health? A recent review of the available literature by Simons-Morton *et al.* (1988) concluded that appropriate (i.e. health-related) physical activity for children involves large muscle groups (e.g. the legs) in dynamic movement for periods of twenty minutes or longer. The types of activity referred to include cycling, swimming, jogging, skating, and dancing. Simons-Morton emphasized that this type of physical activity should take place at least three times per week and that it should be of an intensity which elicits heart rates equal to or in excess of 140 beats/min. As children have, on average, maximum heart rates of about 200 beats/min (Armstrong *et al.*, 1990d) Simons-Morton's endorsement of appropriate physical activities which raise the heart rate to above 70 per cent of maximum is in close relative agreement with the level of physical activity suggested by Morris *et al.* (1987) to be associated with a low incidence of CHD in adults. To put this heart rate threshold in perspective it is worth noting that with children we have found that brisk walking at 6 km/h on the treadmill elicits steady state heart rates in excess of 140 beats/min (Armstrong *et al.*, 1990a). So the current concept is that health-related physical activity involves sustained, regular periods of moderate-intensity physical activity.

THE ESTIMATION OF CHILDREN'S HABITUAL PHYSICAL ACTIVITY

The measurement of adults' habitual physical activity is one of the most difficult tasks in epidemiological research and the assessment of the daily physical activity of free-ranging children is even more problematic. A range of methods for estimating the level of adults' physical activity has been developed and several of these methods have been used in the assessment of children's habitual physical activity without due consideration being taken of the differences between children and adults. With children the technique used must be socially acceptable; it should not burden the child with cumbersome equipment and it should minimally influence the child's normal physical activity pattern. Ideally the relative intensity and duration of physical activity should be monitored and if a true picture of habitual physical activity is required some account should be taken of any day-to-day variation. Bar-Or (1983) has suggested that with children a minimum follow-up of three days, including one weekend day, should be employed. Few studies of British children have satisfied all of the above criteria.

The available methodology can be grouped into three categories: self-report of physical activity, movement analysis (e.g. by observation), and physiological analysis (by monitoring heart rate and/or oxygen consumption). All three methods have been used to estimate British children's physical activity patterns.

Self-report of physical activity

Self-reporting of physical activity is by far the most popular method in epidemiological research due to the ease of implementation, and methods employed with British children have included retrospective questionnaires, questionnaire–interview techniques, and activity diaries. Several researchers have expressed concern over the validity of physical activity questionnaires and the imprecision of self-report methodology even with adults (LaPorte *et al.*, 1979; Washburn and Montoye, 1986). The self-assessment—through retrospective questionnaire—of the intensity and duration of bouts of physical activity by children is especially problematic because they are less time-conscious than adults and tend to engage in physical activity at sporadic times and intensities rather than in consistent bouts. The problem is compounded by leisure-time activity, which is more difficult to quantify than occupational activity, making up a greater proportion of total habitual physical activity in children. Self-administered questionnaires are believed to be less precise than those that are administered by an interviewer and large discrepancies have been demonstrated between the two methods (e.g. Wessel *et al.*, 1965). Physical activity diaries appear to be superior to retrospective questionnaires but the quality of completed diaries is inconsistent with children. Following his longitudinal study of Dutch children's physical activity, Saris (1982) concluded that physical activity diaries were unsuitable for use with children under 16 years of age. It may be, of course, that the task of keeping a diary may substantially influence the volume of physical activity.

We investigated the feasibility of using self-report seven-day recall, interview-administered seven-day recall and activity-questionnaire techniques with 72 12-year-old children using continuous heart-rate monitoring as the criterion measure (Armstrong and Biddle, 1990). The results clearly demonstrated that self-report and interview techniques present serious problems of validity with this age group, especially as far as the recall of relative intensity is concerned. An experience of one of my colleagues during this study illustrates the problems of relying on children's recall. During interview a child claimed not to have exercised on the preceding Wednesday whereas the interviewer knew that she had run to exhaustion on the treadmill in the Research Centre laboratory on the day in question! When challenged the child revealed that she had simply forgotten when the test took place and thought that it had been held during the previous week.

Despite the well-documented methodological problems concerned with children's self-reported activity the vast majority of available data have been generated in this manner and must therefore be interpreted with caution.

Observational analysis of physical activity

The assessment of physical activity through the use of observational techniques has inherent appeal, but observational studies are very time consuming, likely to influence the observee's activity, and are not always socially acceptable. The value of the data collected is of course limited by the inevitable short-term collection period and the technique is not a feasible tool for monitoring the regular physical activity of large numbers of children over several days. Nevertheless at least one study of British children has included observational monitoring.

Physiological analysis of physical activity

As man obeys the law of conservation of energy it may be assumed that physical activity can be quantified in terms of either energy intake or energy expenditure. This assumption is, however, only valid with children when energy intake is measured over an extended period of time (at least seven days) and changes in the growing body mass are taken into account. As recall methods are the only feasible techniques for large studies, accuracy of estimating energy expenditure depends primarily on the subject's ability to recall and describe the kind and amount of food eaten. The problems with children are analogous to those described in the self-report section above. Dietary estimates are also unable to identify the frequency, duration, and intensity of physical activity and they are therefore inadequate as a means of estimating children's habitual physical activity.

If it is assumed that physical activity throughout the day is almost entirely aerobic (see Bar-Or, 1983 or Astrand and Rodahl, 1986 for discussions of the limitations of this assumption) then energy expenditure can be directly measured by determining oxygen consumption (indirect calorimetry). This approach requires a means of measuring expired gas and analysing it for oxygen and carbon dioxide content. Classically it would require the subject to have a Douglas bag fixed to his/her back and although more recent developments have alleviated the problem, the wearing of a face mask or a mouthpiece and nose clip is still obligatory. These requirements make this method unsuitable for use with children and also put into perspective the attempts of researchers to equate activity diaries and questionnaire responses to energy expenditures measured in this manner.

Because of the problems encountered in measuring oxygen consumption under field conditions several investigators have chosen to monitor heart rate to predict children's energy expenditure. The use of heart rate to estimate energy expenditure derives from the demonstration, under laboratory conditions, of a linear relationship between heart rate and oxygen uptake over most of the range for walking, running, and cycling. It is common practice to bring a subject into the laboratory, establish a heart rate–oxygen uptake calibration curve and then use this curve to convert heart rate recorded in the field into oxygen uptake. There are several theoretical objections to this approach as controlled exercise in a laboratory is somewhat different from the real-life situation. Oxygen uptake has three major components: heart rate, stroke volume and arterio-venous oxygen difference (see Bar-Or, 1983 or Astrand and Rodahl, 1986 for detailed analyses of oxygen uptake). Stroke volume and arterio-venous oxygen difference are not constant at different levels of oxygen uptake and, especially at lower levels, the heart rate–oxygen uptake relationship departs significantly from the linear model. Even within the range where heart rate and oxygen uptake are linearly related during controlled, incremental treadmill exercise the sometimes rapid changes of activity intensity in the real-life situation will dissociate the relationship between the two variables. In addition heart rate may be more affected than oxygen uptake by different modes of activity (static vs dynamic), activity with different muscle groups (arms vs legs), the ambient environment, and emotional changes.

The direct measurement of energy expenditure (oxygen consumption) during field conditions is unlikely to reflect children's normal physical activity. The use of heart rate, however, is a feasible unobtrusive procedure that provides a physiological quantification of physical activity, but it is physiologically naïve to extrapolate heart rates recorded in the field to estimates of energy expenditure on the basis of regression equations determined during controlled laboratory exercise tests. Nevertheless, this methodology is commonly used to estimate children's energy expenditure.

THE PHYSICAL ACTIVITY PATTERNS OF BRITISH CHILDREN

The limited data available on British children's physical activity patterns need to be interpreted in the light of the methodological problems discussed above. Bedale's (1923) detailed analysis of the energy expenditure ('heat production') of Hampshire children during selected activities was probably the first attempt to classify the energy expenditure of British children. Her work was, of course, limited by the available technology, and she used Douglas bags to collect expired gas which was subsequently analysed for oxygen and carbon dioxide content using a Haldane apparatus. Miss

Bedale reported her results in terms of 'total heat production in 24 hours' and concluded that boys' values rose from 2,191 calories (9.16 MJ) at 8 years of age to 3,901 calories (16.31 MJ) at 17 years of age. Girls' 'heat production' increased from 2,223 calories (9.29 MJ) at 9 years of age to 3,214 calories (13.43 MJ) at 17 years of age. Although difficult to compare directly her results indicate that boys have a higher 'heat production' at all ages studied.

Over 40 years later Durnin (Durnin, 1971, 1974; Durnin and Passmore, 1967) extended the short-term work of Bedale by investigating the daily energy expenditures of Scottish children through both self-report and indirect calorimetric methods. Durnin's work was a bench-mark study but it is very frustrating to read as he persistently failed to report the precise details of his methodology. Distrustful of the accuracy of much of the information obtained from children by questionnaires, Durnin used a daily diary technique of recording the physical activity, of 102 boys and 90 girls aged 14 years over a seven-day period. The subjects, using a series of simple symbols, noted down the time they began and ended each activity on a special card provided by the research team. The diaries were supplemented by 'sometimes fairly long periods' of observing the subjects to cross-check their personal records and by making 'many measurements' of the energy expended in various activities by indirect calorimetry. In addition, food intake was assessed by weighing the separate foods immediately before they were eaten, and then calculating the nutrient and energy value from tables of food composition. The precise number and length of observations and measurements by indirect calorimetry were not reported and Durnin did not comment upon the effects such a comprehensive series of measurements may have had on the resulting data.

Durnin reported his work both in terms of energy expenditure and duration and intensity of activity. He found that the average daily energy expenditures of the boys and girls were 11.76 and 9.66 MJ/day respectively. He noted that these figures were below the then recommended allowance of 13.02 and 10.92 MJ/day suggested by the Food and Agriculture Organisation of the United Nations Committee on Calorie Requirements for 14-year-old boys and girls and commented that these recommendations may be overestimates of children's needs. In reporting the duration and intensity of activity Durnin excluded light activity from his analysis and arbitrarily divided the remaining activities into moderate, heavy, and very heavy on the basis of the measured level of energy expenditure (by indirect calorimetry) of the particular activity. The classification was carried out according to the level of energy expenditure applicable to a 'standard' man of 65 kg and a 'standard' woman of 55 kg with allowance made for the body weights of the subjects. Moderate activity was defined as 21.0 to 31.1 kJ/min for males and 14.7 to 22.7 kJ/min for females. Heavy activity was defined as 31.5 to 41.6 kJ/min for males and 23.1 to 31.1 kJ/min for females, with energy expenditures of greater than 42.0 kJ/min for males and 31.5 kJ/min for females classified as very heavy activity. The boys were reported to spend 71 minutes in moderate activity, 29 minutes in heavy activity, and 12 minutes in very heavy activity each day. The girls' daily activity was reported as 87 minutes in moderate activity, 10 minutes in heavy activity, and 3 minutes in very heavy activity. During school time the time spent in heavy or very heavy activity was 7 min/day and 2.5 min/day, respectively, for boys and girls. The large standard deviations in all categories were notable. In a subsequent study involving 'roughly' 50 male and 50 female adolescents Durnin (1971) reported that boys spent 165 and 104 minutes respectively in moderate and heavy activity. The corresponding figures for girls were 190 and 61 minutes respectively. The results of the two studies are, however, not comparable as the criteria of 'moderate' and 'heavy' were less stringent in the latter study. No attempt to analyse sustained periods of heavy activity was made in either study.

In a more recent paper Durnin (1982) argued that,

> The measurement of energy consumption in physical activity, apart from nutritional or specialized biochemical studies, is often of little real biological value, and, when it is measured, is open to the possibility of significant error. (p. 10)

He emphasized that the critical things to assess were the amount of physical work a person is able to do and the stress of the work on the cardiovascular system. He commented that, 'it is often of greater value, when comparing different individuals, to measure work capacity and heart rate rather than energy consumption'.

Bradfield *et al.* (1971) fitted heart rate monitors to 54 7- to 10-year-old boys and monitored them throughout a school day. Each boy was monitored for three school days during the winter months. Pilot work with six boys had demonstrated that there were no significant differences between data generated from five days and data from three days. The heart rate monitor used required heartbeats to accumulate as charges on an electrochemical cell, and the cells needed to be changed when periods of physical activity were likely to change—for example during early morning classes, recess period, late morning classes, lunch hour, early afternoon classes, recess, and later afternoon classes. In order to establish an individual regression line between heart rate and oxygen consumption 36 boys had their heart rate and oxygen uptake simultaneously measured, during step-bench exercise, at heart rates of 75 to 90, 120 to 130 and more than 150 beats/min. For those children without individual regressions, the mean slope and mean intercept for age and weight were used. Oxygen consumptions were converted into energy expenditure, presumably assuming that the exercise was exclusively supported by aerobic metabolism. Total energy expenditure for the day was calculated in two ways: first, as a summation of class, recess, and lunch-time energy expenditure; and second, by use of the mean heart rate for the school day (400 minutes) and the individual's regression line. Bradfield noted that there was surprisingly little variation between the two approaches. The mean energy expenditure of the boys was reported as 9.2 kJ/min during morning school, 11.3 kJ/min during afternoon school, and 12.2 kJ/min during lunch-time and play periods. No reference was made to peak energy expenditures or to the frequency and duration of any health-related physical activity. The study is also flawed by the need for regular changes of equipment and limited by the restriction of monitoring activity occurring only during the school day.

A few studies have used heart rate to monitor the physiological load of physical education lessons. Brooke *et al.* (1975) used a 'transitory electrode device' to ascertain the heart rates elicited by a group of 27 girls (13- and 14-year-olds) during a 'demanding' 25-minute netball lesson. The investigators used random sampling techniques to call girls to a centrally placed table where electrocardiograph readings were taken in the seconds immediately after the subject stopped. The mean heart rate during the lessons was 163 beats/min. Using a similar technique one of the same research group (Knowles, 1978) later monitored twenty 11- and 12-year-old boys during a 47-minute gymnastic lesson which embodied what the investigator called 'quality work'. The mean heart rate during the lesson was 123 beats/min. Hale and Bradshaw (1978) studied a group of seven 12- to 16-year-old 'enthusiastic girl participants' (PE teacher's comment) over seven 25-minute practical sessions. They used a telemetry system and averaged the heart rates over the lesson although they acknowledged that this may disguise the true stress of the session. The results indicated that heart rates rarely exceeded 140 beats/min during the sessions and the mean value was 130 beats/min. Although intrinsically interesting, however, these short-term analyses provide minimal information about children's habitual activity in non-structured situations.

Sleap and Warburton (1990) collected information on 1,091 primary schoolchildren using a diary analysis in which they logged data for an average of thirteen hours on each child. All monitoring took place outside of school time, covering school week-days (before and after school), weekends and holidays. In addition their team observed 56 of the children during school break-times, lunch-times, and physical education lessons as well as during the children's free time. On average each child was observed for 268 minutes. They concluded that half of the children took part in no vigorous physical activity and only one in five children engaged in vigorous activity on more than one occasion. The longest period of continuous vigorous activity recorded was eight minutes. They reported contrasting results in that the diary logging revealed that boys took part in more vigorous activity on more occasions and for longer periods than girls, whereas girls were demonstrated to be as active as boys in the observational analysis. Sleap and Warburton's findings, however, need to be interpreted in the light of the limitations of their methodology.

Other surveys of British children's physical activity patterns have relied solely upon self-recall. Several studies (Hendry, 1978; South Western Council for Sport and Recreation, 1984; McCusker, 1985) have simply reported global participation rates in sports whereas others have used sports participation to supplement other activity data (Heartbeat Wales, 1987; Balding, 1988; Williams, 1988).

In a detailed survey of approximately 9,000 boys and 9,000 girls, Balding (1988) asked secondary schoolchildren, through the well-established Health-Related Behaviour Questionnaire, whether they had participated in various activities at least once per week outside school curriculum time. Soccer was identified as the most popular sport for boys with 58.6 per cent, 53.2 per cent, 54.1 per cent, 49.5 per cent, and 41.8 per cent of seventh to eleventh years respectively indicating participation. The pre-eminence of soccer has been confirmed in other surveys (Heartbeat Wales, 1987; Williams, 1988), but the percentage participation rates are not directly comparable due to the use of different criteria. Balding (1988) reported that the other major game for boys, rugby, had a participation rate which fell from 15.3 per cent to 6.3 percent over the secondary school phase. With girls, netball participation fell from 19.4 per cent in year seven to 6.3 per cent in year eleven, and hockey participation fell from 10.1 per cent to 5.7 per cent over the same period. Swimming was shown to be the most popular sport with girls, but participation fell from 41.3 per cent in year seven to 21.8 per cent in year eleven. Swimming was reported to be quite popular with younger boys but participation almost halved during the secondary school phase. With girls, the popularity of dancing was maintained throughout the period analysed with about 25 per cent of all girls being involved at least once per week. Less encouraging was the male participation rate in snooker with 44.8 per cent of seventh year boys participating at least once per week and by year eleven snooker was reported to have overtaken soccer in popularity. Balding (1988) posed the question, 'During the last 2 weeks, have you used a bicycle for enjoyment?'. It was answered with a 'yes' by 48.4 per cent of seventh year boys and 38.4 percent of seventh year girls but by year eleven the positive responses had fallen to 26.6 per cent and 8.7 per cent respectively. This type of analysis is obviously limited in scope, but with the facility to include large numbers of subjects general trends can be indicated.

The Welsh Youth Health Survey (Heartbeat Wales, 1986a, 1987) obtained information on the activity patterns of 6,581 children, aged 11 to 16 years, from 81 secondary schools in Wales. The data were collected through a series of questions concerned with physical activity and sports participation. Vigorous activity was defined as 'games and sports that make you out of breath or sweat'. Of seventh year boys, 80 per cent claimed to take part in vigorous activity outside school at least twice per week but the figure fell to 70 per cent of eleventh year boys making the same claim. The corresponding figures for girls were 63 per cent in year seven and 33 per cent in year eleven. Over a third of eleventh year girls self-reported that they took part in vigorous activity once per month or less.

The Welsh Heart Health Survey (Heartbeat Wales, 1986b), carried out in the summer of 1985, involved contacting a random sample of 21,000 households in Wales and asking those aged 12 to 64 years to complete a questionnaire booklet and return it by post. Almost 22,000 people replied. A 'very active' classification was designed to identify people who take the type of exercise considered to reduce the risks of heart disease and 49 per cent of 12- to 17-year-old males and 19 per cent of females of the same age were reported to fall into this category.

Williams (1988) administered a self-completion questionnaire to 921 year ten children from six schools. She reported that 60.5 per cent of boys and 39.8 per cent of girls participated in some form of physical activity outside school and that boys also tended to be more frequent participants. However, the results of this study should be treated with caution because of large interschool differences. The school with the highest participation rate outside school time (72.7 per cent) was an all-boys school and the school with the lowest female participation rate (16 per cent) contained a large proportion of Muslim girls who had certain restrictions placed upon their movements. In addition, the intensity and duration of activities cannot be ascertained on the basis of the information presented.

Orchard *et al.* (1982) asked a group of 590 children, aged 13 to 18 years, questions about their leisure and sporting activities using an adapted form of a questionnaire developed by Morris *et al.* (1973) for use with adults. The answers were coded 'according to the oxygen consumption and energy output of each activity', based on figures provided by Astrand and Rodahl (1986), and then graded to give a five-point scale. Boys and younger adolescents obtained significantly higher scores than girls and older subjects. The futility of this type of analysis, however, has been demonstrated in the methodology section above.

Gleeson *et al.* (1989) assessed the habitual physical activity of 293 15-year-old Sheffield youngsters by asking them to recall the physical activities they had taken part in during the previous three weeks. For any given subject, a total weekly activity score was derived from the summed product across all reported activities, of the weekly frequency of participation, average duration of the physical activity in minutes, and the averaged perceived intensity of a given activity. The results revealed that 63 per cent of the boys and 82 per cent of the girls failed to engage in exercise above 'minimal habitual activity for health risk reduction'. Children and adolescents are, however, noted for underestimating their level of physical exertion (Bar-Or, 1983) and this effect may have influenced their self-report of physical activity.

Seven-day recall, supported by questionnaires, was used by Riddoch (1990) to evaluate the level of 11- to 18-year-old Northern Irish children's physical activity. He concluded that boys were 'far more active' than girls at all ages studied. He noted that there was a 'marked decline' in activity levels after the age of 13 to 14 years, the rate of which was similar in both sexes.

A more detailed study of children's physical activity patterns was carried out in the West Midlands by Dickenson (1986a, 1986b, 1987). He asked a random sample of 11- to 16-year-olds, a total of 500 from six large comprehensive schools, to fill in a daily questionnaire for one school week to identify the frequency, duration, and intensity of physical activity. Activity which made the children 'sweat or become breathless' was identified as 'vigorous activity'.

Dickenson reported that over 80 per cent of the children did less than five minutes of vigorous activity on any weekday. From 67 to 76 per cent of children self-reported no vigorous activity whatsoever on each day. Only 60 per cent of the children completed the questionnaire for the whole week and 55 per cent of those reported no vigorous activity whatsoever. Dickenson (1987) explained the discrepancy in figures on the basis that those pupils who failed to complete the questionnaire on each day (e.g. through absence) were much more likely to be inactive than those who completed a full attendance. When the data were broken into sex and year groupings it was demonstrated that girls' level of activity decreased steadily with age, 45.5 per cent of 11-year-olds reported no vigorous activity during the week analysed whereas 80 per cent of 16-year-olds reported no vigorous activity. The boys' results indicated an increase in activity around 14 to 15 years, with only 28.5 per cent reporting no vigorous activity, but this was followed by a sharp decrease at 16 years when 52.5 per cent of the boys claimed no vigorous activity during the week studied. These results, however, although they are widely quoted to support the premise of children's low levels of activity (e.g. Sports Council, 1988; Almond, 1989) must be interpreted very cautiously because some of the sample sizes were extremely small (e.g. only fifteen 16-year-old girls and only nineteen 16-year-old boys) and this fact is not noted in the published versions of the report (Dickenson, 1986a, 1986b).

Dickenson followed up his questionnaire by interviewing 100 of the original sample to verify the results and to elicit information about weekend activity. The interviewees were asked to describe their regular recreational activities to identify if any form of physical activity featured in their lifestyle. Only 16.8 per cent mentioned any form of vigorous activity after school hours, closely reflecting the data derived from the questionnaire. The results of questions concerning physical activity at weekends indicated that the children were even less active at weekends with only 18 per cent of the sample claiming to take part in any vigorous activity.

It was pointed out earlier that the technique used to monitor children's physical activity must be socially acceptable, it should not burden the child with cumbersome equipment, and it should only minimally influence the child's normal physical activity pattern. The relative intensity and duration of activity should be monitored and the period of monitoring should be at least three days, including one weekend day. Although the limited information on British children's physical activity patterns is generally consistent, none of the studies of British children prior to the Physical Education Association (PEA) Research Centre Studies satisfied the above criteria either in terms of technique or of length of study. Whether British children regularly experienced health-related physical activity was therefore unknown.

PEA Research Centre Studies

With the development of self-contained, computerized telemetry systems the use of continuously monitored heart rate became a feasible method of assessing the relative intensity and duration of physical activity. Léger and Thivierge (1988) carried out a detailed analysis of the most popular commercially variable heart rate monitors and concluded that the Sport Tester 3000 was first choice as 'in addition to having excellent validity and stability it permits almost total freedom of motion'. The Sport Tester 3000 consists of a lightweight transmitter and a receiver/microcomputer. The transmitter is fixed to the chest with electrodes and the receiver/microcomputer is worn as a watch on the wrist. The Sport Tester 3000 is capable of storing minute-by-minute heart rates for up to sixteen hours. The interpretation of continuous heart rate is complex, however, because it reflects not only the metabolism of the child but also the transient emotional state, the prevailing climatic conditions, and the specific muscle groups which perform the activity (Armstrong, 1989). In the light of the previous discussion it was felt important to monitor the number and length of sustained periods with heart rate equal to or above 140 beats/min (health-related physical activity). If the Sports Tester is interfaced with a microcomputer the development of a simple programme will allow sustained periods of pre-determined length, with heart rates at or above 140 beats/min, to be readily identified and recorded. The PEA Research Centre Studies utilized this facility to investigate whether British children regularly experienced health-related physical activity.

The volume (frequency, duration, and intensity) of physical activity of 163 girls and 103 boys, aged 11 to 16 years, was estimated from continuous heart rate monitoring over three weekdays. Each child was monitored from about 0900 until 2100 during a normal school day. The receivers were retrieved, replaced, and refitted the next morning and the process repeated over three days. In addition 212 of the children were monitored from 0900 until 2100 on a Saturday (Armstrong et al., 1990b). Only four boys and one girl experienced a daily period of physical activity of the length and intensity defined by Simons-Morton et al. (1988) as health-related physical activity. Of the boys, 77 per cent failed to experience a single twenty-minute period at the intensity equivalent to health-related physical activity over three days of monitoring; the figure for girls was 88 per cent. Over a third of the boys and over half of the girls failed to experience a single ten-minute period with their heart rate maintained at or above 140 beats/min during the weekday monitoring, with 71 per cent of the boys and 94 per cent of the girls failing to experience a single ten-minute period with their heart rate at or above 140 beats/min during Saturday monitoring. This report provided the first objective evidence of British children's low levels of habitual physical activity. A comparison of the level of physical activity of girls and boys revealed that girls were significantly less active than boys and that, unlike boys, girls' volume of physical activity gradually decreased from the age of 11 years through 15 years.

These findings stimulated the researchers to study a group of 42 primary schoolchildren, aged 10 years, from the same catchment area as some of the secondary schoolchildren, mean age 13 years, already surveyed (Armstrong *et al.*, 1990c). A comparison of physical activity patterns revealed that although there was no significant difference between the volume of physical activity of primary schoolboys and secondary schoolboys, the primary schoolgirls were significantly more active than the secondary schoolgirls. Furthermore, no significant difference between the volume of health-related physical activity of the primary schoolboys and the primary schoolgirls was detected. This prompted a more in-depth analysis of primary schoolchildren's physical activity patterns (Armstrong and Bray, 1991). A study of the three-day activity patterns of 67 boys and 65 girls, aged 10 years, confirmed that there was no significant difference between the health-related physical activity patterns of girls and boys. Very few primary schoolchildren, however, experienced daily periods of twenty minutes or longer with their heart rates above the recommended thresholds. It appears that sustained periods of physical activity for this length of time are not features of young children's habitual physical activity. A similar analysis of ten-minute periods also revealed that only a minority of children experienced a daily session with their heart rate above the recommended level. However, when five-minute periods were examined it was demonstrated that 90 per cent of the boys and 85 per cent of the girls experienced daily sessions of this length with their heart rate above 139 beats/min. Relatively short periods of health-related physical activity appear to be typical of primary schoolchildren.

All of the PEA Research Centre studies were carried out throughout the school year, but in order to investigate whether there was any difference between physical activity levels during the autumn and summer terms 24 children were monitored for three days in the autumn term 1989 and three days in the summer term 1990 (Armstrong and Bray, 1990). No significant differences were detected.

This series of studies has shown that British children have surprisingly low levels of habitual physical activity and that many children seldom experience the intensity and duration of physical activity associated with health-related outcomes.

HEALTH-RELATED PHYSICAL ACTIVITY TRACKING FROM CHILDHOOD INTO ADULT LIFE

The hypothesis that participation in health-related physical activity and/or sport at school increases the likelihood of such participation as an adult has been advanced by many writers. The hypothesis is intuitively plausible but remains to be unequivocally proven.

Some researchers (e.g. Montoye *et al.*, 1959; Dishman, 1988) have indicated that the level of physical activity in adults is no different in former school athletes and non-athletes. Whereas others (e.g. Harris, 1979; Fardy *et al.*, 1978) have reported that active adults were more likely than sedentary adults to have been members of high school or college athletic teams or participants in college physical activity programmes. Powell and Dysinger (1987) reanalysed Paffenbarger's epidemiological study of 16,396 Harvard University alumni (Paffenbarger *et al.*, 1984) in the context of

physical activity patterns. They concluded that the data suggest that those who participate in varsity and intramural sports in college are more likely to continue a beneficial
physical activity pattern throughout their later years.

This type of analysis is, however, flawed on several counts. The use of college
students as the base population is probably not valid if the results are to be extrapo-
lated to children as physical activity patterns are likely to be well established by the
college years. The comparison of 'athletes' with 'non-athletes' introduces selection
bias, for example on the basis of genetic endowment. The generic use of 'athletes' is
probably inappropriate as activities that do not require a team may be more readily
performed throughout life. Similarly, the often early specialization of successful
young athletes may be achieved at the expense of developing a broader base of
fundamental motor skills which in turn may affect adult participation (Armstrong,
1990).

The United States National Adult Fitness Survey (Clarke, 1974) surveyed a rep-
resentative sample of 3,875 persons aged 22 years or above using personal interview
techniques. The respondents were asked if they ever took physical education when
they were in school and if they 'are now doing' any of a list of specific activities
(walking, cycling, swimming, jogging, lifting weights, calisthenics) or some other
activity. Those who had participated in two or more school sports during any phase of
their education were two to five times more likely to be 'now doing' all of the
activities, apart from walking, than those who had not participated in any school
sports. Similarly, those who took physical education at any time in school were also
likely to be 'now doing' common exercises when compared to those who did not take
physical education. These data suggest that participation in school sports or physical
education may predispose one to participate in exercise or sports as an adult.

Sofranko and Nolan (1972) and Yoesting and Burkhead (1973) studied adult participation in outdoor activities in relation to childhood participation and concluded
that the activity level of an individual as a child seems to have a direct effect on the
activity level of that individual as an adult.

In what appears to be the only published prospective longitudinal study of physical
activity from childhood through to adulthood Engstrom (1986) interviewed 2,454
randomly selected Swedish 15-year-olds about their sport activities during leisure time
and followed the same group through mailed questionnaires five, ten and fifteen years
later. The attrition rate was only 19 per cent so a full set of data was obtained on 2,000000072
individuals. The results clearly indicated that 'early experiences of physical activity are
important for psychological readiness to participate in keep-fit activities in later life'
(Engstrom, 1986, p. 89).

The definitive study of physical activity tracking from childhood into adult life has
yet to be carried out, but the weight of evidence supports the hypothesis that children's physical activity patterns persist into adulthood and reinforces the importance
of adopting an active lifestyle during childhood.

THE ROLE OF PHYSICAL EDUCATION IN PROMOTING HEALTH-
RELATED PHYSICAL ACTIVITY

The evidence presented in this chapter has clearly demonstrated that despite a decade
of teachers supposedly emphasizing the importance of health-related fitness (Arm-

strong, 1984, 1987) in the physical education curriculum, British children's current level of physical activity is a cause for grave concern. Many children seldom experience the intensity and duration of physical activity that are believed to promote health-related outcomes. It appears that participation in health-related physical activity as a child increases the likelihood of such participation as an adult. Children must therefore be encouraged to adopt and maintain active lifestyles—the development of 'activity independence' (Armstrong, 1990). In order to achieve 'activity independence' children need to understand the principles underlying health-related physical activity and the role that appropriate physical activity can play in a balanced lifestyle (Armstrong and Biddle, 1991). Through their physical education programme children need to experience a wide variety of individual, partner, and team activities, with the emphasis placed upon developing a sound foundation of motor skills, which can contribute to successful and enjoyable physical activity experiences both in the present and the future. These activity experiences need to be placed within a suitable theoretical framework which integrates with other foundation subjects and cross-curricular themes in the National Curriculum (National Curriculum Council, 1990).

Heads of physical education departments have been reported to regard health-related fitness (physical development) as the second most important objective of physical education but their curricula do not explicitly reflect this emphasis (Physical Education Association, 1987). In accord with the British Association of Sports Sciences/Health Education Authority/Physical Education Association Working Group (Armstrong *et al.*, 1990e) this writer therefore believes that the most effective way of achieving the objective that 'pupils should develop a knowledge and understanding of the beneficial effects of health-related physical activity and the ways in which these benefits can be achieved and sustained' (Armstrong *et al.*, 1990e, p. 225) is for health-related physical activity to be a core component of physical education in the National Curriculum. The issue is too important not to address and if physical educators miss the opportunity to firmly and explicitly establish health-related physical activity as part of the National Curriculum they will have performed a great disservice to our children.

NOTE

1 Tracking is the maintenance over time of the relative ranking of an individual with respect to his/her peers (Webber *et al.*, 1980).

REFERENCES

Almond, L. (1989) Do children take enough exercise? In Coronary Prevention Group, *Should the Prevention of Coronary Heart Disease Begin in Childhood?*, pp. 29–36. London: Coronary Prevention Group.

Armstrong, N. (1984) Why implement a health-related fitness programme? *British Journal of Physical Education* **15**, 173–5.

Armstrong, N. (1987) Health and fitness in the curriculum. *Perspectives* **31**.

Armstrong, N. (1989) Children's physical activity patterns and coronary heart disease. In Coronary Prevention Group, *Should the Prevention of Coronary Heart Disease Begin in Childhood?*, pp. 37–44. London: Coronary Prevention Group.

Armstrong, N. (1990) Children's physical activity patterns: the implications for physical education. In N. Armstrong (ed.), *New Directions in Physical Education* 1, pp. 1–15. Champaign, IL: Human Kinetics.

Armstrong, N., Balding, J., Gentle, P., and Kirby, B. (1990a) The estimation of coronary risk factors in British schoolchildren—a preliminary report. *British Journal of Sports Medicine* **24**, 61–6.

Armstrong, N., Balding, J., Gentle, P., and Kirby, B. (1990b) Patterns of physical activity among 11 to 16 year old British children. *British Medical Journal* **301**, 203–5.

Armstrong, N., Balding, J., Bray, S., Gentle, P., and Kirby, B. (1990c) The physical activity patterns of 10 and 13 year old children. In G. Beunen, J. Ghesquiere, R. Reybrouck and A. L. Claessens (eds), *Children and Exercise* XIV, pp. 152–7. Stuttgart: Ferdinand Enke.

Armstrong, N., Balding, J., Gentle, P., Williams, J., and Kirby, B. (1990d) Peak oxygen uptake and habitual physical activity in 11 to 16 year olds. *Pediatric Exercise Science* **2**, 349–58.

Armstrong, N., Bellew, B., Biddle, S., Bray, S., Gardonyi, P., and Winter, E. (1990e) Health-related physical activity in the National Curriculum. *British Journal of Physical Education* **21**, 225.

Armstrong, N. and Biddle, S. (1990) The assessment of children's physical activity patterns: continuous heart rate monitoring, self-report and interview recall technique. *Journal of Sports Sciences* **8**, 291.

Armstrong, N. and Biddle, S. (1991) Health-related physical activity in the National Curriculum. In N. Armstrong (ed.), *New Directions in Physical Education* 2: *Towards a National Curriculum*, Champaign, IL: Human Kinetics.

Armstrong, N. and Bray, S. (1990) Primary schoolchildren's physical activity patterns during autumn and summer. *Bulletin of Physical Education* **26**, 23–6.

Armstrong, N. and Bray, S. (1991) Physical activity patterns defined by continuous heart rate monitoring. *Archives of Disease in Childhood* **66**, 245–7.

Astrand, P. O. and Rodahl, K. (1986) *Textbook of Work Physiology*. New York: McGraw-Hill.

Balding, J. (1988) *Young People in 1987*. Exeter: Health Education Authority Schools Health Education Unit.

Bar-Or, O. (1983) *Paediatric Sports Medicine for the Practitioner*. New York: Springer-Verlag.

Bedale, E. M. (1923) Energy expenditure and food requirements of children at school. *Proceedings of the Royal Society (London)* **94**, 368–404.

Bradfield, R. B., Chan, H., Bradfield, N. E., and Payne, R. R. (1971) Energy expenditures and heart rates of Cambridge boys at school. *American Journal of Clinical Nutrition* **24**, 1461–6.

Brooke, J. D., Hardman, A. E., and Bottomley, F. A. (1975) The physiological load of a netball lesson. *Bulletin of Physical Education* **11**, 31–42.

Clarke, H. H. (1974) National adult physical fitness survey. *Physical Fitness Research Digest* **4**(2).

Dickenson, B. (1986a) Report on children's activity patterns and their perceptions of physical education and activity. *British Journal of Physical Education* **17**, ii.

Dickenson, B. (1986b) The physical activity patterns of young people—the implications for P.E. *Bulletin of Physical Education* **22**, 36–9.

Dickenson, B. (1987) A survey of the activity patterns of young people and their attitudes and perceptions of physical activity and physical education in an English local education authority. Unpublished M.Phil. thesis, Loughborough University of Technology.

Dishman, R. K. (1988) Supervised and free living physical activity: no differences in former athletes and non-athletes. *American Journal of Preventive Medicine* **4**, 153–60.

Durnin, J. V. G. A. (1971) Physical activity by adolescents. *Acta Paediatrica Scandinavica* (Suppl. 217), 133–5.

Durnin, J. V. G. A. (1974) A cross-sectional nutritional and anthropometric study, with an interval of 7 years on 611 young adolescent school children. *British Journal of Nutrition* **32**, 169–79.

Durnin, J. V. G. A. (1982) Energy consumption and its measurement in physical activity. *Annals of Clinical Research* **14**, 6–11.

Durnin, J. V. G. A. and Passmore, R.(1967) *Energy, Work and Leisure*. London: Heinemann.

Engstrom, L.-M. (1986) The process of socialisation into keep-fit activities. *Scandinavian Journal of Sports Science* **8**, 89–97.

Fardy, P. S., Maresh, C. M., Abbot, R., and Kristiansen, T. (1978) A comparison of habitual lifestyle, aerobic power, and systolic time intervals in former athletes and non-athletes. *Journal of Sports Medicine and Physical Fitness* **18**, 287–99.

Fentem, P. H., Bassey, E. J., and Turnbull, N. B. (1988) *The New Case for Exercise*. London: Sports Council and Health Education Authority.

Gleeson, N., Tancred, B., and Banks, M. (1989) Psycho-biological factors influencing habitual activities in male and female adolescents. *Physical Education Review* **12**, 110–24.

Hale, T. and Bradshaw, F. (1978) Heart rates during female physical education lessons. *British Journal of Sports Medicine* **12**, 22–6.

Harris, D. V. (1970) Physical activity history and attitudes of middle-aged men. *Medicine and Science in Sports* **2**, 203–8.

Heartbeat Wales (1986a) *Welsh Youth Health Survey 1986*. (Heartbeat Report No. 5).

Heartbeat Wales (1986b) *The Pulse of Wales: Preliminary Report of the Welsh Heart Health Survey 1985*. (Heartbeat Report No. 4).

Heartbeat Wales (1987) *Exercise of Health*. (Heartbeat Report No. 23).

Hendry, L. (1978) *School Sport and Leisure*. London: Lepus Books.

Knowles, J. E. (1978) The assessment of the physiological load of curricular activities. *Research Papers in Physical Education* **3**, 4–9.

LaPorte, R. E., Kuller, L. H., Kupfer, D. J., McPartland, R. M., Mathews, G., and Casperson, C. (1979) An objective measure of physical activity for epidemiological research. *American Journal of Epidemiology* **109**, 158–68.

Léger, L. and Thivierge, M. (1988) Heart rate monitors: validity, stability, and functionality. *Physician and Sports Medicine* **16**, 143–51.

McCusker, J. (1985) Involvement of 15–19 year olds in sport and physical activity. In L. Haywood and I. Henry (eds), *Leisure and Youth*. London: Leisure Studies Association Conference Report No. 17. Cited by B. Dickenson (1987) A survey of the activity patterns of young people and their attitudes and perceptions of physical activity and physical education in an English local education authority. Unpublished M.Phil. thesis, Loughborough University of Technology.

Montoye, H. J., Van Huss, W., and Zuidema, M. (1959) Sports activities of athletes and non-athletes in later life. *Physical Education* **16**, 48–51.

Morris, J. N., Chave, S. P. W., Adam, C., Sirey, C., Epstein, L., and Sheehan, D. J. (1973) Vigorous exercise in leisure time and the incidence of coronary heart disease. *Lancet* i, 333–9.

Morris, J. N., Everitt, M. G., and Semmence, A. M. (1987) Exercise and coronary heart disease. In D. Macleod, R. Maughan, M. Nimmo, T. Reilly, and C. Williams (eds), *Exercise Benefits, Limits and Adaptations*, pp. 4–17. London: E. and F. N. Spon.

National Curriculum Council (1990) *Curriculum Guidance 3. The Whole Curriculum*. York: National Curriculum Council.

Orchard, T. J., Hedley, A. J., and Mitchell, J. R. A. (1982) The distribution and associations of blood pressure in an adolescent population. *Journal of Epidemiology and Community Health* **36**, 35–42.

Paffenbarger, R. S., Hyde, R.T., Wing, A. L., and Steinmetz, C. M. (1984) A natural history of athleticism and cardiovascular health. *Journal of the American Medical Association* **252**, 491–5.

Physical Education Association (1987) *Physical Education in Schools*. London: Ling Publishing House.

Powell, K. E. and Dysinger, W. (1987) Childhood participation in organised school sports and physical education as precursors of adult physical activity. *American Journal of Preventive Medicine* **3**, 276–81.

Powell, K. E., Thompson, P. D. Casperson, C. J., and Kendrick, J. S. (1987) Physical activity and the incidence of coronary heart disease. *Annual Reviews of Public Health* **8**, 253–87.

Riddoch, C. (1990) *Northern Ireland Fitness Survey—1989*. Belfast: Queen's University.

Saris, W. H. M. (1982) *Aerobic Power and Daily Physical Activity in Children*. Meppel, Netherlands: Kripps Repro.

Simons-Morton, B. G., Parcel, G. S., O'Hara, N. M., Blair, S. N., and Pate, R. R. (1988) Health-related physical fitness in childhood. *Annual Reviews of Public Health* **9**, 403–25.

Sleap, M. and Warburton, P. (1990) *Physical Activity Patterns of Primary Schoolchildren: An Interim Report*. London: Health Education Authority.

Sofranko, A. J. and Nolan, M. F. (1972) Early life experiences and adult sports participation. *Journal of Leisure Research* **4**, 6–18.

South Western Council for Sport and Recreation (1984) *From School to Community*. Crewkerne: Sports Council.

Sports Council (1988) *Children's Exercise, Health and Fitness*. London: Sports Council.

Washburn, R. A. and Montoye, H. J. (1986) The assessment of physical activity by questionnaire. *American Journal of Epidemiology* **123**, 563–76.

Webber, L. S., Srinivasen, S. R., Voors, A. W., and Berenson, G. S. (1980) Persistence of levels for risk factor variables during the first year of life: the Bogalusa Heart Study. *Journal of Chronic Diseases* **33**, 157–67.

Wessel, J. A., Montoye, H. J., and Mitchell, H. (1965) Physical activity assessment by recall method. *American Journal of Public Health* **55**, 1430–6.

Williams, A. (1988) Physical activity patterns among adolescents—some curriculum implications. *Physical Education Review* **11**, 28–39.

Yoesting, D. R. and Burkhead, D. L. (1973) Significance of childhood recreation experience on adult leisure behaviour. An explanatory analysis. *Journal of Leisure Research* **5**, 25–36.

Chapter 10

Promoting Health-Related Physical Activity in Schools

Stuart Biddle

There can be little doubt that the greater recognition given to health/fitness issues in physical education (PE) in the past few years has been one of the most striking features of the subject during this period. Despite the use of several terms used to describe this aspect of PE—health-related fitness, health-related exercise, health-related physical activity, health focus, health-based PE—the rationale given has been characterized by an emphasis on preventive health. In other words, the rationale has been (a) children are not active and/or fit enough, therefore (b) children need either more activity and/or education for health/fitness, because (c) physical inactivity has been shown to be related to increased risk of some chronic diseases in adulthood.

This preventive health approach (a 'physiological' rationale; see Armstrong, 1987) is a justifiable and powerful one. However, teachers have recognized that simply imparting facts about the outcomes of exercise, or teaching the health benefits of physical activities, does not necessarily increase involvement in sports and exercise by children. The concept of 'health' is likely to be abstract to many children, and the health outcomes may not be particularly meaningful, at least from a motivational standpoint.

A second aspect of the work of teachers in health/fitness has been in the design and implementation of programmes. These have usually focused on the components of health-related fitness: cardiopulmonary exercise, muscular strength and endurance, flexibility, and body composition. Little has been said about the promotion of such activities or how individual pupils are taught self-regulatory skills or lifestyle planning in order that the likelihood of such activities being pursued is increased.

For these reasons it is important that teachers consider issues in addition to physiological outcomes that are concerned with health-related physical activity (HRPA) for children and youth aged 5–18 years.

The purpose of this chapter, therefore, is to outline three issues associated with the promotion of HRPA in school-aged children. Specifically, individual behaviour-change strategies will be discussed with a view to providing guidance for teachers. Second, strategies relevant to institutional change will be considered, and finally, aspects of school and community links and exercise promotion will be discussed. In short, the chapter focuses not on the outcomes of HRPA but on the interventions thought likely to promote greater participation.

INDIVIDUAL BEHAVIOUR CHANGE

Although a greater recognition of social influences on health and physical activity patterns is emerging (Sparkes, 1989, and Chapter 13 in this book), there is a wealth of evidence on psychological and social psychological antecedents of exercise and physical activity (Biddle and Fox, 1989; Biddle and Mutrie, 1991; Dishman, 1988).

A number of 'models' or 'theories' have been proposed and subsequently applied to HRPA. These include models of attitudes and beliefs, as well as motivation and self-perceptions. Such models provide a framework for research and for guiding intervention strategies (see Dishman, 1990). However, the theoretical background to these models will not be discussed in any detail here, although summaries are available (Sonstroem, 1988). The practical interventions that stem from these and other approaches, however, will be considered.

Interventions

Self-regulatory skills

Although there is little systematic research evidence on the effects of self-regulatory skills in the promotion of physical activity in children, there is sufficient information from a number of sources to suggest that this is an important area for consideration. Self-regulatory skills are those skills that can be learned and developed by the individual for gaining greater control over the adoption and maintenance of desired behaviours. A variety of different strategies may be applicable, including goal-setting, self-reinforcement and monitoring, attribution and perceived control, and self-efficacy (confidence) enhancement.

Goal-setting

The goal-setting process can be complex but does hold important implications for motivation (Wraith and Biddle, 1986). Goal-setting has been used with some success in industrial settings and more recently in sport (Hall and Byrne, 1988; Harris and Harris, 1984; Locke and Latham, 1985). It provides a focus and direction for actions which, if reached, provide a sense of achievement and satisfaction for the participant. This in itself is likely to provide further motivation.

The following guidelines are provided and it is the belief of this author that these should be taught to children within a course on 'how to exercise'.

1   Goals should be set for the short, medium and long term: consider the goal-setting process as a stairway with the long-term goal at the top of the stairs (see Figure 10.1). Short-term goals can be achieved more easily and appear more achievable.

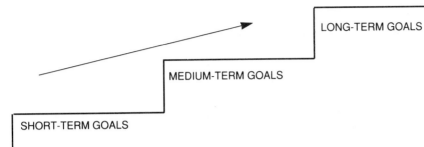

Figure 10.1 *A stairway approach to goal-setting.*

2 Goals should be specific: general, vague 'do-your-best' goals are not specified in a way that directs action. Specific goals should state not only what you want to achieve, but how you are going to achieve it.
3 Goals should be realistic but challenging: this is not always easy to do and may come about through trial and error more than systematic planning. Nevertheless, goals must act as a stimulus and should therefore be neither too hard nor too easy.
4 Set goals that relate to the process of exercise rather than solely the product. That is to say the emphasis should be on participation not outcome, at least in the initial stages of involvement and for those unfit or uncomfortable with exercise. Sustained involvement is the goal, therefore the targets should reflect this. Rejeski and Kenney (1988) suggest that at the start of an exercise programme fitness improvement should actually be discouraged. This is to prevent unpleasant experiences of over-rigorous sessions and also to encourage the adoption of the right behaviour patterns in preference to transient gains in fitness.
5 Goals should be flexible: as stated, setting goals at the appropriate level is difficult. Therefore, the pupil and teacher must be prepared to be flexible and alter goals, upwards or downwards, if they appear to be inappropriate. A study by Martin *et al.* (1984) showed that when subjects were allowed to modify their exercise goals they had a greater adherence rate than those with fixed goals.
6 Goals must be accepted by the participant and he/she must be committed to achieving them: these can be enhanced by having the individual participate in the goal-setting process. Goals set externally by the teacher, without involving the pupil, may be less effective. Goal-setting 'contracts' can also help whereby the individual signs a commitment to the goal.
7 Regular feedback should be given about progress towards the goals: this can be done through external feedback from the teacher or internal feedback through self-monitoring. This should also allow for flexible goal-setting and a reappraisal of inappropriate goals, as discussed in 5 above.

Reinforcement and monitoring

Reinforcing physical activity increases the likelihood that it will be repeated. Punishment is designed to have the opposite effect. Regrettably, many have experienced exercise as an aversive experience and teachers have used physical activity as punishment. This legacy remains even today and provides a major stumbling block to the promotion of HRPA in schools and in the community at large.

The consequences of some forms of exercise, of course, may not be immediately pleasant and indeed do have the potential to be punishing. However, the teacher should avoid using exercise in this way and substitute more desirable experiences if long-term involvement is an objective. The individuals who may experience most discomfort in exercise, such as the obese, are those who stand to benefit the most from sustained involvement. Sensitive strategies are essential here.

In addition to modifying the exercise routine, such as lowering the intensity and increasing the length of warm-up, teachers can introduce other interventions such as music.

Knapp (1988) suggests that shame and embarrassment can be reduced with 'unconditional positive regard' for pupils. In other words, the 'worth' of the pupil should not be dependent on exercise performance.

Positive reinforcement is an important concept in promoting HRPA. This is the presentation of a desirable reward, and the sooner it is presented after the behaviour the more powerful its influence will be. Negative reinforcement, however, is the withdrawal of an unpleasant event or stimulus. Negative comments from a teacher can act as negative reinforcement as one tries to escape the comments. They are seldom effective in behaviour change.

In addition to the positive reinforcement that can be given by the teacher, pupils should be aware of the importance of self-reinforcement. This can include goal-setting, self-monitoring (such as through a diary), and decision balance sheet (DBS) procedures (Wankel, 1984). DBS involves individuals writing down the potential costs and benefits of physical activity. The strategies best suited to the adoption and maintenance of HRPA are then considered and chosen. It is advocated that children in schools have the opportunity of experiencing this.

Other behaviour change strategies might include behavioural contracts, extrinsic rewards (see pp. 159–60), and social support. This latter strategy has been found to be very important for adults recovering from a heart attack. The support of others, and in particular that of the spouse, predicts adherence to post-myocardial infarction exercise rehabilitation programmes (Oldridge, 1988).

Attributions and perceived control

The way we think about exercise and physical activities can have a strong influence on subsequent behaviour. One important aspect of this is the way we perceive events and the reasons or causes we give for their occurrence. The process of attributing reasons and causes is referred to as the 'attribution' process. For example, after receiving positive feedback on performing a particular exercise routine to music, a child may think it was due to his/her effort and personal practice. Alternatively, 'failure' may be attributed to not trying hard enough or believing one has limited ability. This process is discussed more fully in my chapter on motivation in this volume. It is important that teachers encourage students to take responsibility for their successes and positive experiences in exercise, but it is also important that they encourage students to look for solutions to negative situations or 'failure'. This means avoiding attributing failure to factors that appear uncontrollable, such as lack of ability. All children can take part in exercise regardless of ability.

Rewards, motivation and control

In a section on self-regulatory skills, it should be obvious that strategies which reduce perceived control over events should be avoided. Ironically, in some situations the use of extrinsic rewards can have this effect. This has been discussed elsewhere and therefore will only be summarized here (see Biddle, 1984; Deci and Ryan, 1985; Fox and Biddle, 1988).

Originally, it was thought that people with high levels of intrinsic motivation would benefit automatically from the use of rewards, or extrinsic motivation. These rewards might include money, badges, prizes, etc. However, research with children in the classroom has shown that when children were told they would be rewarded for continuing with a task already intrinsically interesting to them, participation actually declined. This was not so, however, for those who received a reward later on but did not expect the reward to be given (Lepper *et al.*, 1973).

Subsequently, Deci and Ryan (1985) have formulated the 'Cognitive Evaluation Theory' (CET) to help explain this phenomenon. CET proposes that if people receive a reward and perceive this to be a recognition of their competence and 'a job well done', then intrinsic motivation should be enhanced. However, if the reward is seen to be the reason for participation, then long-term involvement could decline. In other words, if rewards 'take over' and dominate then intrinsic motivation may be reduced—play becomes more like work.

The implication of this is that rewards *can* stimulate involvement in HRPA, but only if they are used as a reward for competence. The American 'Physical Best' scheme has a structure that promotes three types of rewards. These are outlined in Table 10.1.

Table 10.1 *The 'Physical Best' recognition system.*

Award	Behaviour
Fitness Activity Award	Recognition of the student's participation in physical activities outside of school physical education. Student keeps an 'activity log/diary' and sets personal goals and activities in consultation with the teacher.
Fitness Goals Award	Recognition for obtaining individual fitness and exercise goals, set in consultation with the teacher. Goals can be set in cognitive, psychomotor and affective learning domains.
Health Fitness Awards	Recognizes the attainment of fitness levels associated with minimal risk or risks of health problems. Students have to attain the standards for all six items (distance run, skinfold measures, body mass index, sit and reach flexibility test, sit-up, and pull-up).

Source: American Alliance for Health, Physical Education, Recreation and Dance (1988).

Some (e.g. Corbin *et al.*, 1988) have called for a greater emphasis on the rewarding of participation in exercise ('process' awards). However, this reward system is also open to the problems already outlined, although one would have thought it would allow for greater numbers of pupils to be able to be rewarded for their competence.

Self-confidence

The HMI document *Physical Education from 5–16* specifies that one of the eleven aims of physical education is to 'develop self-confidence through understanding the capabilities and limitations of oneself and others' (HMI, 1989, p. 2). Certainly the development of self-confidence in physical activity settings would appear to be an important strategy for the promotion of HRPA.

The most influential perspective on self-confidence has been the theory of 'self-efficacy' (SE) proposed by Bandura (1977, 1986). Essentially, he suggests that SE is the belief or conviction one has in being able to carry out a particular behaviour. In other words, it is situation-specific self-confidence. It is not the same as being a generally confident individual (personality trait), nor is it confidence in the outcome of a particular action. For example, Bandura distinguishes between efficacy expectations—the expectation that one can or cannot carry out a specific behaviour, such as an exercise programme—and outcomes expectations. These are expectations about whether the behaviour will produce certain effects, such as weight loss in the case of exercise. SE is about the actual behaviour itself rather than the outcomes of that behaviour.

SE has been found to be a good predictor of exercise behaviour in many contexts, including medical rehabilitation, the workplace, and community fitness programmes (see Biddle and Mutrie, 1991). For a review of self-confidence in sport, see Feltz (1988).

Bandura proposes four main mechanisms or sources of information for the development of SE and these are illustrated in Figure 10.2. The four sources are performance attainment (or prior performance on the task or related tasks), imitation and modelling of others in the same situation, verbal and social persuasion about performance, and judgements of coping via physiological responses such as heart rate.

Performance attainment is thought to be the most powerful source of SE as it is based on personal experience of success and failure. The way pupils think about such successes and failures (attributions) will influence their expectations and behaviours, as already suggested in an earlier section of this chapter and elsewhere in this volume (see Chapter 6, pp. 102–4). Confidence gained in one situation may generalize to another, but the strongest gains in SE will occur when the behaviours are closely matched. For example, confidence in one's ability to continue a jogging programme may not predict very well one's confidence in continuing with a weight-training programme. This suggests that pupils require a wide range of exercise experiences to develop SE across exercise modes.

The role of learning through imitation and modelling is highlighted in SE theory. Observing others succeed or fail can affect subsequent perceptions of personal capabilities, particularly if the model is seen to be similar to oneself. This suggests that the use of elite sport models may be inappropriate for those who require greater SE in exercise. Similarly, Bandura has suggested that imitative learning will be more

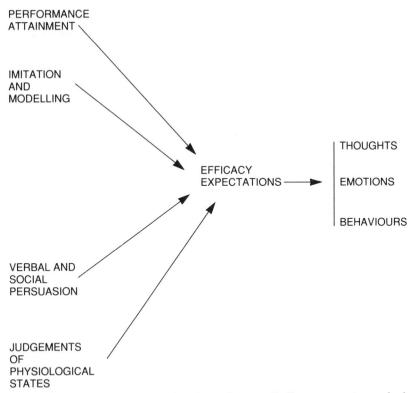

Figure 10.2 *The major sources of information thought to influence self-efficacy expectations and subsequent thoughts, emotions, and behaviours* (adapted from Feltz, 1988).

powerful for those with limited or no experience of the task in question because the model becomes more salient in such situations.

The use of verbal and social persuasion can enhance SE, although the strength of this effect is likely to depend on the source of such persuasion. The highly respected physical educator will, of course, have greater influence than a teacher who is seen in a less favourable light.

Finally, SE theory proposes that confidence may also be related to emotional arousal and perception of internal physiological states. The original SE theory was developed from research into phobic behaviours, hence the role of physiological arousal may be more important there than in exercise and health behaviours.

SE theory predicts, therefore, that HRPA will be promoted via enhanced SE through the mechanisms of prior perceived success in various exercise settings, appropriate modelling of exercise by people to whom pupils can 'relate', and positive verbal and social persuasion by significant others and respected authority figures.

Summary of interventions for individual behaviour change

This part of the chapter has suggested that HRPA can be promoted in schools by allowing students to be involved in the learning of self-regulatory skills, such as goal-setting and self-reinforcement. Issues associated with perceived control and rewards, as well as self-efficacy or confidence were also discussed in the belief that they need highlighting for physical educators. Those involved in the promotion of HRPA require an understanding and awareness of these issues.

INSTITUTIONAL BEHAVIOUR CHANGE

The individual strategies and interventions outlined will, of course, have a reduced impact within an environment that fails to support such behaviour change. For this reason, the role of the institution becomes important. Conflicts within the institution can arise that offset positive educational influences from teachers. One example that regularly features in questions from teachers on health-related exercise courses is that of school meals. Too often it is reported that pupils go from a lesson on 'healthy eating' into the school hall where they can easily choose an unhealthy option, albeit one that is commercially successful for the school or local meals service.

Organizational change, therefore, is required to support more discrete curricula changes. Parcel *et al.* (1987) studied four schools in the USA in terms of both physical activity and diet. Their data suggested that school lunches were excessive in fat and salt and that physical education lessons and break periods contained low levels of physical activity. Consequently, four stages of institutional change were suggested. These were institutional commitment, structured alternatives in school policies and practices, changes in the practices and roles of individual staff, and the implementation of learning activities for students. The example of aerobic exercise is given in Figure 10.3 to illustrate this approach.

Figure 10.3 shows that institutional commitment should come from support at 'area' level, such as that supported by advisers or school consortia. Similarly, 'key' personnel in the school must be persuaded that such changes are desirable. Given that physical education can be considered a 'marginal' subject by some staff, due to its physical location and/or subject status (see Sparkes *et al.*, 1990), involving other staff in the work of the department may help. For example, staff themselves may be interested in obtaining advice on exercise. Bringing them 'into' the department may be a positive step towards encouraging institutional commitment (see Fox *et al.*, 1987).

Policies and practices must also change, such as revising aspects of the curriculum to reflect a greater awareness of health issues. Similarly, implementing courses in aerobic exercise rather than simply assuming that learning about this aspect of fitness and health will occur through more 'traditional' courses, such as team games, will also need to occur. This is where 'real' change can take place over and beyond 'mere' policy statements or intentions.

Downey *et al.* (1987) have also described a model for institutional intervention in health. This is the 'Heart Smart' programme developed within the Bogalusa study in Louisiana, USA. One of the goals of the 'Heart Smart' programme is to develop an effective cardiovascular risk reduction and health promotion programme that 'positively influences predisposing factors (knowledge, attitudes, beliefs, values) and enabling factors (skills)' (Downey *et al.*, 1987, p. 99). Part of this programme is to promote the adoption of regular exercise to increase cardiovascular fitness. A simpli-

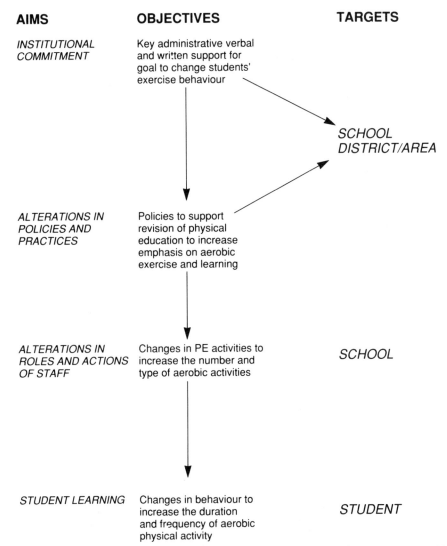

AIMS

INSTITUTIONAL COMMITMENT

ALTERATIONS IN POLICIES AND PRACTICES

ALTERATIONS IN ROLES AND ACTIONS OF STAFF

STUDENT LEARNING

OBJECTIVES

Key administrative verbal and written support for goal to change students' exercise behaviour

Policies to support revision of physical education to increase emphasis on aerobic exercise and learning

Changes in PE activities to increase the number and type of aerobic activities

Changes in behaviour to increase the duration and frequency of aerobic physical activity

TARGETS

SCHOOL DISTRICT/AREA

SCHOOL

STUDENT

Figure 10.3 *A school health promotion model applied to the promotion of aerobic exercise* (adapted from Parcel *et al.*, 1987).

fied version of the model proposed by Downey *et al.* (1987) is shown in Figure 10.4 on p. 164.

The foot of Figure 10.4 shows that the overall intervention is aimed at changing behaviour and subsequently health and social outcomes via intermediate variables identified as determinants of behaviour, including predisposing factors, enabling factors, and reinforcing factors.

One of the problems with such interventions is the assessment of its impact. Downey *et al.* (1987) suggest three forms of evaluation. 'Process evaluation' involves a qualitative assessment of the overall intervention, the 'impact evaluation' assesses short-term changes in factors such as attitudes and fitness, and 'outcome evaluation' involves the assessment of longer-term changes. Regrettably, few such interventions

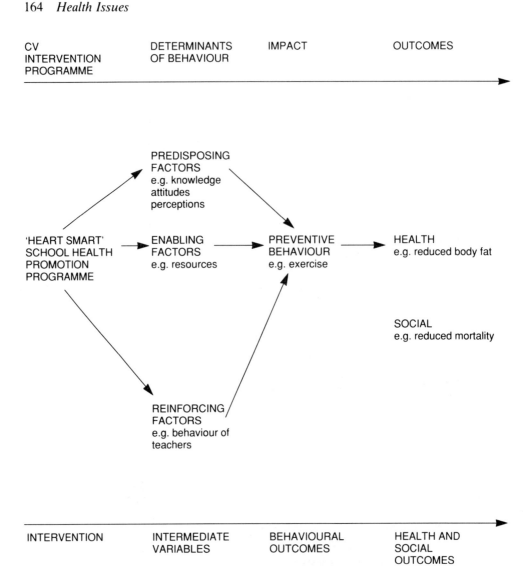

Figure 10.4 *A school cardiovascular health promotion model* (adapted from Downey *et al.*, 1987).

in schools are properly monitored or evaluated, often for very good reasons such as lack of resources. At least a minimal assessment should take place, such as a process evaluation.

Daily physical education

The school Sport Forum (1988) recommended that:

> as part of a school health policy, there should be a daily session of vigorous physical

activity in each primary school as part of the physical education programme or as a supplement to it. A local education authority should be asked to set up a pilot scheme to determine the value of a similar policy in the secondary school. (p. 15)

Such intervention, at first sight, may seem appealing. However, it raises the fundamental point in physical education of whether the goals of such an intervention are short-term physiological goals or goals of a longer-term educational nature. Indeed, the claims made about daily PE have often outstripped the evidence. For example, it has been claimed that academic performance may be enhanced by such an intervention, but no supportive evidence was found in a study of daily PE in South Australia (Dwyer *et al.*, 1983). Similarly, a study conducted in Scotland (Pollatschek and O'Hagan, 1989) showed superior fitness test performance after daily PE (compared with 'normal' PE of one period per week) on only five of twelve post-intervention analyses. Indeed, the one test most likely to be relevant to health outcomes (endurance run) showed no difference between the two groups. This may reflect the problematic nature of field tests of endurance exercise performance as much as anything else (Armstrong and Biddle, 1991).

The key issue in daily physical education is not transitory changes in fitness or exercise performance, since these can often be achieved outside the educational environment by non-professionals. If we value our status as professional educators we must set educational objectives which allow students the opportunity to increase their chance of long-term behaviour change.

LINKING SCHOOL AND COMMUNITY

Having discussed individual and institutional intervention strategies it would appear appropriate to conclude the chapter by considering some issues associated with long-term involvement in physical activity and exercise in the community. The link between school and community, therefore, becomes very important.

Many of the issues already raised are important in developing a positive feeling about exercise for school leavers. For example, White and Coakley (1986) found that in a group of school leavers who had decided not to take part in community sport and recreation, prior experience of physical education was an important factor in their decision not to participate. In particular, negative experiences such as embarrassment, perceived incompetence, negative peer evaluation, and unattractive facilities contributed to these youths being 'turned off' physical activity. This appeared to be particularly so for girls.

One objective for the physical educator, therefore, is not only to promote links between school and community opportunities, but to enhance the PE environment and overall experience. Unfortunately, data suggest that people put physical activity quite low on their list of priorities. The Canada Fitness Survey (1983) showed that physical activity was seen as less important for health than adequate sleep, good diet, medical/dental care, not smoking, maintaining weight, and control of stress. Physical educators have a role in emphasizing the importance of physical activity in health promotion.

If school physical education has as one of its objectives the enhancement of participation in community activities, either for pupils after school hours or after they have
left school, then a rethink on the type of activities taught in schools may be required.
Although some activities, such as gymnastics and team games, are wholly appropriate
for children, it is questionable how relevant these are for adults. They are not the type
of activities adults readily participate in during their leisure time. At what stage,
therefore, should the curriculum introduce adolescents to sports and other activities
that have 'carry-over value' for adulthood (see Simons-Morton *et al.*, 1987; Simons-
Morton *et al.*, 1988)? This is not an easy question to answer, but certainly the teaching
of health/fitness courses would appear to be essential if school students are to be
prepared adequately to become independent lifetime exercisers.

Fitness/exercise marketing

Similar issues must be addressed when looking at the promotion of health/fitness
activities. Eadie and Leathar (1988) investigated the understanding that Scottish
adults had of the words 'fitness' and 'health', what factors were thought to influence
these concepts, and how media campaigns might influence people's ideas about fitness
and health. The study was an attempt to produce marketing strategies that would
increase community participation. It provides some results that might have important
implications for the way physical educators promote or 'market' their product.

From interviews with 140 people, Eadie and Leathar found that fitness was viewed
as a physical ability enabling people to carry out daily tasks, and was associated with
positive leisure activity such as sport and exercise. However, it was also viewed as a
concept involving improvement and one that was controllable, although few exercised
this control. When exercise was viewed as involving effort and commitment it was also
perceived as unenjoyable.

Health, on the other hand, was seen in terms of illness, disease, and problems, and
was more complex than fitness. Health was viewed as being about maintenance rather
than improvement, and was believed to be less controllable than fitness.

The same subjects said that information and persuasion campaigns could be effective in promoting exercise but would need to be positive and not 'over-persuasive';
authoritarian messages were disliked.

Eadie and Leathar's research produced four main guidelines for promoting fitness
and exercise in the community and these have implications for schools:

1 Fitness should have positive appeal as it was viewed as unimportant by most
   subjects. Negative fear appeals should be avoided and the emphasis should be
   placed on more immediate and pleasurable physical, mental and social outcomes.
2 Greater 'universal representation' is required to make fitness and exercise socially
   acceptable rather than appeal only to those with higher levels of fitness or sporting
   ability.
3 Promotion campaigns must recognize individuality by allowing a wide range of
   activities to choose from.
4 Fitness marketing should highlight the informal nature of participation. Many

people are likely to be put off by highly structured and professionalized activities, yet often these are the kinds of activities that dominate school curricula. For example, the strict enforcement of 'dress codes' in recreational sports and exercise adds to the structured nature of these activities and may therefore reduce their appeal to some individuals.

Barriers to participation

A recognition of the major barriers to regular exercise may help in the promotion of HRPA. Data from the Canada Fitness Survey (1983) showed that perceived lack of time and poor motivation were seen as the major obstacles to exercise. Both these barriers can be tackled through the procedures outlined in the first section of this chapter on individual strategies. For example, perceived lack of time may be the result of poor time management. Goal-setting could be one way that this problem is tackled. No study has shown that exercisers have more time available to them than non-exercisers. It has also been suggested that access to community facilities may be less of a problem than once thought.

A breakdown of the Canada Fitness Survey data shows that men perceive time as a barrier more than women, but the reverse is true for the motivation factor. It is difficult to distinguish clearly between these two barriers. For example, perceived lack of time may be a *post-hoc* rationalization for 'not liking sweaty exercise'. Similarly, motivation may be related to the time needed to travel to a facility or the effort required to sustain aerobic exercise.

When asked 'what would increase their activity levels' only 6 per cent said that this would be achieved with more information on the benefits of activity. Information on its own is unlikely to be very beneficial. Indeed, many people probably already know of the potential benefits of physical activity. However, they may be less aware of the self-regulatory skills required to adopt and maintain participation.

CONCLUSION

This chapter has attempted to raise a number of issues for contemporary physical education by addressing the important topic of *promoting* HRPA. The health outcomes of habitual physical activity and exercise are now well documented (see Bouchard *et al.*, 1990), yet the activity levels of children and adults remain low (Armstrong *et al.*, 1990; Stephens *et al.*, 1985). This suggests that a greater emphasis should be placed on the understanding of the adoption and maintenance of HRPA. Interventions at individual and institutional levels offer guidelines for this. However, it is the belief of this author that a radical shift in emphasis from the product of exercise outcomes to the process of exercise participation is required by teachers before activity levels will change and the associated health benefits be recognized in the community.

REFERENCES

American Alliance for Health, Physical Education, Recreation and Dance (1988) *Physical Best*. Reston, VA: Author.

Armstrong, N. (1987) Health and fitness programmes in schools: a physiological rationale. In S. J. H. Biddle (ed.), *Foundations of Health-Related Fitness in Physical Education*, pp. 19–27. London: Ling Publishing House.

Armstrong, N., Balding, J., Gentle, P., Williams, J., and Kirby, B. (1990) Peak oxygen uptake and physical activity in 11- to 16-year-olds. *Pediatric Exercise Science* **2**, 349–58.

Armstrong, N. and Biddle, S. J. H. (1991) Health-related physical activity in the National Curriculum. In N. Armstrong (ed.), *New Directions in Physical Education* 2. Champaign, IL: Human Kinetics.

Bandura, A. (1977) Self-efficacy: toward a unifying theory of behavioural change. *Psychological Review* **84**, 191–215.

Bandura, A. (1986) *Social Foundations of Thought and Action: A Social Cognitive Theory*. Englewood Cliffs, NJ: Prentice-Hall.

Biddle, S. J. H., (1984) Motivational issues in health-related fitness: a note of caution. *British Journal of Physical Education* **15** (1), 21–2.

Biddle, S. J. H. and Fox, K. R, (1989) Exercise and health psychology: emerging relationships. *British Journal of Medical Psychology* **62**, 205–16.

Biddle, S. J. H. and Mutrie, N. (1991) *Psychology of Physical Activity and Exercise: A Health-Related Perspective*. London: Springer-Verlag.

Bouchard, C., Shephard, R. J., Stephens, T., Sutton, J. R., and McPherson, B. D. (eds) (1990) *Exercise, Fitness and Health: A Consensus of Current Knowledge*. Champaign, IL: Human Kinetics.

Canada Fitness Survey (1983) *Fitness and Lifestyle in Canada*. Ottawa: Author.

Corbin, C. B., Whitehead, J. R., and Lovejoy, P. Y. (1988) Youth physical fitness awards. *Quest* **40**, 200–18.

Deci, E. L. and Ryan, R. M. (1985) *Intrinsic Motivation and Self-Determination of Human Behaviour*. New York: Plenum.

Dishman, R. K. (ed.) (1988) *Exercise Adherence: Its Impact on Public Health*. Champaign, IL: Human Kinetics.

Dishman, R. K. (1990) Determinants of participation in physical activity. In C. Bouchard, R. J. Shephard, T. Stephens, J. R. Sutton, and B. D. McPherson (eds), *Exercise, Fitness and Health: A Consensus of Current Knowledge*, pp. 75–101. Champaign, IL: Human Kinetics.

Downey, A. M., Frank, G. C., Webber, L. S., Harsha, D. W., Virgilio, S. J., Franklin, F. A., and Berenson, G. S. (1987) Implementation of 'Heart Smart': a cardiovascular school health promotion programme. *Journal of School Health* **57**, 98–104.

Dwyer, T., Coonan, W. E., Leitch, D. R., Hetzel, B. S., and Baghurst, R. A. (1983) An investigation of the effects of daily physical activity on the health of primary school students in South Australia. *International Journal of Epidemiology* **12**, 308–13.

Eadie, D. R. and Leathar, D. S. (1988) *Concepts of Fitness and Health: An Exploratory Study*. Edinburgh: Scottish Sports Council.

Feltz, D. L. (1988) Self-confidence and sports performance. *Exercise and Sport Sciences Reviews* **16**, 423–57.

Fox, K. R. and Biddle, S. J. H. (1988) The child's perspective in physical education: II. Children's participation motives. *British Journal of Physical Education* **19**, 79–82.

Fox, K. R., Whitehead, J. R. and Corbin, C. B. (1987) Getting started in health-related fitness. In S. J. H. Biddle (ed.), *Foundations of Health-Related Fitness in Physical Education*, pp. 82–93. London: Ling Publishing House.

Hall, H. K. and Byrne, A. T. J. (1988) Goal setting in sport: clarifying recent anomalies. *Journal of Sport and Exercise Psychology* **10**, 184–98.

Harris, D. V. and Harris, B. (1984) *Athletes' Guide to Sport Psychology*. Champaign, IL: Leisure Press.

HMI (1989) *Physical Education from 5 to 16*. London: HMSO.

Knapp, D. N. (1988) Behavioural management techniques and exercise promotion. In R. K.

Dishman (ed.), *Exercise Adherence: Its Impact on Public Health*, pp. 203–35. Champaign, IL: Human Kinetics.

Lepper, M. R., Greene, D. and Nisbett, R. E. (1973) Undermining children's intrinsic interest with extrinsic reward: a test of the 'overjustification' hypothesis. *Journal of Personality and Social Psychology* **28**, 129–37.

Locke, E. A. and Latham, G. P. (1985) The application of goal-setting to sports. *Journal of Sport Psychology* **7**, 205–22.

Martin, J. E., Dubbert, P. M., Katell, A. D., Thompson, J. K., Raczynski, J. R., and Lake, M. (1984) Behavioural control of exercise: studies 1 through 6. *Journal of Consulting and Clinical Psychology* **52**, 795–811.

Oldridge, N. B. (1988) Compliance with exercise in cardiac rehabilitation. In R. K. Dishman (ed.), *Exercise Adherence: Its Impact on Public Health*, pp. 283–304. Champaign, IL: Human Kinetics.

Parcel, G. S., Simons-Morton, B. G., O'Hara, N. M., Baranowski, T., Kolbe, L. J., and Bee, D. E. (1987) School promotion of healthful diet and exercise behaviour: an integration of organizational change and social learning theory interventions. *Journal of School Health* **57**, 150–6.

Pollatschek, J. L. and O'Hagan, F. J. (1989) An investigation of the psycho-physical influences of a quality daily physical education programme. *Health Education Research: Theory and Practice* **4**, 341–50.

Rejeski, W. J. and Kenney, E. A. (1988) *Fitness Motivation*. Champaign, IL: Life Enhancement Publications.

School Sport Forum (1988) *Sport and Young People: Partnership and Action*. London: Sports Council.

Simons-Morton, B. G., O'Hara, N. M., Simons-Morton, D. G., and Parcel, G. S. (1987) Children and fitness: a public health perspective. *Research Quarterly for Exercise and Sport* **58**, 295–302.

Simons-Morton, B. G., Parcel, G. S., O'Hara, N. M., Blair, S. N. and Pate, R. R. (1988) Health-related physical fitness in childhood: status and recommendations. *Annual Review of Public Health* **9**, 403–25.

Sonstroem, R. J. (1988) Psychological models. In R. K. Dishman (ed.), *Exercise Adherence: Its Impact on Public Health*, pp. 125–53. Champaign, IL: Human Kinetics.

Sparkes, A. C. (1989) Health-related fitness: an example of innovation without change. *British Journal of Physical Education* **20**, 60–2.

Sparkes, A. C., Templin, T. J., and Schempp, P. G. (1990) The problematic nature of a career in a marginal subject: some implications for teacher education programmes. *Journal of Education for Teaching* **16**, 3–28.

Stephens, T., Jacobs, D. R., and White, C. C. (1985) A descriptive epidemiology of leisure-time physical activity. *Public Health Reports* **100**, 147–58.

Wankel, L. M. (1984) Decision-making and social support strategies for increasing exercise involvement. *Journal of Cardiac Rehabilitation* **4**, 124–35.

White, A. and Coakley, J. J. (1986) *Making Decisions: The Response of Young People in the Medway Towns to the 'Ever Thought of Sport?' Campaign*. London: Greater London and South East Region Sports Council.

Wraith, S. C. and Biddle, S. J. H. (1986) Goal-setting in sport and exercise. *British Journal of Physical Education* **17**, 208–10.

Chapter 11

Health-Related Physical Activity in the Primary School

Sue Bray

In the early years of the century physical education was mainly referred to as 'physical training' although as early as 1909 the term 'physical education' began to be used within documents produced by the Board of Education. The first official syllabus of physical training for schools was issued at the beginning of the century and was based on a series of Swedish exercises which had been used by the British Armed Forces (Board of Education, 1904). Children were not encouraged to think for themselves or expected to enjoy the programmes. The value was thought to be in the formal nature of the work and the beneficial effect on the physiological functioning of the body. The syllabus was slightly altered in 1905 and revised in 1909 by the Medical Department (Board of Education, 1909).

In 1908 physical education became the responsibility of the Medical Department of the Board of Education and part of the curriculum in all public elementary schools. The Board was beginning to move away from the purely disciplinary approach favoured by the early military influence and recognized that physical training could contribute towards the development of a healthy body. 'The object of Physical Education and Training is to help in the production and maintenance of health in body and mind' (Board of Education, 1909, p. 9). However, Williams (1988) recognized that 'the "health" which was the aim of early physical education programmes was rather basic compared with the concept of health for which we aim today' (p. 1). The main health focus was on short-term fitness and keeping the body free from disease.

The 1909 syllabus was in essence therapeutic and emphasized the contribution that physical activity could make to both the physical and mental health of children. General principles of physiology of exercise and hygiene were outlined for teachers and some recreative exercises were included to encourage enjoyable pupil participation. The 1909 syllabus formed the foundation of physical education in the majority of elementary schools up to and throughout the First World War.

The shift of emphasis from the military character of earlier syllabuses was clearly demonstrated by the Board. As Johnson (1981) observed:

> Physical training was to belong to the family of education as an integral part of the overall scheme for improving child health and welfare. (pp. 101–2)

By 1919 the concept of physical education had broadened since it was recognized that healthy physique, keen intelligence, and sound character were benefits of physical education. For the first time also there appeared evidence of the Board being concerned not only with the growth and development of children during their school years but also with fostering habits for the future:

> What the Board desire to secure is the careful and well balanced development of the physical powers of each individual, not only in reference to his immediate bodily and mental growth, but also with a view to encouraging the formation of habits of recreation which will be of value in the future.   (Board of Education, 1919, p. 4)

This is the first evidence of the concept of physical education preparing children for active adult lifestyles, which 70 years later has re-emerged as an objective of physical education programmes.

It is of interest to note that it was around this time that Saltykov (1915) first called attention to the paediatric origins of atherosclerosis when he stated that 'the so-called fatty changes in the arteries of childhood and youth, especially in the aorta are nothing less than the beginning of atherosclerosis'. Certainly the Board of Education was changing the emphasis it placed on the value of physical education programmes for young children, although no mention was made of heart disease in any syllabus.

The advice from the Board of Education in 1919 was sound, but in reality the picture was rather different since lack of funds during the inter-war years limited the provision of adequate facilities in the majority of schools. The development of physical education varied throughout the country mainly because the provision of resources and expertise was patchy. The Chief Medical Officer tried to convince schools of the therapeutic value of physical education and of its contribution to preventive medicine. This was an inexpensive way of addressing the issue of child health as it avoided the real issues of malnutrition and disease which required radical changes in social policy. However, the philosophy of George Newman, Chief Medical Officer, was considered by some historians (McIntosh, 1981; Smith, 1974) to be ahead of its time.

In 1922 the Board of Education instigated economies in education in the form of a bill which became known as the Geddes Axe. However, physical education remained in the curriculum because local authorities were encouraged to support its development for its therapeutic value.

The case for the inclusion of physical education in school was stated by the Board of Education (1926):

> Exercise in fresh air conditions and proper food, are the two primary factors that govern growth and health, and by attention to these two matters we strike at the root of disease. Measures directed to the prevention of particular diseases or to the early treatment of disease, although important can never yield the same result to the State.   (p. 90)

However, not all were convinced, and social reformers who had contributed significantly to the development of physical education understood that children needed sound nutrition and adequate medical care as prerequisites to any physical training (Smith, 1974).

In 1925 the National Playing Fields Association was formally inaugurated and made great efforts to provide adequate facilities for games and recreation for every section of the community. It was recognized that, if people were to enjoy physical activity in their leisure time, then facilities needed to be improved (Board of Education, 1926).

This did not directly affect provision in elementary schools but offered more opportunities to the community to enjoy physical activity.

By 1930 the Chief Medical Officer of the Ministry of Education proclaimed that physical training and health education were intimately related and universally an integral part of school life. The aims of the Board (Board of Education, 1930) were stated:

> for our aim should be to produce men and women able to work out for themselves a way of life, full of wisdom and understanding and not turn out drilled automatons crammed with facts who will some few years hence overcrowd the waiting room of the insurance doctor, fill the tuberculosis sanatorium or swell the hospital waiting list.   (p. 69)

One of the aims of the *Syllabus of Physical Training for Schools* (Board of Education, 1933) was to encourage safe and systematic teaching of all activities likely to promote a healthy way of living. It was devised for children up to the age of 12 but could be adapted for 14-year-olds. It included gymnastics, games, swimming and dancing, sports, free play, walking and school journeys, and those pursuits which might create an appreciation of fresh air and a healthy way of living.

The Board of Education (1933) emphasized the importance of teachers applying the syllabus to suit the needs of their particular classes. Previous syllabuses had demanded mindless repetition of prescribed movement with little regard to the nature of the individual. This syllabus relied more on the initiative of the teacher to motivate the children and to provide an interesting and effective programme. One of the objectives was to encourage good posture in rest and action:

> the child who has learnt to stand up straight and hold his head up has, other things being equal, a better chance of making his way in life than his stooping weak kneed brother.
> (p. 12)

Inspectors judged teachers' effectiveness by the smart appearance of their class and general good posture of the pupils. Emphasis was pplaced on the importance of flexibility and control of tension in the body, and it was stressed that good posture was necessary for all round physical development and would develop good habits for the future.

The 1933 syllabus recommended a daily lesson of twenty minutes activity, to include three periods of formal lessons and others to cover activities such as games and swimming. It is interesting to note that in 1933 it was believed that 'physical training is by now a sufficiently well established part of the curriculum for the daily lesson to be accepted in all schools' (p. 19). Fifty-four years later, the physical education profession was still striving to encourage daily physical education in primary schools (The Physical Education Association of Great Britain and Northern Ireland, 1987). Physical education has been included in the National Curriculum as a foundation subject (Department of Education and Science (DES),1989b) in all state primary schools but with no recommendation as to the amount of time that should be allocated to the subject.

In 1933 open-air teaching was encouraged, not only to provide children with increased oxygen to supply their muscles during increased exertion, but also to lay the foundation of the habit of seeking outdoor pursuits and enjoyment in taking part in physical activities after school. This recommendation may have been made in the light of lack of indoor facilities.

Teachers were advised to encourage children to discard some of their outer garments to enjoy freedom of movement. Few could afford special clothing for these sessions, and yet attention was drawn to the importance of suitable footwear and clothes for physical education. There is, however, no evidence of financial support to families to supply suitable clothing.

In compiling the *Syllabus of Physical Training for Schools*, the Board of Education (1933) had considered the issues of the health and fitness of children both during their school lives and in their future. The emphasis was clearly on physiological training for all children under 14 years (Williams, 1988). However, in order to fulfil the objectives of the syllabus, neither the teachers nor the pupils were expected to understand these concepts. Instead, it was thought to be important that children enjoyed physical activities and consequently formed habits of recreation which would be valuable to them throughout their lives. Williams (1987) recognized the conditions of the time precluded many from enjoying these benefits:

> despite this far reaching policy, the reality for many state school pupils was rather different. Social conditions of the 1930s insured that few had time or opportunity to pursue recreational activity into adult life. (p. 104)

The international crises in the mid-1930s drew the nation's attention to the poor state of fitness of the youth of the country. The government made attempts to improve facilities for physical education and training, and after 1934, authorities made great efforts to instigate changes, but the Second World War arrived before many of those changes could be implemented. A popular view held by Opposition MPs was that the government was still failing to address the real problem of physical neglect and malnutrition of the young. Smith (1974) reported a view at the time that physical activity should be sought by the young for pleasure and that health should not be the main objective but a by-product. This was not the general consensus of opinion. In the late 1930s (Board of Education, 1938) the emphasis remained on physical training for both boys and girls:

> The training promotes the steady physiological development of the whole body, preventing defects of posture, cultivates poise, strength, mobility and agility and aims at building up a sound physique. In addition, physical education wisely conceived and intelligently directed contributes also to the child's mental and social development. (p. 29)

The war inevitably affected the development of education in schools as many teachers had to join the armed forces and general disruption was caused by children being evacuated. Smith (1974) suggested that there was no decline in the health and fitness of children during the war and perhaps the main contributing factors to this were the introduction of school meals, free milk, and communal feeding which improved general nutrition.

THE BEGINNING OF THE PRIMARY/SECONDARY DIVIDE

The 1944 Education Act established the right of children to receive a sound secondary school education and marked the end of elementary schools. Local education authorities (LEAs) were encouraged to improve the provision of facilities for physical training and recreation for older pupils and this probably had a positive effect on provision in primary schools as more funds became available.

In 1945 responsibility for physical education was transferred from the Chief Medical Officer to the Senior Chief Inspector of the Ministry of Education and this heralded a dramatic change of focus for physical education in schools. The emphasis moved away from the inclusion of the subject on remedial and therapeutic grounds, and physical educationalists leaned towards justification of their subject in the curriculum for social, moral, intellectual, and cognitive reasons—a legacy physical educationalists have been struggling to justify ever since.

The influence of the military was again felt in schools after the war, but in a different way from that at the beginning of the century (Johnson, 1981). Primary schools took ideas for new equipment from apparatus used in commando and combat training by the forces. Children were encouraged to develop their strength by hanging, climbing and swinging on ropes, rope nets and logs which appeared in many playgrounds. This was the beginning of equipment being introduced into schools for the prime purpose of promoting such activities, which later became more purpose-built and sophisticated. Teachers began to adopt a more child-centred approach, since children were encouraged to interpret their own solutions in response to a given task. This new approach encompassed the philosophies of Dewey and Piaget whose theories had a major impact on primary schools across the curriculum.

Rudolf von Laban and Lisa Ullman made a significant contribution to the teaching of dance from 1944 and this influence spread more widely in the development of 'movement' education in the late 1940s and early 1950s. Wright (1977) suggested that extravagant claims were made that these principles of movement embraced all aspects of physical education. Men returning from their National Service favoured an approach to teaching physical education which included exercises for their anatomical and physiological effects. In addition, they preferred direct teaching of skills and agilities and rejected the movement approach which they considered had neglected these aspects of physical education (Smith, 1974; Groves, 1977; McIntosh, 1977).

In 1952 the Ministry of Education published the first of a two-part publication *Physical Education in the Primary School* called *Moving and Growing* (Ministry of Education, 1952); it certainly reflected a different approach to that adopted in earlier government publications. It gave advice to primary school teachers on landmarks in children's growth and physical development and explained how these might affect the development of movement. The text was supported by a wealth of photographs showing children of all ages involved in a rich variety of physical activity. Even though two chapters were devoted to physical education as a general term the Ministry considered the physical education curriculum to be games, swimming, dance, dramatic movement, and 'PT'. In the section devoted to 'PT' the Ministry compared gymnastics in the secondary school with 'PT' in the primary school. It was emphasized that a wider range of activities ought to be offered to younger children rather than exercises which merely developed the muscles, which had been the narrow view of gymnastics at that time.

The compensatory or remedial movements in this publication were quite different from those in early publications which had been more concerned with specific aspects of fitness. Reference was now made to the all-round development of the child and the need for teachers to observe and recognize any lack of skill of fitness in their pupils during games, dance, or swimming lessons and to practise techniques and fitness training in the PT lesson. This was referred to as grammatical movement:

> Grammatical movement implies practice in diverse forms of movement which are held to serve as a basis of healthy living, and of the enjoyment of skill in various fields.   (p. 76)

No other reference was made to healthy living and no specific activities were offered to influence particular aspects of fitness. In the following year a similar guidance book was produced by the Ministry of Education to support primary school teachers in their teaching of physical education, this publication was called *Planning the Programme* (Ministry of Education, 1953) and was part two of *Physical Education in the Primary School*. In Appendix 1 of this book teachers were offered a nucleus of material from which to plan their own programme of physical training. The activities were well illustrated and aims were clearly stated so that teachers were left in no doubt about the physical effect certain activities would have on the body. Guidance was given in the chapter 'Framework of the Lesson' for lesson structure, and major consideration was given to mobility, and strengthening and agility exercises. No reference was made to the health of the school child which is remarkable as, only eight years earlier, responsibility for physical education teaching in schools had been under the direction of the Chief Medical Officer and presumably had been the main justification for inclusion of the subject in the curriculum. Teachers began to base their claims for the subject on educational grounds, citing moral, social, and psychological benefits alongside the anatomical and physiological effects.

CHANGING SOCIAL CONDITIONS: PHYSICAL EDUCATION AND HEALTH EDUCATION DRIFT APART

Rowe (1978) attributed the changing social conditions and consequent improved well-being of the nation to the decline in the overall concern for health. He also blamed the lack of unanimity among physiologists and the medical profession at the time in their opinions about the positive contribution physical activity could make towards health.

During the early 1950s the links between physical education and health lingered within the curriculum. It was the emergence of new social problems during the late 1950s and early 1960s that went some way towards changing the focus of health education in schools. Society was becoming aware of the problems associated with drugs, sex, and alcohol misuse and a national response was required.

In 1968 the Health Education Council (HEC) was formed and part of its function was to develop health education in schools. Certainly by this time physical education and health education had drifted apart.

DEVELOPMENTS IN PHYSICAL EDUCATION

The next guidance in physical education for primary school teachers was the government publication *Movement—Physical Education in the Primary Years* (DES, 1972), which paid very little attention to either health or fitness. It was noted that gymnastics was often associated with physical development and fitness but, in the primary school, gymnastics was to be regarded for its creative contribution to a child's development.

> Vigorous effort leading to increased strength and endurance should be a normal part of physical education. Maximal physical effort should be encouraged, and is almost unavoidable in games, athletics and swimming. But it is in the development of versatility and sensitivity, and in the ability to apply skill and control in purposeful creative and imaginative situations that the true values of physical education lie.   (p. 14)

The major focus of the publication was on the application of general educational principles to the teaching of physical education. It was stressed that movement as a mode of expression gave physical education a more central place in the curriculum, offering children opportunities for individual exploration and creative learning. Wright (1977) has suggested that educationalists might well have compromised their responsibility and concern for pupils' physical welfare in attempting to cater for a wider range of pupil needs. Developing the ideas of others (Dearden, 1968; Williams, 1959), he highlighted the false dichotomy that was created in which physical needs were seen as being apart from and in opposition to educational needs. Recognizing that some primary schools managed to provide a balanced programme of physical education, he questioned how many teachers had considered the importance of children understanding the value of physical activity in 'its diverse individual and social contexts as contributory factors to their continuing total health and well-being long after school days have passed?' (p. 81).

DEVELOPMENTS IN HEALTH EDUCATION

As far as health education in schools was concerned during the 1970s, Her Majesty's Inspectors (HMI) and Medical Advisers (DES, 1977) stated:

> health education is neither recognised, nor recognisable, in the school curriculum in the sense that mathematics is recognised and recognisable. But health education is unavoidable, even if its presence is denied.   (p. 29)

The DES proposed methods by which health education could be implemented in primary schools and implied that teachers may unintentionally influence children's attitudes and habits when working across the curriculum:

> so in a fragmented way health education happens to boys and girls in all schools without anyone necessarily being aware of its totality. Nowadays, however, a growing number of schools adopt a more positive approach.   (p. 4)

Assumptions were often made that if teachers were providing children with experience in the arts and physical activity then health education was taking place regardless of the quality of teaching:

> If so ancient an educational aim as the development of a healthy mind in a healthy body is accepted, the contributions of teachers of all expressive and creative arts, and of gymnastics, games and sports are self evident.   (p. 4)

This statement by the DES seemed to imply that primary school teachers naturally linked health education with teaching of physical education. It seemed to suggest that through their experience of gymnastics, games, and sports children would be prepared to make decisions about their lifestyles which would affect their health. This gave the impression that teachers were able to relate these concepts from a position of knowledge. However, it is questionable as to whether primary school teachers were competent or confident in the teaching of health education or physical education. Studies (MacDonald Wallace, 1962; Head *et al.*, 1975) have shown that only a limited number of training colleges offered health education as an essential subject and many students completed their training unable to teach health education with confidence as they felt their knowledge was inadequate (Williams and Roberts, 1985).

The survey by HMI, *Primary Education in England* (DES, 1978), reported on some aspects of work of 7, 9 and 11-year-old children in 542 primary schools in England.

HMI found that the extent and quality of work in physical education varied considerably and the balance of the programme depended on the types of facilities available and the interests and skills of individual teachers. HMI made no effort to discover whether children had any understanding of the value of physical activity or if it linked with other areas of the curriculum. The focus of the survey was clearly on the content of the curriculum and the performance of the children.

This survey had little to say about health education, although it did reveal that only 17 per cent of the 542 primary schools had written guidelines for health education. Health education appeared in the curriculum in the form of assemblies, lessons on hygiene, sex issues, visits, and keep-fit.

DEVELOPMENTS IN PRIMARY SCHOOL TEACHER TRAINING

The 1978 survey highlighted the value of schools utilizing the expertise of members of staff in support of their colleagues in developing particular aspects of the curriculum. These curriculum leaders were expected to keep up to date with developments in their subject and to provide ongoing support to teachers in that area of the curriculum. HMI discovered that posts of responsibility for games, swimming, and gymnastics were often allocated, which, it was suggested, reflected additional organizational duties often associated with these subjects. The survey revealed that the majority of teachers with posts of special responsibility had little influence on the work of their teacher colleagues, and HMI recommended that students in initial training needed to be well prepared to advise and help other teachers who might have different strengths.

About this time the main associations interested in physical education in schools, the Physical Education Association of Great Britain and Northern Ireland (PEA) and the British Association of Lecturers and Advisers in Physical Education (BAALPE), expressed concern about the apparent erosion of time devoted to physical education in the initial training of primary school teachers. An investigation by the PEA (1984) into the nature of initial training in the teaching of physical education for non-specialist primary school teachers revealed an immense variability in time allocation. As a result of the survey, the PEA recommended that a minimum of 60 hours be devoted to physical education for students preparing to teach children of primary school age. BAALPE (1979) issued a statement supporting the notion of curriculum leadership in physical education in the primary school which emphasized the need to help teachers plan and deliver progressive programmes of physical education. The statement reflected developments in physical education at the time as it emphasized that curriculum leaders would need expertise in gymnastics and games, but no mention was made of integrating physical education with other areas of the curriculum. Mawer (1984) identified the potential of the primary school physical education curriculum leaders in coordinating health education programmes and guiding colleagues to resources to enable them to include health and fitness issues in the curriculum. He reported that the PEA recommended that initial training courses for primary school teachers should offer compulsory courses in the teaching of health education. However, at this time there was a certain amount of confusion surrounding the place and role of health education in primary schools.

As Williams (1979) had observed:

> in many ways the problems surrounding health education mirror those experienced in physical education; for it is a subject which has undergone considerable change over a period of time with regard to its aims and objectives, content area, methods of teaching, and means by which success or failure in it are to be evaluated.   (p. 113)

SURVEYS

In 1981 the Health Education Unit of the University of Southampton took a random sample of 12½ per cent of all state schools in England and Wales to determine what was happening with regard to health education in schools and to find out the views of senior members of staff about what might be included in health education during initial teacher training. A total of 1,463 primary schools returned their questionnaires and the survey also included 288 secondary schools (as the focus of this chapter is on primary schools the secondary school results will not be discussed here). In this national survey of schools Williams and Roberts (1985) found that only 30.7 per cent of primary schools had planned programmes of health education throughout the school, whilst 54 per cent left the planning to the individual class teacher. Only 18 per cent of the primary schools in the survey had a teacher on the staff with responsibility for health education. The picture that emerged was that health education in these primary schools was rarely based on developmental programmes, although 87 per cent of primary schools taught and valued health education. The help of outside agencies was enlisted by 98 per cent of schools in their teaching of health education and 47 per cent of the sample used television programmes in the context of their health education syllabus. Of the teachers who responded, 98 per cent agreed that health education should be included as a core subject in initial teacher training education.

The survey did throw some light on the practice of health education in primary schools. It certainly identified the number of schools teaching health education, those with planned programmes and those with a member of staff with responsibility for health education. It provided an insight into the number of schools who used outside agencies and television programmes in their teaching of health education, but it did not provide any information about the actual content of health education in primary schools.

By the 1980s, later surveys undertaken by HMI found that most schools were aware of the need for education about health in its broadest sense and that there was a wide interpretation of health education and a variety of opportunities for the teaching of the subject. There was ample evidence of schools incorporating health education into the curriculum at classroom level but little evidence of coordinated programmes of health education. Certainly HMI found that the quality of work in health education reflected the interest and leadership of headteachers who were usually the initiators of written policies for health education (DES, 1983a, 1983b).

During the 1980s the Health Education Council (HEC) funded a different but significant development which was designed for use in schools with children in the upper primary age range. This was the My Body Project (HEC, 1983), an initiative adapted from America, wherein the focus was on the human body—in particular on the respiratory system. The origin of the project was concerned with the prevention of smoking. The central theme was concerned with enabling children to make decisions which might benefit their physical, mental, and social well-being (McLeavy, 1986). The project was based on active, participatory learning and aimed at encouraging children to choose healthy ways of living. Williams (1986) reported that in the mid–1980s the My Body Project provided the major resource for junior and middle school teachers in England and Wales, and that it had a positive influence on the development of health policies in schools.

In response to the reports by HMI in 1983 and the National Survey of primary schools, the team from Southampton set out in 1984 to develop a flexible curriculum guide to encourage primary schools to produce coherent and broad-based programmes of health education. The HEC supported this project and the initial research phase involved 138 primary schools in eleven LEAs (Williams *et al.*, 1987).

The views of pupils, parents, teachers, and all others professionally involved in the care of school children were sought. Central to the project was the notion of the school as a health-promoting institution. The perceptions of healthy living were investigated in young children aged from 4 to 8 by using a draw and write technique. Children were asked to respond by pictures and writing to the question 'What do you do that makes you healthy and keeps you healthy? A total of 9,584 children took part in the study.

It is of interest to note that from the age of 5, boys put exercise as the major theme. Girls, up to the age of 7, considered food the major theme but at age 7 onwards this was overtaken by exercise. The exercise category was divided into subcategories according to the response of the children. Jogging was the subcategory of exercise most frequently depicted by both boys and girls from the age of 6 to 8 years. After jogging, the activities mentioned by girls as contributing to a healthy life were swimming, walking, cycling, games, weight-lifting, gymnastics, dance, and press-ups in that order. Specific activities most mentioned by boys reflected a different emphasis, with weight-lifting featuring as second choice (after jogging) followed by games, cycling, swimming, press-ups, walking, gymnastics, and dance.

The research team put forward some possible explanations for the persistence and growth of the theme of exercise from 4-to 8-year-old children:

- children see people exercising on their way to and from school
- fun runs, charity walks, sponsored physical exercise abound in children's own expeerience and in television programmes
- well-known people are often involved
- sports programmes feature strongly on television and in day-to-day conversation

- much of today's news—television, radio, newspaper—is concerned with the lifestyle of sports personalities and their supporters
- the children,as they move towards age 8, begin to be involved in more physical activity in and out of school. Games, especially team games, begin to be important, as is family support and encouragement to 'make the team'
- there is an increase in family orientated exercise and leisure centres
- much fashionable clothing, often worn to school, has its roots in sportswear and is spoken of in sports terms, 'trainers', 'jogging suit', 'leotard'.   (pp. 86–7)

Most of these views were purely speculative as there is no evidence in this country of children being more active at age 8 than at any other age or any studies which have sought to discover how the media and the press influence children's attitudes towards exercise. However, the high profile given to physical activity by children during these early years prompted the research team to suggest that there is a need for others to capitalize on this early and lasting link between physical activity and young children's perception of being healthy.

Williams and his colleagues (1987) highlighted the need for:

- a physical education programme in which children are enabled to be aware of exercise and its impact on their bodies and on their feelings of health
- an extension of the theme of exercise to take in rest, safety, responsibility, awareness of others
- relating physical well-being to other aspects of becoming and being healthy.

(p. 87)

This survey had concentrated on children aged 4 to 8 years, but the team from Southampton were also interested in the views of children in the 7- to 10-year-old age range. In this instance the work of the Health Education Unit at the University of Exeter was acknowledged as being of value for use in their field studies. The *Just a Tick* questionnaire (Balding, 1986) was already in an advanced state of development and was used to identify priorities for inclusion in the primary curriculum in the areas of personal development, health, and social education. Children aged from 7 to 10 and adults were presented with the same list of 43 health or personal development topics. Children were asked to indicate their level of interest in each one, and the adults were asked to indicate their perceived importance of the topics for inclusion in the primary school curriculum. A total of 10,984 children from the eleven regions which had been involved in the 1981 National Survey were invited to express their levels of interest by putting a tick in one of four columns for each of the topics. They were asked to indicate whether they were:

> very interested: I would like to find out more about this subject
> quite interested: If somebody talked about this I would be quite interested to hear what
>   they had to say
> not sure: I don't know if I am interested or not. I am not sure
> no: I definitely do not want to know more about this topic.   (p. 2)

For the topic of physical fitness teachers helped the children to complete the questionnaire by offering the words, 'The kind of activity you do and the exercise you take to make you stronger and healthier'.

The results of the inquiry have not yet been published in full. The results shown in

Tables 11.1 and 11.2 indicate that both boys and girls in each age group cared strongly about physical fitness as a topic. The boys appeared to be more interested than the girls (Balding *et al.*, 1989). These results may reflect that boys have a genuinely greater interest in physical fitness as a topic than do girls. However, the advice from the teacher could have influenced the response with the use of words like 'exercise' and 'make you stronger'. It had been seen from the survey of infant children that boys favoured activities with a focus on strength.

Table 11.1 *Results of* Just a Tick *Questionnaire—Fitness topic*.

Physical Fitness: 'The kind of activity you do and the exercise you take to make you stronger and healthier'

	Very interested				Quite interested				Not sure				No!			
	7+	8+	9+	10+	7+	8+	9+	10+	7+	8+	9+	10+	7+	8+	9+	10+
Physical Fitness Boys (%)	67	66	68	66	15	16	18	20	11	10	9	10	7	7	5	4
Girls (%)	62	58	58	57	18	21	26	29	14	15	11	11	6	6	4	3

Source: Balding, Code, and Redman, 1989, p. 14.

Table 11.2 *The five most interesting* Just a Tick *topics to pupils in the junior/middle age range**

Boys 7+	8+	9+	10+
Food and health	Care of eyes	Care of eyes	Care of eyes
Physical fitness	Food and health	Food and health	Food and health
Safety at home	Physical fitness	Physical fitness	Physical fitness
Safety in traffic	Safety at home	Safety at home	Safety at home
Water safety	Safety in traffic	Safety in traffic	Safety in traffic

Girls 7+	8+	9+	10+
Care of hair, teeth, skin	Care of hair, teeth, skin	Care of hair, teeth, skin	Care of hair, teeth, skin
Physical fitness	Physical fitness	How a baby is made	How a baby is made
Understanding the needs of old people	Understanding the needs of old people	Physical fitness	Physical fitness
Safety at home	Safety at home	Safety at home	Safety at home
Water safety	Safety in traffic	Water safety	Water safety

Source: Balding, Code, and Redman, 1989, p. 22.
* Rankings are based on the percentage of pupils responding in the 'very interested' column of Table 11.1. The topics are in questionnaire order.

The HEA survey (Williams *et al.*, 1987) revealed that children of this age are keen to learn more about fitness and this perhaps reinforces the need to capitalize on the interest of children of primary school age in developing programmes of physical education with a focus on health.

With regard to general health education in primary schools during the 1980s HMI (DES, 1986) reported similar findings to that of the 1981 National Survey, which suggested that health education in primary schools remained fragmented and patchy. Schools adopted a variety of approaches if they addressed health education at all. This was in spite of the fact that many authorities had been recommending that health education should be planned and structured (DES, 1986, 1983a, 1983b; Johnson, 1981).

It was against the background of lack of training and direction that resources were developed to help teachers adopt a positive, structured approach to health education. Williams (1986) emphasized the value of resources and materials and stressed the importance of a sensitive balance of teaching styles and methods in teaching health education. He also added that the ideal approach was to encourage children to make decisions to enhance their lives through physical, mental, and social well-being. It is widely recognized (DES, 1977, 1986; McLeavy, 1986) that education for health begins in the home where habits and attitudes become firmly established. In schools, strategies are required to promote health education which sensitively acknowledge the influence of home life and seek to develop children's awareness of healthy lifestyles. Acknowledging that health education is organized and practised in a variety of ways in primary schools, the DES (1986) indicated that by the end of the primary phase of education children should have achieved a 'simple knowledge and understanding' of:

- the human body
- the conditions which promote healthy growth and development, i.e. fresh air; exercise; personal care; sleep; rest; a healthy diet
- health hazards
- safety
- knowledge of the function of health and safety services in the community
- circumstances which affect environment and social conditions and the interdependence of man and other living things. (p. 7)

PHYSICAL EDUCATION AND HEALTH EDUCATION LINKS IN THE PRIMARY SCHOOL

The obvious links of health education with physical education in the DES (1986) health document were reserved for the secondary phase:

> In physical education important health matters arise in a variety of ways, not least through its focus on body management and control. Some aspects of hygiene are suitably stressed, including changing into appropriate clothing and footwear for lessons. Showering should be the general expectation for all pupils after physical activity. Many PE teachers stress the importance of looking after one's own body and the need for suppleness, stamina and strength, and in recent years there has been a growth in work explicitly concerned with keeping fit. This work can with benefit include discussion about fitness; discovering how muscles work; the possible relationship between exercise, health and fitness; and encouragement to pupils to continue some form of physical activity when they leave school. (p. 13)

There seems to be nothing in this statement that could not have been applied to the primary phase of education. Many schools use the body as a focus for topic work in the early years and primary school teachers are spared some of the difficulties experienced by secondary school colleagues associated with interdepartmental communication, rigid timetabling and examinations.

In guidance issued by HMI, *Physical Education from 5–16* (DES, 1989a) also highlighted the links between physical education and health issues but again the focus was for secondary specialist teachers of physical education:

> The importance of diet and care of the body are concerns of health education, home economics and physical education. Practical work in physical education can extend and apply the information and knowledge about health acquired in other lessons.   (p. 15)

If one of the aims of physical education is to enable children to develop an understanding of the importance of exercise in maintaining a healthy life then it would seem sensible for this process to begin in the first six years of schooling during the primary phase of education.

Young children are curious to find out about themselves and this enthusiasm for discovery can provide a sound foundation from which teachers can help children to begin to understand the relationship between physical activity, good health, and fitness. Primary school teachers are constantly interrelating other areas of the curriculum and yet physical education is often perceived as an isolated subject with opportunities often being missed to facilitate other curriculum issues through physical education.

A topic which is popular in primary schools is 'Ourselves' or 'My Body': more opportunities need to be created to reinforce some health issues addressed in the classroom through the physical education curriculum. It is not enough for children to be taught about the value of physical activity as a contribution to their health and fitness. They already have a notion that the reason for engaging in physical education is to affect their general physical and mental well-being. The physical education programme should offer variety and challenge and should allow children plenty of time to develop skill, quality, and a sense of personal satisfaction and achievement. It should lay the foundations for children to seek pleasure from involvement in physical activity through childhood and into adulthood. During the primary phase of education children should be taught to understand very simply the effects of exercise on their bodies. They should be encouraged to exercise and play safely. They need to know what to wear, how to warm-up, what are considered to be undesirable exercises and how to cool down after vigorous activity. They should be taught to lift and carry safely to lessen their chances of back injury in later life. Children who have learnt to recognize unnecessary tension in their body and how to release it are likely to cope well if faced with stressful situations. Children should be taught simple techniques of relaxation, so that they are able to develop personal strategies to calm down. It is also important that children begin to understand that body composition is dependent upon the balance between heredity, nutrition, and activity. These issues can be addressed through practical activities in the physical education programme (Bray, 1991). The primary school environment is ideal because teachers have responsiblity for all aspects of the curriculum and can encourage children to make natural links between the theory and practice of health-related activity. I would suggest that if these issues are left to the secondary phase of education, then it is too late.

Lifestyles in the United Kingdom have changed—since the beginning of the twentieth century, advances in medical research have mainly eliminated the infectious diseases which beset the nation at that time. The development of technology has led society to adopt more sedentary lifestyles than those experienced by men, women, and children in the early years of the century. This has resulted in the nation being vulnerable to hypokinetic diseases which are caused by or are related to lack of regular physical activity. Educationalists have responded to prevailing social conditions, although curriculum change has taken time to become established.

During the first 50 years of this century the primary school physical education curriculum reflected a focus on discipline and short-term fitness. Health education was closely linked with physical education and was developed in response to poor living conditions and diseases which existed during those years.

From the 1950s onwards physical education and health education drifted apart. Primary school teachers were encouraged to adopt different teaching styles and to apply general educational principles to the teaching of physical education. More emphasis was placed on the acquisition of movement skills than underlying the principles of fitness and health. Health education re-emerged in response to the 'permissive' society of the 1960s and 1970s. During the 1970s, other countries became aware of the health problems associated with modern-day living.

However, it was not until the mid-1980s that health-related fitness programmes were designed to help young people to understand the principles underlying health and fitness and to encourage them to develop and monitor their own individual fitness regimes throughout their lives. They were developed in response to the evidence which suggested that many hypokinetic diseases were preventable with regular physical activity, a balanced diet, and moderation in lifestyles. All the emphasis in this curriculum development was in the secondary phase of education; little was provided for the primary phase, which is a pity because these are the years when lifetime habits are likely to be formed.

A review of the North American, Australian, and European literature revealed a concern for the health and fitness of the citizens of these nations which, at the time, was not evident in the United Kingdom (Bray, 1991). These nations recognized the value of instigating positive habits and attitudes towards physical activity from the early years of schooling. In efforts to promote the health of their citizens several projects have been initiated which involved children of primary school age. The most prominent of these have been reviewed elsewhere (Sleap, 1990; Bray, 1991) and reflected a concern about laying the foundations and sowing the seeds of healthy lifestyles from an early age. Sleap (1990) noticed that two particular approaches were discernible in primary education which were aimed at increasing physical activity levels of primary schoolchildren:

1   integrated heart health programmes which aimed to influence lifestyles by providing education about diet, smoking, and physical activity; and
2   physical activity programmes in addition to the normal curricula.

Both these approaches were attempts at modifying heart disease risk factors from an early age.

The emergence of coronary heart disease (CHD) has been a special cause for concern, the evidence suggesting that the roots of the disease are established during childhood and that it is preventable. Although there is no clear understanding of the mechanisms involved, an active and fit way of life appears to be one way of preventing or delaying CHD. 'Appropriate physical activity' has been identified as a contributing factor in the prevention of CHD. That is, physical activity maintained at 70 per cent of maximal heart rate (i.e. above 139 beats/min), three times a week for a period of twenty minutes (see Chapter 9).

Very little is known about the habitual physical activity of children of primary school age. Our own investigations (Armstrong and Bray, 1991) have indicated that children rarely engage in physical activity of that intensity for that amount of time or duration. However, our study of 10-year-olds, in which 132 children took part, identified five-minute periods with heart rates above 139 beats/min as a regular feature of their physical activity. More research is necessary to establish the effect this prescription of physical activity might have on the developing cardiopulmonary systems of young children. The study did highlight, however, the low level of physical activity children of primary school age experienced.

Physical education in the primary phase of education needs to provide children with a rich and varied programme through which they have opportunities to acquire a foundation of motor skills, gain confidence in themselves, and begin to understand simple concepts about exercise and its contribution to good health and fitness. It is also vital that children are offered an enjoyable and exciting programme of physical education in which they can achieve success and form positive attitudes about physical activity. There is some evidence that activity patterns track from childhood into adulthood (reviewed in Chapter 9) which accentuates the importance of the experiences in physical education during those early years of a child's life being both stimulating and pleasurable.

This will require teachers to be well prepared to plan balanced progressive and enjoyable programmes of physical education. Teachers need sound initial training in physical education. It is important that as individuals they are encouraged to value the subject and recognize the unique contribution of physical education to the growth and development of the young child. Physical education has increasingly been afforded a low profile in terms of time allocation in initial teacher education (PEA, 1987). Physical education courses must be underpinned by a sound theoretical component to enable potential primary school teachers to understand the needs of children, to plan physical education lessons which are challenging and meaningful and which stimulate children to seek pleasure from physical activity in their leisure time.

Many primary school teachers admit that they feel inadequately prepared to teach physical education and declare fears about safety and anxieties about the content of the curriculum (Williams, 1980). In the past curriculum resources have been scarce but they are now being developed. The main initiative relating physical activity and health in this country is the Happy Heart Project (Mawer and Sleap, 1987). The main concern of the project is the promotion of active lifestyles of children of primary school age. It is based on the concept of creating an active school, with all concerned encouraging children to enjoy physical activity and enabling them to begin to understand the relationship between physical activity and health. Resources are available in the form of classroom workpacks for work related to physical activity (HEA, 1989a, 1989b) and guidelines have been developed to help teachers bring a health focus into the physical education programme. The information is designed for both infant and junior classes. A playground games pack has also been produced which has been received enthusiastically by primary school teachers and supervisory staff. This initiative has been supported by the National Children's Play and Recreation Unit. The pack provides clear and concise details of a variety of active, easily organized games which could be played by children of all ages in the primary school. It offers supervisory staff a wealth of material from which to select simple ideas which might encourage active participation during break-time.

Other aspects of the project are designed to offer teachers guidelines to promote physical activity in an exciting way in the form of 'Happy Heart Days' and schools are also encouraged to form links with other agencies to promote active lifestyles within the school and community.

Sleap (1990) also suggested that one way of implementing the curriculum might be to focus on health-related activity for a half-term block of work in the physical education programme. The resources which have been developed for this project have been well received by teachers. Although the project has yet to be fully evaluated this is clearly one way forward in teaching children about the value of exercise in promoting good health.

THE NATIONAL CURRICULUM

The National Curriculum Council (NCC) (1990a) has identified health education as a cross-curricular theme essential to the whole curriculum for children aged 5–16. The guidance for health education (NCC, 1990b) sets out a framework for a health education curriculum. Nine components form the framework and include health-related exercise, safety, food and nutrition, environmental and psychological aspects of health education, all of which could be addressed through the physical education programme of children beginning at key stages 1 and 2.

Although the National Curriculum working party for physical education has not yet reported, primary school teachers have been obliged to teach the National Curriculum core subjects of English, Mathematics and Science since 1989. Primary schools were encouraged to explore the possibilities for cross-curricular themes in the planning and delivery of topic work. *Science in the National Curriculum* (DES and the Welsh Office, 1989) provided scope for primary school teachers to teach children about the value of physical activity. In attainment target three, 'Processes of Life,' pupils are expected to gain a knowledge and understanding of the organization of living things and of the processes which characterize their survival. Level two requires pupils to:

> know that personal hygiene, food, exercise rest and safety are important.
> Be able to give a simple account of their own day.   (p. 8)

What better way than through the physical education curriculum? If teachers are knowledgeable about health-related physical activity and have resources to enable them to achieve these attainment targets within the physical education pro-gramme then the cross-curricular links might be established and rich and meaningful programmes developed.

The British Association of Sport Sciences, the HEA, and the PEA have recognized the potential contribution of health-related physical activity to the National Curricu-lum and in a joint statement (Armstrong *et al.*, 1990) recommended that 'health-related physical activity should be an attainment target within physical education in the national curriculum' (p. 225).

These Associations acknowledged that a comprehensive body of knowledge concerned with the adoption and maintenance of health-related physical activity is now available and should be passed on to children.

The advent of the National Curriculum has offered an opportunity to reappraise the contribution of physical education and health education to the lives of young children. It has also secured the place of physical education in the curriculum at key stages 1 and 2. The Department of Education and Science must recognize that primary school teachers need adequate preparation in physical education during initial training if they are to cope with delivering effective programmes of physical education in schools. It is unfortunate that the government rejected the recommendation of the Schools Sports Forum (1988) that the initial training of primary school teachers should include a basic course in physical education of at least 100 hours (DES and Department of the Environment, 1989). It is essential that teachers in initial training and those already in post have adequate support in planning rich programmes of physical education. Curriculum development is an important focus of attention in the early 1990s and teachers are challenged to consider the essential concepts, knowledge, and skills their pupils will need to survive in this ever-changing world.

There is no doubt that there is a need for a change of focus in the primary school physical education curriculum and primary school teachers need to be well prepared for such a challenge. Colleges and universities concerned with the initial training of teachers need to provide students with a sound knowledge base from which they will be able to plan broad, balanced, and coherent programmes of physical education which will prepare children for life in the twenty-first century.

REFERENCES

Armstrong, N., Bellew, W., Biddle, S., Bray, S., Gardonyi, P., and Winter, E. (1990) Health-related physical activity in the National Curriculum. *British Journal of Physical Education* **21**, 225.

Armstrong, N. and Bray, S. (1991) Physical activity patterns defined by continuous heart rate monitoring. *Archives of Disease in Childhood* **66**, 245–7.

Balding, J. (1986) *Just a Tick—A Personal Development and Health Education Enquiry.* Exeter: Health Education Authority, Health Education Unit, University of Exeter.

Balding, J., Code, T., and Redman, K. (1989) *Health Education Priorities for the Primary School Curriculum.* London: Health Education Authority, Schools Health Education Unit.

Board of Education (1904) *The Syllabus of Physical Exercises for Schools.* London: HMSO.

Board of Education (1909) *The Syllabus of Physical Exercises for Schools.* London: HMSO.

Board of Education (1919) *Syllabus of Physical Training for Schools.* London: HMSO.

Board of Education (1926) *The Health of the School Child.* Annual Report of the Chief Medical Officer. London: HMSO.

Board of Education (1930) *The Health of the School Child.* Annual Report of the Chief Medical Officer of the Board of Education. London: HMSO.

Board of Education (1933) *Syllabus of Physical Training for Schools.* London: HMSO.

Board of Education (1938) *The Health of the School Child.* Annual Report of the Chief Medical Officer. London: HMSO.

Bray, S. (1991) Health-related physical activity and primary schoolchildren. Unpublished M.Ed. thesis, University of Hull.

British Association of Advisers and Lecturers in Physical Education (1979) (BAALPE) *Physical Education in the Primary School. Curriculum Leadership.* British Association of Advisers and Lecturers in Physical Education Publication.

Dearden, R. F. (1968) *The Philosophy of Primary Education.* London: Routledge & Kegan Paul.

DES (1972) *Movement—Physical Education in the Primary Years.* London: HMSO.

DES (1977) *Health Education in Schools.* London: HMSO.

DES (1978) *Primary Education in England, A Survey by H.M. Inspectors of Schools.* London: HMSO.

DES (1983a) Report by HM Inspectors on *A Survey of Health Education in Fifteen Primary Schools in Avon.* Middlesex: DES.

DES (1983b) Report by HM Inspectors on *A Survey of Health Education in Some Primary Schools in Nottingham, Nottinghamshire.* Middlesex: DES.

DES (1986) *Health Education from 5 to 16. Curriculum Matters 6.* London: HMSO.

DES (1989a) *Physical Education from 5–16.* London: HMSO.

DES (1989b) *National Curriculum—From Policy to Practice.* London: DES.

DES and Department of the Environment (1989) The government's response to the School Sports Forum Report.

DES and the Welsh Office (1989) *Science in the National Curriculum.* London: HMSO.

Groves, L. (1977) Twenty-five years of PE. *British Journal of Physical Education* **8**, 69.

Head, M. J., Tones, B. K., and Uffindall, D. K. (1975) Health education and teacher training. A survey of health education in colleges of education. *Journal of the Institute of Health Education* **13**, 41–5.

Health Education Authority (HEA) (1990a) *Happy Heart: 1—Resources for 4–7 Year Olds.* Walton-on-Thames: Nelson.

Health Education Authority (HEA) (1990b) *Happy Heart: 2—Resources for 7–11 Year Olds.* Walton-on-Thames: Nelson.

Health Education Council (HEC) (1983) *My Body Project.* London: Heinemann Education.

Johnson, J. C. (1981) Physical training in the army and its influence on British schools. In D. McNair and N. Parry (eds), *Readings in the History of Physical Education,* pp. 95–102. Hamburg: Czwalina.

MacDonald Wallace, J. (1962) Health education in the training of teachers. *Health Education Journal* **20**, 9–15.

McIntosh, P. C. (1977) Jubilee for PE—a historical perspective. *British Journal of Physical Education* **8**, 68.

McIntosh, P. C. (1981) Games for two nations in one. In P. C. McIntosh, J. G. Dixon, A. D. Munrow, and R. F. Willetts, *Landmarks in the History of Physical Education,* pp. 185–215. London: Routledge & Kegan Paul.

McLeavy, D. (1986) Helping children to make their own decisions—the 'My Body' Project. *Health Education Journal* **45**, 30–1.

Mawer, M. (1984) Education for an active healthy lifestyle: physical education and health education in the primary school. In M. Mawer and M. Sleap (eds), *Physical Education within Primary Education,* pp. 38–41. London: The Physical Education Association of Great Britain and Northern Ireland.

Mawer, M. A. and Sleap, M. (1987) Educating primary schoolchildren about the relationship between physical activity and health: the Happy Heart Project. *Perspectives* 31, pp. 88–100. Exeter: University of Exeter.

Ministry of Education (1952) *Moving and Growing.* London: HMSO.

Ministry of Education (1953) *Planning the Programme.* London: HMSO.

National Curriculum Council (1990a) *Curriculum Guidance Three. The Whole Curriculum.* York: National Curriculum Council.

National Curriculum Council (1990b) *Curriculum Guidance Five. Health Education.* York: National Curriculum Council.

Physical Education Association of Great Britain and Northern Ireland (PEA) (1984) *Professional Courses in Physical Education for Non-specialist Primary and Middle School Teachers 1977–1983.* Report of the 1982/83 survey of initial training institutions by the study group on Primary PE. London: Physical Education Association of Great Britain and Northern Ireland.

Physical Education Association of Great Britain and Northern Ireland (PEA) (1987) Report of a commission of enquiry. *Physical Education in Schools*. London: Physical Education Association of Great Britain and Northern Ireland.

Rowe, M. (1978) What ever happened to physical education? *British Journal of Physical Education* **9**, 7.

Saltykov, S. (1915) Jugendliche und beginnende Atherosclerose. *Korrespondenzblatt für Schweizer Aerzte* (Basel) xlv, 1057. Cited by R. D. Voller and W. B. Strong, Pediatric aspects of atherosclerosis, *American Heart Journal* **101** (1981), 815.

School Sports Forum (1988) *Sport and Young People*. London: Sports Council.

Sleap, M. (1990) Promoting health in primary school physical education. In N. Armstrong (ed.), *New Directions in Physical Education* 1, pp. 17–36. Champaign, IL: Human Kinetics.

Smith, D. W. (1974) *Stretching Their Bodies—A History of Physical Education*, pp. 106–62. London: David & Charles.

Williams, A. (1980) Intention versus transaction—the junior school physical education curriculum. *Physical Education Review* **3**, 96–104.

Williams, A. (1987) Health and fitness in the physical education curriculum: regression or progress? *Health Education Journal* **46**, 103–7.

Williams, A. (1988) The historiography of health and fitness in physical education. *British Journal of Physical Education Research Supplement* **3**, 1–4.

Williams, G. (1979) Physical education and health education, necessary or contingent connection? *Physical Education Review* **1**, 111–17.

Williams, J. F. (1959) *The Principles of Physical Education*. Philadelphia: Saunders.

Williams, T. (1986) School health education 15 years on. *Health Education Journal* **45**, 3–7.

Williams, T. and Roberts, J. (1985) *Health Education in Schools and Teacher Education Institutions. A Compilation of the Survey Reports of the Health Education Council Project: Health Education in Initial Teacher Education*. University of Southampton. Teacher Education Publication.

Williams, T., Wetton, N., and Moon, A. (1987) *A Picture of Health—What Do You Do That Makes You Healthy and Keeps You Healthy?* Southampton: Health Education Authority, Health Education Unit.

Wright, J. (1977) Total health—a jubilee perspective. *British Journal of Physical Education* **8**, 80–1.

Chapter 12

Chronic Illness: The Implications for Physical Education

Bryan Woods

Modern medical care in Great Britain has greatly reduced the incidence of childhood sickness. Immunization and vaccination have practically excluded acute conditions such as tuberculosis, poliomyelitis, and diphtheria which in the past would annually be epidemic and responsible for a significant number of childhood deaths. Similarly, measles, chickenpox, mumps, and influenza are gradually becoming less common because of prophylaxis, and the majority of children can now expect to pass through their early childhood unaffected by serious illness. Inevitably they will suffer from colds and other upper respiratory tract infections from time to time and perhaps the occasional gastric upset but these are relatively trivial and rarely require the child to be kept away from school for more than a day or so. However, although the incidence of acute disorders appears to be decreasing, some chronic conditions are still very evident and may even be increasing in their frequency. By definition a chronic disease is one of long duration in which progress is slow. Sometimes the disease is punctuated by acute episodes of variable length and although symptoms can be alleviated there is no overall cure. In some instances a chronic disease may eventually resolve, and in others it may gradually become worse.

The three chronic disorders that are most commonly seen in schools are asthma, diabetes, and epilepsy. Their occurrence is such that all teachers will inevitably have contact with children with these complaints. In all three instances 'attacks' or acute episodes can occur and it is therefore important that teachers have at least sufficient knowledge to enable them to determine what is happening and what they can do in the emergency situation.

ASTHMA

Asthma is the commonest chronic disease in industrialized society (Stuttaford, 1990). In this country one in ten children are affected to some degree by asthma (Heal *et al.*, 1987) and similar statistics apply to America and Australia. In many countries there appears to be a steady increase in asthmatic incidence, for which it is difficult to account. Increasing levels of atmospheric pollution may be a contributory cause which, of course, relates to the fact that asthma tends to be an urban rather than a rural complaint. It may be that more cases are actually being diagnosed. Epidemiological studies related to asthmatic incidence (Milner, 1986) agree that in the past asthma has frequently been under-diagnosed. Milner indicates that some parents show reluctance to take a wheezy child to the doctor unless there has been an occasion of severe breathlessness. Doctors are also aware that a diagnosis of asthma imposes an acute anxiety on some parents who probably have had experience of a relative or friend who has been severely affected. This may cause them to use an alternative 'label' such as a 'wheezy cold' or 'bronchitis'. It also makes the point that it is essential that time should be spent in educating parents and convincing them that asthmatic symptoms respond very well to appropriate medication and that their child should not be treated like a semi-invalid. Inevitably, genuine mis-diagnosis may occur when mild asthma is confused with a chest infection.

The range in the severity with which asthma can occur may also give rise to confusion. A surprising number of people will display mild asthmatic symptoms if exposed to an appropriate stimulus. For example, some people become wheezy during or immediately after aerobic exercise. This passes off very quickly and the person never really experiences any real inconvenience and seldom realizes that they suffer from a minimal exercise-induced asthma. At the other end of the scale, acutely affected people with advanced asthma can have attacks lasting for a number of days in which the symptoms are so severe that talking, eating, and even sleeping are not possible and the situation can be life-threatening.

To understand what asthma is we should perhaps briefly review the structure and function of part of the respiratory system. Asthma is a condition which affects the respiratory tract below the level of the larynx. This consists of the trachea which splits into the right and left bronchus, each of which subdivide into secondary bronchi. The secondary bronchi in turn divide and so the process of subdivision continues until the smallest air passages, the bronchioles, eventually make their connection with the alveoli which collectively form the respiratory surface. The wall of the larger air passages is composed of connective tissue, elastic tissue and involuntary muscle, some of which is laid down in a circular pattern. Incomplete rings of cartilage occur regularly and serve to keep the airway open. At bronchiole level there are no cartilaginous supporting rings, there is little or no elastic tissue, and the wall consists essentially of circular involuntary muscle fibres. The whole of the airway is lined with mucous membrane. Goblet cells within this membrane exude mucus onto the surface of the respiratory tract. This layer of mucus is normally kept moving upwards by cilial action up to the level of the oesophagus where it can be swallowed. The involuntary musculature throughout the tract is extensively supplied by the sympathetic and parasympathetic elements of the autonomic nervous system. Stimulation of the sympathetic supply will bring about relaxation of the circular muscle which has the effect of opening up the airways. Parasympathetic stimulation produces the converse effect, causing a contraction of the muscle and therefore a reduction in the bore of the air passages. The functional effect of this bronchoconstruction or bronchospasm will be most marked where the bronchioles have a large amount of muscle in their makeup and where the size of the air pathway is relatively small. Normally the patency of the airways is maintained by a controlled interplay between the sympathetic and parasympathetic systems which is dictated by respiratory demand. In an asthmatic attack there is a disruption in this control mechanism and parasympathetic activity predominates, which brings about bronchospasm which drastically impedes the normal process of respiration. Although we are aware of a range of factors that will trigger off an asthmatic attack we are not entirely sure why they should do so. Accompanying bronchospasm there can be an inflammation of the mucous membrane. This inflammatory reaction causes the mucosa to swell and also stimulates the production of mucus. Both effects will compound the problem of bronchospasm. The swelling will further reduce the bore of the bronchioles and the increase in mucus will cause plugging, preventing air from reaching the respiratory surface.

Normally, on inspiration the diaphragm and intercostal muscles contract, which brings about an increase in thoracic volume and an associated decrease in intrapleural pressure. This negative pressure causes air to be drawn in. It will also cause a slight expansion of the smaller bronchioles and alveoli. On exhalation there is a relaxation of the respiratory musculature and the intrapleural pressure will increase as the elasticity of the thorax and lung tissue returns the thoracic cavity to its preinspiratory volume. The increase in intrapleural pressure also has the effect of slightly compressing the bronchioles and alveoli. During an asthmatic attack it will be seen that difficulty is experienced in breathing in but actually there is considerably more difficulty in breathing out which is due to the fact that exhalation is essentially a passive action involving no musculature and depends upon the natural recoil of stretched structures and tissue. If the person cannot breathe out they obviously cannot breathe in and the sufferer literally fights in the effort to increase inspiration.

How then does the asthmatic attack develop? Premonitory signs are not uncommon. The patient will often experience a sense of restlessness and a growing feeling of constriction described as 'tightness' in the chest. Sometimes an itching of the skin develops on the back or chest. As the attack progresses the feeling of tightness increases, producing the onset of wheezing on breathing out. As inflammation develops, breathing becomes laboured and wheezing is evident on breathing in and breathing out and there may be a certain amount of coughing. The person will show signs of lack of oxygen. The face is pale and sweaty and the lips blue (cyanosed). The heart will attempt to compensate by beating faster and pulse rates can increase dramatically. The person will look anxious and may well be fearful of dying if the attack is severe. Considerable tension is evident in the muscles around the neck. The sternocleidomastoids and the scaleni are being used as accessory muscles in an attempt to improve inspiration. The person will prefer to sit up or even stand and will sometimes try to support his arms on something high up. In this position the pectoral muscles can be brought into play as emergency inspiratory muscles. Sometimes the attack will terminate with a bout of coughing in which a considerable amount of watery sputum is coughed up.

If attacks are frequent and long-lasting, changes occur within the lungs and in the person's posture. The mucosa thickens and the walls of the smaller bronchioles hypertrophy, which will increase the effect of bronchospasm. The alveoli may eventually become overdistended and their walls atrophy, producing a condition known as emphysema. Mucus plugging may cause some alveoli to collapse. The elasticity of the lung tissue becomes reduced, which hampers exhalation, and the capillary supply to the respiratory surface becomes impaired. All these changes will result in a reduced oxygen uptake which will require the right side of the heart to work much harder in compensation. The chest becomes barrel-shaped and the shoulders hunched; the neck muscles are tight, which gives an impression of the neck being short. The chest appears to be in a constant state of inspiration. A degree of kyphosis is commonly evident and the thorax becomes rigid, losing its normal range of expansion.

What then precipitates the asthmatic attack? As has been stated earlier, authorities are unsure as to the fundamental cause of asthma. So far it has not been possible to identify a specific characteristic or aetiological factor which is common to all sufferers of asthma, consequently it tends to be explained in broad descriptive terms such as:

> A state of hyper-responsiveness of the bronchi, which renders them liable to undergo muscle constriction and/or mucosal inflammation when provoked by certain exogenous or endogenous stimuli that have no such effects in normal bronchi, these processes causing intermittent or persistent reduction in the calibre of the airways and increased resistance to airflow which can be abolished by therapy. (Gregg, 1987, p. 473)

However, there is a general understanding as to the factors that may precipitate an attack. Five such factors are listed below.

1 Allergy

Asthma is frequently described as an allergic condition and this is undoubtedly true though it should be remembered that not all asthmatics have allergies. Allergy is probably more common in children than in those people that develop asthma later in life.

Common allergens are:

- Dust, or rather the microscopic dust mites that exist in dust.
- Pollen.
- Animals—dogs, cats, horses, etc.
- Bird or animal products—feathers, fur, etc.
- Food—certain proteins may trigger an attack, e.g. cheese.

2 Irritants

- Gases such as ozone, sulphur dioxide, oxides of nitrogen and chlorine. It is significant that most of these exist as industrial atmospheric pollutants and their effect will be more pronounced in conditions of smog or fog.
- Smoke—including cigarette smoke.
- Paint.
- Moulds.

3 Exercise

Shortness of breath and wheezing following exercise has been recognized practically since medical history began. Hippocrates described it as did Aretaeus the Cappadocian in AD 200. More than 80 per cent of asthmatic children will experience some symptoms following aerobic exercise. The severity of the reaction is directly related to the intensity and the duration of the exercise. Anderson *et al.* (1975) reported that exercise-induced bronchospasm is most likely when the intensity of the exercise is between 60 and 85 per cent of the predicted maximum oxygen consumption and the duration of effort is from 6 to 8 minutes. If the exercise is extended the reaction can occur during the exercise, as in distance running. Otherwise it tends to occur from 3 to 15 minutes post exercise (Scanlon, 1987) and can last from a few minutes up to several hours. A late phase reaction can sometimes occur. This follows after the immediate reaction has resolved and can last for some hours. It is thought that the early reaction is essentially one of bronchospasm whereas the late reaction is due to inflammation. Exercise-induced asthma is greatly influenced by the ambient humidity and temperature (Anderson *et al.*, 1982). Cold dry air is much more likely to evoke a reaction than warm humid air. These conditions, combined with the increased pulmonary flow during exercise, tend to increase water loss from the respiratory tract thus cooling it and in so doing are likely to precipitate an attack. It is noticeable that asthmatics swimming in a heated indoor swimming pool can generally tolerate vigorous exercise and people suffering from a mild exercise-induced asthmatic attack will sometimes experience relief when taken into the warm humid atmosphere of a shower.

Asthmatics sometimes find that a period of low level activity lasting for about fifteen minutes will induce mild symptoms. If this is followed by vigorous exercise the symptoms do not get worse and may even get better. It may be that this phenomenon of 'breaking through' might be utilized in preparing an asthmatic for more intense exercise of long duration.

4 Infections

Viral infections affecting the upper respiratory tract will very frequently cause exacerbations of asthma in young children. Colds inevitably will 'go to the chest'.

5 Psychological factors

Asthma is not a psychosomatic disorder but there is no denying that emotional factors can provoke an attack. Excitement, laughing, crying, anxiety, and anger may all be triggering agencies.

It is fortunate that asthma responds to medication, and mild and moderate sufferers will obtain immediate and lasting relief. Control is obtained by the administration of three types of drugs. The first of these are $beta_2$ adrenoceptor stimulants, the best known of which are salbutamol (Ventolin) and terbutaline (Bricanyl). These act as bronchodilators and are usually given by aerosol inhalation, though they can be given in tablet form or by injection. Corticosteroids are often given in conjunction with $beta_2$ adrenoceptors. These probably bring relief by reducing the bronchial mucosal inflammatory state and modifying the allergic reaction. Corticosteroids are normally administered as a preventative and are taken three times a day over a protracted period. The commonest corticosteroid is beclomethasone—marketed as Becotide or Becloforte—taken either as an aerosol inhalation or as a fine powder which is administered through a 'spinhaler' or similar device. Sodium cromoglycate (Intal) is the third drug that is used. This acts as a prophylactic which can reduce the incidence of asthmatic attacks and permit the reduction of the dosage of bronchodilators and corticosteroids that are being given concurrently. Like the corticosteroids, sodium cromoglycate can be given either by aerosol inhalation or insufflation.

What then are the responsibilities that teachers in school should have towards asthmatic children in their classes? First, they should be aware who they are. Asthmatics are usually identified soon after arrival at a school either by themselves or by their parents or at the first school medical. It might be that a minimally affected child has escaped diagnosis but shows symptoms during activity at school. This should preferably be discussed with the school nurse who will contact the parents recommending that they seek the advice of their general practitioner. In most schools these days a list is circulated to all teachers alerting them to those children who are suffering from chronic disorders. Teachers should find time to have a chat with asthma sufferers. It is very reassuring for a child to know that teachers are aware of their problems and that they will be given sympathetic help if they have a difficulty.

Asthmatic attacks in school will most likely occur during or after physical education lessons and PE teachers should be especially aware of this. Exercise-induced asthma affects the majority of sufferers and will be aggravated by the allergens and irritants which are usually present in the working environment. An attack can be prevented by the child using a bronchodilator inhaler before the lesson starts. Advice varies as to how long before, but two inhalations ten minutes before activity will normally give protection. Children should be allowed to carry their inhalers at all times rather than having them left with a teacher or nurse. Some schools have in the past been reluctant to allow this, being concerned with possible overdosage or even other children 'trying out' the inhaler. Fortunately these dangers are minimal and even primary age children can be taught to administer their own medication responsibly and safely. This immediate availability of the inhaler is very important because inhalation becomes progressively more difficult as an episode develops. Taken very early the attack will be aborted but the inhaler may be less effective or not effective at all if the attack progresses. Children are generally reluctant to make themselves conspicuous or appear different when with their peers. Consequently they may not want to ask for an inhaler held by a staff member or even use an inhaler in full view of their friends and so it is quite possible for an attack to become serious before it is recognized. Not only should the suffering child be educated, also there is an obvious need for the class as a whole to be made aware of the condition, with the teacher making it clear to all pupils that apart from the recurring attacks the sufferer is in every other way normal. Asthmatics are certainly not invalids and in a well-controlled situation they can follow a normal life.

Parents of asthmatic children are well aware of the effects of exercise and will sometimes actively discourage them from taking part in PE lessons. The children themselves may associate discomfort with exercise, particularly if they are not using an inhaler or if their inhaler technique is poor. It might well be that they also have a low tolerance to exercise because they exercise infrequently. All of these factors may militate towards the avoidance of any form of exercise. Every effort should be made to convince them that suitably medicated they can cope with many forms of exercise and, as far as possible, they should join in normal class activity. It is worthwhile pointing out to them that a large number of well-known athletes and sports people suffer from asthma. In fact, 11 per cent of the US track and field team at the Los Angeles Olympic Games were asthmatics (Voy, 1986), but this did not prevent 60 per cent of them from winning medals. If for some reason an attack becomes established and acute, medical assistance should be quickly sought. A severe asthmatic attack can be life endangering. It should be remembered that more than 2,000 people die every year in this country from asthma. The majority of these may well be elderly but a significant number will be children. The severity of an attack is gauged by the difficulty that the person experiences in breathing. If taking the inhaler is difficult or appears to be not having effect, if the person is having difficulty in talking, if there is cyanosis and if the pulse rate is over 120, medical assistance must be obtained. It is better if a doctor can be brought to see the child, rather than taking the child to the doctor.

When an attack starts encourage the child to use the inhaler, remove to a quiet comfortable room and be as calm and reassuring as possible. Avoid developing an atmosphere of emergency or crisis. Encourage the child to breathe out fully and to try and relax in a comfortable position. Do not leave the child unaccompanied.

There is no doubt that children will profit from taking regular exercise. As exercise tolerance increases they will find that the frequency and intensity of attacks decreases and that they feel less distressed during an attack. Exercise-induced attacks occur less frequently and are less easily provoked. They will experience that increased sense of well-being that exercise brings to everyone and self-confidence is enhanced.

There is considerable variation in the tolerance to different types of exercise. Nearly all sufferers will react to extended aerobic activity such as cross-country running. However, activities in which there are bursts of work punctuated by periods of rest or low activity are generally acceptable and this will include the majority of games. The variability between individuals is such that it is difficult to draw up rigid guidelines and ultimately individuals will know what they can and cannot contend with. Teachers should be aware of this and be careful about pressing asthmatic children beyond their capabilities.

DIABETES

The British Diabetic Association reports that about 2 per cent of the United Kingdom population is affected by diabetes and of the 600,000 that have been diagnosed approximately 30,000 are under 20 years old. It is also estimated that there are probably 250,000 cases that are undiagnosed. The incidence of diabetes in children, therefore, is in the order of one in 500, and consequently schools can expect to have the occasional diabetic child. It is unusual if a diabetic child is not identified by the parents on joining a school. The dramatic nature of a hypoglycaemic attack from which the child might possibly suffer makes it imperative that these conditions can be immediately identified and correctly dealt with.

Diabetes is a condition in which there is a breakdown in the mechanism that normally controls the mobilization and uptake of glucose. This process is dependent upon the hormone insulin which is secreted by the beta cells in the islets of Langerhans found in the pancreas. Insulin acts to reduce the level of blood glucose which it does in a number of ways. It speeds up the process by which glucose passes from the bloodstream into cells, especially voluntary muscle fibres. It accelerates the production of glycogen from glucose, and it also slows down the hydrolysis of glycogen to glucose and inhibits the production of glucose from protein and fat (Tortora and Anagnostakos, 1990).

There are two sorts of diabetes: Type 1 or juvenile diabetes which is also known as insulin-dependent diabetes, and Type 2 diabetes, non-insulin dependent or maturity onset diabetes.

Type 1 diabetes is characterized by a marked decrease in the amount of insulin that is produced. In some cases, there is no insulin at all and unless insulin is administered to these people they will die. Type 1 diabetes comes on suddenly and is commonest in people under the age of 20. It is thought that although there may be a genetic predisposition to this condition, it is generally triggered off by a viral infection or by malfunction of the auto-immune system.

In the absence of insulin large amounts of glucose build up in the circulation. This eventually finds its way into the urine which is normally glucose free. The lack of glucose in the tissues stimulates the liver to release more glucose and secondary sources of energy such as fat and protein are mobilized. Over a period of time this will lead to loss of weight. The increase in circulating lipids may cause atherosclerosis which eventually may give rise to a range of circulatory disorders resulting from impeded circulation such as ischaemic heart disease, disease of the peripheral circulation, gangrene, and renal failure.

Type 2 diabetes, although much more common, tends to occur in people who are over 40 and overweight. In general its symptoms are less severe and it can be controlled more easily. Although Type 2 diabetes may be evident in other staff members, schoolteachers will rarely find it in children in their classes.

The onset of Type 1 diabetes is somewhat variable as is the severity of symptoms which generally appear over a period of a few weeks but can come on very quickly or may, conversely, take a number of months to become established. Characteristic symptoms are:

- Thirst and a dry mouth
- Passing of large amounts of urine
- Tiredness
- Itching of the genital organs
- Blurring of vision
- Weight loss   (British Diabetic Association, 1990)

Without treatment the symptoms become progressively worse, leading to vomiting and drowsiness and eventually coma. The symptoms of Type 2 diabetes are similar but their onset is much more gradual and they do not generally lead to diabetic coma.

The person suffering from Type 1 diabetes needs to follow a regular daily regimen in order to lower the abnormally high blood sugar level. The blood sugar level is primarily controlled by self-administered injections of insulin twice a day but this must be balanced against dietary intake and exercise. Imbalance can lead to either hypoglycaemia or hyperglycaemia. Hypoglycaemia will occur when the level of blood sugar drops below normal; it may be due to taking too much insulin but is more likely to be caused by lack of dietary carbohydrate or perhaps by an unusually high level of activity or exercise. Hyperglycaemia generally results from taking too little insulin or perhaps from eating too much carbohydrate which allows the blood sugar level to rise. Both of these conditions can lead to unconsciousness and an emergency situation. Of the two, a hypoglycaemic reaction is more common and might well occur at school, particularly during PE lessons. Teachers should, therefore, be familiar with the signs and symptoms of an attack and know how to treat it. As with asthma, if an attack can be anticipated or treated quickly, severe symptoms will be prevented and the person can rapidly return to normal activity. Diabetics are familiar with the signs of an oncoming 'hypo' and generally know exactly what to do to prevent it, but sometimes an attack can develop rapidly before preventive measures can be applied.

During a hypoglycaemic reaction diabetics will appear pale and sweaty and confused and be unable to concentrate. They may complain of feeling faint, of being weak and tremulous and cry or even become aggressive. Eventually they will become unconscious. The treatment is to administer sugar as quickly as possible in a form that can be rapidly absorbed. Two teaspoonfuls of sugar dissolved in a glass of water, a glass of fruit juice or milk, proprietary soft drinks such as Coke, Fanta, etc. are suggestions made by the British Diabetic Association. Recovery will occur in about ten minutes. Sweets, chocolate or glucose tablets will have the same effect but will take a little longer to act.

As always, reassure the child and keep calm. Sit victims down and do not rush them to the medical room. Bring help to them rather than take them to help. After the worst is over encourage them to eat some carbohydrate such as biscuits or a sandwich. This will raise the blood sugar level and prevent them from dropping into hypoglycaemia again. If unconsciousness ensues sufferers should be placed in the recovery position. Make sure that the neck is fully extended and that there is no blockage to the airway. No attempt should be made to administer sugar in any form by mouth, and a doctor should be summoned immediately. Although this may be very alarming the response to injected glucose is rapid with sufferers returning to normal very quickly.

A hyperglycaemic attack is far less likely to be encountered because its onset is very gradual. Victims will usually feel unwell and be able to identify familiar symptoms that will lead them to seek medical assistance. Symptoms may start as excessive thirst together with frequent urination which eventually will lead to a decrease in the circulating blood volume. As this hypovolemic state becomes more profound the pulse will become weak and rapid and breathing will be heavy and laboured. The breath characteristically smells 'sweet and fruity' and the person becomes confused and may complain of headache. The condition is reversed by administering insulin and treating the dehydration. This will of course require medical attention and there are no simple first-aid measures that can be applied that will be helpful.

If there is doubt as to whether a person is hypoglycaemic or hyperglycaemic, sugar should be given. Hypoglycaemia will respond rapidly whereas there will be no change if the person is hyperglycaemic. The small additional amount of sugar that is given will have little effect on an already high blood sugar level.

Provided that a child is under medical supervision and a balance has been established between insulin, dietary intake and exercise, a fairly normal school life should be able to be followed. Of these three factors, exercise is potentially the most variable, as insulin and diet are more easily controlled. Physical education lessons will be most likely to produce a drop in blood glucose levels and increase the chances of a 'hypo' occurring, but occasions such as field study trips, school outings, parties, etc. might all have the same effect. As the intensity and duration of physical activity increases so will the chances of hypoglycaemia. If the increased activity can be anticipated steps can be taken beforehand to prevent imbalance occurring. Less insulin might be taken or diet can be increased. Of the two possibilities, adjustment of the diet is to be preferred. More carbohydrate should be eaten in the meal before activity and the child should be prepared, if necessary, to take some form of quickly absorbable sugar immediately prior to exercise. If the exercise is sustained more sugar might have to be taken to maintain stabilization. Glucose tablets or Dextrosol sweets are a convenient way of doing this and diabetics commonly carry these with them.

Ultimately, the choice of whether a child should take part in PE lessons or not will depend upon the wishes of the child's parents but every effort should be made to encourage the parents to discuss this issue with their doctor so that both they and their child are reassured that, with care, exercise is both safe and desirable. Incumbent with the policy of inclusion of diabetics in the normal school programme is the responsibility of all teachers to know who is at risk, what is likely to precipitate a hypoglycaemic reaction, and what to do if one occurs.

EPILEPSY

After strokes, epilepsy is the second most common neurological disorder that affects people of all age groups. The National Society for Epilepsy (1990) report that a prevalence rate of 1 in 200 is usually quoted for the UK, but following recent American and Australian studies a rate of 1 in 100 may be a more accurate estimation.

Epilepsy is characterized by fits or seizures which are caused by random irregular discharges of impulses from neurones within the brain. The sites of origin can vary, therefore so will the nature of the attack as motor, sensory, and psychological manifestations can occur either independently or combined. A seizure may be triggered off by some factor that is extrinsic to the brain such as an abnormally high temperature in young children, anoxia, or hypoglycaemia. Many people experience such an attack some time within their life but this does not constitute epilepsy. Epilepsy is the condition in which a person experiences repeated fits that are due to intrinsic neuronal malfunction. Such is the variety of the clinical manifestations, the sites of origin, and the possible causes of the seizure that epilepsy presents itself as a condition of great variability and complexity.

Diagnosis of epilepsy poses problems because in some instances the symptoms are so minimal and pass so quickly that they may never be noticed. Additionally, there is no permanent neurological disorder and, therefore, no lasting symptoms; this means that between seizures the person appears to be perfectly normal. A decision, therefore, is made on the basis of witness accounts of a number of fits. The sufferer may see evidence of having experienced a fit but might not have any recollection at all of the fit itself. Testing procedures may produce corroborative evidence but in themselves be inconclusive.

Epilepsy is generally seen as one of two forms. These are described nowadays as minor or major epilepsy. Minor epilepsy can easily pass unnoticed because the symptoms are not dramatic and are of short duration. The person becomes pale, the eyes are fixed or staring, and the impression is given of day-dreaming. This quickly passes and the person continues what they were doing as if nothing has happened. However, staring can be accompanied by strange behaviour such as interrupted speech, lip smacking, playing in an absent way with clothing or saying odd things; these symptoms are known as automatisms and, again, are of short duration. There may be a brief period of lack of awareness of what has happened and the person appears to be detached and 'out of touch'. If such an attack is noticed there is not a great deal that can be done or needs to be done. Be reassuring and talk quietly and don't leave the person until there is complete recovery.

There can be no mistaking major epilepsy. The symptoms are dramatic, alarming, and can persist for some minutes. The attack starts with the person suddenly falling to the ground. This is frequently accompanied by an unusual cry. The body then becomes rigid for a brief period and the person appears to have stopped breathing. This causes the face to become suffused and the lips cyanosed. The general body rigidity then passes off and convulsive movements follow. These can involve all the limbs and the head and can be violent and frightening. Breathing becomes difficult because the jaw is clenched. Froth can come from the mouth which might be stained with blood if the tongue, lips, or cheek have been bitten. Double incontinence can occur. Eventually the convulsive movements stop and the body becomes relaxed; the subject slowly regains consciousness but may remain confused and be quite unaware of what has happened.

Very little can be done to help a person during an attack and the most that one can do is to prevent self-injury during the convulsive stage. Victims should be moved away from any source of danger and a space cleared about them to prevent objects from violently contacting the head or limbs. If possible, place something soft under the head. Sufferers should not be forcibly restrained as this too may lead to injury; do not try to force anything between the clenched jaws. There might well be difficulty with respiration but little can be done about this until the convulsions subside, when sufferers can be placed in the recovery position until they regain consciousness. Stay with sufferers until they are fully recovered and are capable of looking after themselves. Alarming though an attack might be to anyone watching, it is not considered to be an extreme emergency. Nevertheless, the sufferer should see a doctor as soon as possible. An attack is usually over within ten minutes and if it extends beyond that time medical help is needed. Occasionally, a number of fits can follow on one after another and this also requires medical assistance.

Children witnessing an epileptic seizure are likely to be very distressed and this should be avoided if at all possible. Do not allow the class to gather round and, if possible, get them right away from the immediate area. Help will be needed and should be sent for as soon as the seizure is recognized.

Epileptics who suffer from major attacks sometimes have a premonition of an impending attack and they can prepare themselves. If a warning can be given to the teacher beforehand, quick preparations can be made like getting the person to lie down, loosen a tight collar, and to clear the rest of the class. If the teacher can show sympathy and understanding it will increase the likelihood of a child giving a forewarning.

It is difficult to anticipate situations that might lead to a seizure. In the majority of instances they are spontaneous events which have no clear cause. Some people, however, do know that certain things might precipitate a fit. Rapidly flickering lights, like strobes, or sometimes television screens are known to be a triggering factor. This does not mean that they cannot watch television. If the ambient light level is high and they are not too close to the screen they are unlikely to be affected. Fatigue, lack of sleep, anxiety or boredom or too much alcohol are also known to be causative factors.

Epilepsy responds to medication and it is estimated that 70 per cent of cases can be completely controlled. Tablets have to be taken on a regular daily basis. Most drugs are taken two or three times a day which will necessitate a child taking tablets while at school. As with diabetes and asthma, children should be made responsible for their own medication as soon as possible.

Determining what epileptic children can or cannot do at school depends entirely upon the severity of their condition. If they are mildly affected and under medical control they can enjoy a completely normal school life. Each situation has to be individually assessed and both parents and teachers will depend very much on the guidance that they are given by the doctor. If a child is more severely affected it is important that the PE teacher in particular knows what the child should not do. The National Society for Epilepsy stresses the importance of not being overprotective and of allowing the child to live as normal and active a life as possible. Activities like boxing or subaqua diving are not recommended and field sports which could involve injury to the head might have to be given very careful consideration, but there is no reason why most other activities cannot be enjoyed as long as the person is being supervised or is accompanied by a responsible friend.

It can be seen therefore that although the effects of asthma, diabetes, and epilepsy upon children are very different and can vary in degree, they can all display acute episodes if a suitably provoking situation occurs. The potential element of danger that may be associated with these occasions requires a prompt assessment of the situation by the supervising teacher and the ability to apply appropriate measures to contend with the emergency until medical assistance can be obtained.

In summary, the following points can be made:

1 All teachers should be informed about those children that suffer from any chronic condition, particularly if that condition may have acute episodes that could lead to an emergency situation.
2 The school should encourage parents to allow their child to lead as normal a school life as possible. If limitations have to be imposed these should be made by the child's doctor and should be clearly understood by both parents and teachers.
3 All teachers should be familiar with the signs and symptoms of an acute asthmatic attack, a hypoglycaemic reaction and an epileptic seizure.
4 All teachers should know how to cope with these acute situations.
5 There should be a clearly understood procedure that teachers should follow in regard to these emergencies.
6 Physical education teachers should be particularly aware that physical activity might increase the chances of an acute episode or, as in the case of epilepsy, involve some element of risk.

7   Teachers should find time to have a private word with those children that have a chronic condition. They should be understanding, sympathetic and, above all, approachable and encourage children to come to them if they experience premonitory signs at any time.

8   Anticipation or quick action might well prevent an acute episode or reduce its severity.

9   It is unrealistic to treat chronic sufferers as completely normal children. They are not, and they know it. However, everything possible should be done not to isolate them or make them appear different in front of their peers.

10 Teachers should appreciate that a considerable range in severity exists in chronic conditions. What one child can manage might be beyond the capability of another.

11 Children with chronic disorders should carry a card which gives information about their condition. Apart from information about how parents/doctors can be contacted there can be a description of symptoms, how long they last, what to do, and whether an antidote is carried—in fact, anything that would assist a person that is giving help.

REFERENCES

Anderson, S. D., Schoeffel, R. E., and Follet, R. (1982) Sensitivity to heat and water loss at rest and during exercise in asthmatic patients. *Journal of Respiratory Disorders* **63**, 459–60.

Anderson, A. D., Silverman, M., and Godfrey, S. (1975) Exercise induced asthma. *British Journal of Diseases of the Chest* **69**, 1–39.

British Diabetic Association (1990) Pamphlets: *What is Diabetes? Introducing Diabetes Mellitus. Helping a Diabetic Person with an Insulin Reaction.* London: British Diabetic Association.

Gregg, I. (1987) Importance of asthma to the general public. *The Practitioner* **231**, 473–5.

Heal, D., O'Halloran, S., and Reynolds, M. (1987) The asthmatic child at school. A practical guide. *Health at School* **3**, 414–15.

Milner, A. D. (1986) Concepts of childhood asthma. *The Physician* **1**, 579–82.

National Society for Epilepsy (1990) Pamphlets: *Fits. Explaining Epilepsy. Epilepsy, Diagnosis and Management. Epilepsy and Leisure. Epilepsy at School.* London: National Society for Epilepsy.

Scanlon, R. T. (1987) Exercise induced asthma and exercise induced anaphylaxis. *Seminars in Adolescent Medicine* **3**, 193–6.

Stuttaford, T. (1990) The rising tide of asthma. *The Times*, 18 July.

Tortora, G. J. and Anagnostakos, N. P. (1990) *Principles of Anatomy and Physiology* (6th edn). New York: Harper & Row.

Voy, R. O. (1986) The U.S. Olympic committee experience with exercise induced bronchospasm. *Medicine and Science in Sport and Exercise* **3**, 328–30.

FURTHER READING

Brown, S. P. and Thompson, W. R. (1989) The therapeutic role of exercise in diabetes mellitus. *The Diabetes Educator* **14**, 202–6.

Cash, J. E. (1959) *A Textbook of Medical Conditions for Physiotherapists.* London: Faber & Faber.

Croucher, N. (1951) *Outdoor Pursuits for Disabled People.* Cambridge: Woodhead Faulkner.

Haseldine, P. (1987) *Epilepsy*. Wellingborough: Thorsons.

Hill, R. A., Britten, J. R., and Tattersfield, A. E. (1987) Management of asthma in schools. *Archives of Disease in Childhood* **62**, 414–15.

Hill, R. A., Standen, P. J., and Tattersfield, A. E. (1989) Asthma, wheezing and school absence in primary schools. *Archives of Disease in Childhood* **64**, 246–51.

Hopkins, A. (1984) *Epilepsy*. Oxford: Oxford University Press.

McGeorge, S. (1990) *Physical Activity for those Children with Asthma or Diabetes*. The Health Education Authority in Conjunction with the Physical Education Association. Newsletter no. 24.

Routon, J. R. and Sherrill, C. (1989) Attitudes towards physical education and self concepts of asthmatic and non asthmatic children. *Perceptual and Motor Skills* **68**, 1320–2.

Seligman, J. and Wilson, L. (1989) Getting a grasp of asthma's grip. *Newsweek* (September), 60–1.

Speight, A. N. P., Lee, D. A., and Hey, D. N. (1983) Underdiagnosis and undertreatment of asthma in childhood. *British Medical Journal* **286**, 1253–6.

Storr, A., Barrell, E., and Lenney, W. (1987) Asthma in primary schools. *British Medical Journal* **295**, 251–2.

Thomas, P. (1980) Dealing with asthmatic and diabetic athletes. *Lifesaver U.K.* **7**, 20–1.

Usherwood, T. (1986) Management of acute asthma in children. *The Physician* **1**, 484–5.

Vranic, M. and Berger, M. (1979) Exercise and diabetes mellitus. *Diabetes* **28**, 147–51.

Chapter 13

Alternative Visions of Health-Related Fitness: An Exploration of Problem-Setting and its Consequences

Andrew C. Sparkes

INTRODUCTION

> problems are not just 'out there', like objects of nature; they are socially constructed and preserved by society's members.
> (Lawson, 1984, p. 49)

It is extremely difficult to gain a firm grasp of the health-related fitness (HRF) movement which has emerged within physical education (PE) in recent years because it is a phenomenon that is international, multidimensional, multifaceted, ambiguous, and shifting.[1] Bearing this in mind this chapter has modest intentions and focuses upon one particular aspect of the HRF movement with a view to gaining an insight into how it has developed during the last decade and the directions it might take in the future.[2] The key issue I want to explore, drawing upon the work of Lawson (1984), is the manner in which different groups within this movement have engaged in a process of problem-setting that, by definition, has led each of them to emphasize certain aspects of health while ignoring others. Problem-setting in this sense can be viewed as a form of social editing that eliminates a range of possible problems from consideration while foregrounding others that become the focus of attention for the development of solutions. Therefore, how we define problems in relation to health determines to a large extent the solutions we seek and the ways in which we come to understand this complex phenomenon in our society.

By focusing upon the nature of problem-setting I hope to indicate that no single approach or perspective is able to provide the 'answer' to the many complex issues of health since *all* approaches to health will have their blind spots, their strengths and weaknesses, with each framing the problem in different ways and advocating different solutions. For example, with regard to Figure 13.1, some approaches might emphasize health choices while others might emphasize the social and physical environment as the major determinant of health. As a consequence, I believe that there is much to be gained by those involved in the HRF movement adopting a more holistic and reflective stance regarding the process and products of problem-setting in order to gain a greater awareness of the inevitable selectivity inherent in their own views and the views of others so that each can be subjected to critical evaluation.

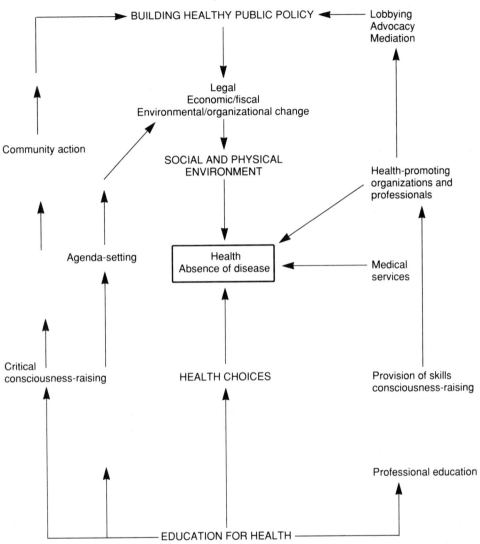

Figure 13.1 *The contribution of education to health promotion* (source: Tones, 1989, p. 261).

With this in mind I attempt, early on in the chapter, to raise some questions regarding the ways in which problem-setting has taken place within the two approaches that, to date, have dominated the contemporary HRF scene. These are the *traditional* and the *educational* approaches. According to Tones (1986) the traditional approach to health education in general has had as its focus the individual, and its goal has been to *persuade* the individual to adopt a particular lifestyle and thus reduce mortality and morbidity in the population. This approach is taken to be entirely consonant with orthodox preventive medicine. In contrast, the educational approach moves beyond the naïve expectation that simply providing information about health issues is sufficient to bring about behaviour change. Based on a concern for rationality and freedom of choice it has as its primary goal the facilitation of informed decision-making irrespective of the nature of the decision which might finally be made. In terms of Figure 13.1, both these approaches focus upon health choices.

Having problematized some of the basic assumptions of these two approaches in general terms by looking at how problem-setting has taken place within their boundaries, I then give attention to how problems are framed differently within what Tones has called the *radical* approach. Here, the focus in terms of Figure 13.1 is on the social and physical environment. In comparing these various approaches my intention is not to prescribe one as better than another, but simply to highlight the manner in which each frames health issues differently and how each has their particular blind spots that impact upon their chosen solutions to the problem of health.

THE NATURE OF CRITIQUE

Throughout the chapter I draw on a range of examples from areas that often seem far removed from HRF in schools. This is intentional because I think that important insights can be generated by comparing events in other domains and thereby locating the HRF movement in a wider socio-historical framework. My questions are raised in a spirit of critique that is intended to stimulate debate and enhance our understanding of health in society. Having said this, it is unfortunate that the term 'critique' is often misunderstood by many within the PE community. As Kirk and Tinning (1990) note:

> We lack a critical tradition in our field, and tend to view conflict and criticism as always destructive, intensely personal, rarely objective and never constructive ... Critique is more than mere criticism in the sense of 'destructive comment'. We use this term here to refer to the effort to stand back from events and practices that are very familiar to us as physical educators, in an effort to gain sufficient analytical space to see beyond the obvious and the everyday. Once we have been able to penetrate the sometimes opaque layers of meaning in social life, critique then enables us to position the events under scrutiny within the larger context of which they are a part.   (pp. 2–9)

With regard to this issue Dewar (1990) emphasizes that critique is not about proportioning blame but is to do with understanding *how* our practices within PE are constructed, *why* they have been constructed in certain ways, and *who* or *what* categories of individuals benefit from these decisions. In keeping with the critical tradition Dewar suggests that a *relational* analysis is particularly appropriate for interrogating these questions. However, she recognizes that this form of analysis is often seen by many as irrelevant to the actual practices that constitute PE programmes in educational institutions because they appear to be abstract, impersonal, and unable to offer practical guidelines for change: 'The problem we face in doing relational work is that it is necessary to understand the complex connections that exist between individual practices, programmes and the social relationships of power and privilege before it is possible to develop alternative anti-oppressive practices' (p. 74).[3] Likewise, Tinning (1990a) notes:

> many of us have an aversion to what I might call abstract forms of understanding (abstract in the sense of not obviously relating to the world of practice). In relation to the teaching

of physical education, many of us search only for what is obvious, 'up front' and easily recognisable. Many of us have 'empiricist' ways of viewing the world, in the sense that we trust only the obvious, the things we can feel with our senses, and we distrust the non-concrete, the abstract. But herein lies a potential problem, *for not all of what is relevant or important in teaching is obvious. Some of the things which have considerable influence on what we do as teachers and learners is subtle, covert and extremely difficult to recognise . . . In order to understand our educational practice in physical education, and to improve it, we must begin to recognise the not-so-obvious.*   (p. 3; my italics)

The forms of question raised by critique tend to fracture the not-so-obvious since they focus upon the networks of unconscious, unreflective, and taken-for-granted assumptions that people hold about the world that in turn shape what they think, say, and do.[4] This focus on implicit ideologies can act as a useful tool in exploring and revealing how people are often unwittingly engaged in practices that have negative consequences for others. The mere act of considering that aspects of what we do in good faith and with the best of intentions for others, may actually operate in subtle and covert ways to oppress them, is disturbing and unsettling. Consequently, Evans (1989) is fully aware that raising critical questions about the ideological content of HRF initiatives, along with their social, cultural, and political origins and consequences as well as the purposes they are required to serve, 'may be difficult and unsettling and difficult to cope with at times, yet in the end it must be of great value' (p. 189).

Evans (1989) goes on to say that debating such issues is important because it would be all too easy—and I would add much more comfortable—for the ideas associated with HRF to simply degenerate into a kind of folklore or new orthodoxy which practitioners uncritically pass on to each other 'believing that they have at last discovered how PE really ought to be . . . The more constructive debate we have about HRF the firmer will be the foundations of this development' (p. 189). Therefore if we believe as I do that the initiatives related to HRF within PE represent something important, significant, and potentially worthwhile then the debate should welcome comments from a variety of perspectives be they critical or otherwise. With this in mind this chapter remains unashamedly in the abstract and it raises more questions than it can possibly hope to answer. Indeed, I want to move one step back from 'answers' to ask, 'If HRF is the solution—what is the problem?'.

THE DOMINANT VIEW OF THE PROBLEM

A brief review of the HRF literature over the last decade suggests to me that for many in the HRF movement the problem so far has been defined in terms of the perceived sedentary lifestyle of children in a modern 'affluent' society and the associated dangers this has for the health of the individual, particularly in relation to diseases of the heart.[5] Indeed, coronary heart disease (CHD) is located as a key feature within the dominant discourse of HRF. It provides a central form of justification in terms of researching into children's activity patterns and the development of motivational strategies to promote an active lifestyle. As Armstrong (1987) notes, in providing a *physiological* rationale for HRF programmes in schools:

> We live in a sedentary culture and although the battle against infectious diseases is being won the occurrence of hypokinetic diseases—those related to or caused by the lack of

regular physical activity—continues to rise at an alarming rate . . . Even more serious is
the tragedy of atherosclerotic coronary heart disease which is annually responsible for the
death of 180,000 Britons . . . Health and fitness programmes designed to change the
lifestyles of children, their parents and their teachers must be initiated.   (pp. 19–23)

Common sense would tell us that this is as it should be. After all, CHD has been
portrayed as the modern killer in Western societies. It is the largest single category of
fatal illness amongst men and also the disease responsible for most of the inequality
between social classes in life expectancy. For many, it has reached epidemic pro-
portions and it has been defined as *the* disease of our affluent times and the current
discourse on heart disease prevention in the media takes on the appearance of a moral
panic. However, the issue of CHD is not as simple as it seems and Brandt (1988)
reminds us, 'Disease is not merely a biological phenomenon; it is shaped by powerful
behavioural, social, and political forces. Social values affect both the way we come to
see and understand a particular disease and the interventions we undertake' (p. 415).
In this view, disease is *socially constructed*.

But how does this work and what relevance does it have to the manner in which
problem-setting has taken place within HRF? To explore this issue and begin to make
connections in the web I want to weave I will start by drawing heavily on a paper by
Bartley (1985) entitled 'Coronary Heart Disease and the Public Health 1850–1983'.
While it will be left to others more capable than myself to dispute Bartley's interpretations, for my purposes his work is significant because it provides important insights
into the process of problem-setting and the manner in which once a 'problem' is
defined in a certain way it leads to a focus on specific solutions that have certain
ideological consequences. As Apple (1982) reminds us, 'macroeconomically our work
may serve functions that bear little resemblance to even our best intentions' (p. 13).
That is, ideologies can work behind the backs of people without them being aware of
it.

GETTING TO THE 'HEART' OF THE MATTER

Bartley (1985) engages in a historical and sociological re-reading of the literature on
the post-Second World War epidemic of CHD in Britain. In doing so he highlights the
ways in which public health texts may be analysed as official portraits of social
problems. Furthermore, he is concerned with the ideological consequences of the
ways in which disease is 'discovered' at death (and on other occasions). Surprisingly,
in terms of our common-sense beliefs about CHD, Bartley claims that the literature
does not in fact yield any consistent evidence to the effect that 'the coronary arteries
of the nation deteriorated over the period we are examining, let alone that such
deterioration was more prevalent in those being classified at death as cardiac victims'
(p. 302). He also notes that with regard to heart disease that similar discussions about
'epidemics' took place in the inter-war period of the 1920s and 1930s where government health statistics indicate there was a much faster rise in heart disease death than
in the post-war period.

These issues are explored by him in an analysis that focuses upon the way in which
one disease category has been woven together against a period of social conflict and
change. Bartley's analysis drawing on a variety of sources, including the Registrar

General's annual Statistical Reports and the Reports of the Chief Medical Officer of the Ministry of Health, is extensive, and it is impossible for me to do justice to it in the space available. In essence, he suggests the epidemic of CHD is a *social construction* related to the expansion of this category by the medical profession, particularly in terms of defining the reasons for death as evidenced in the changing rules for coders on death certificates over the years. For example, in the Registrar General's statistical review for 1926 (HMSO, 1928) the Registrar commented:

> However, 'arteriosclerosis' is rapidly replacing 'old age' in certification. And similarly, myocardial degeneration is much oftener mentioned now than in former years on the death certificate of sufferers from chronic bronchitis etc. As one of the current rules of classification prefers heart to respiratory disease if the two appear on the same certificate, this change in vogue of certification results in the transfer of all deaths from bronchitis etc, to heart disease. (p. 86)

In relation to this Bartley goes on to draw our attention to the fact that from 1929 onwards, along with another change in the International Coding of Death coding rules, death certificates stating 'myocardial degeneration with arteriosclerosis' were coded to *heart disease, rather than to diseases of the blood vessels generally*. As such, the heart began to become the focus for a disease process that had been observed and speculated on for some time but was formally diffused throughout the body. It was the heart that now became the focus for much of the former 'bronchitis' and the former 'arteriosclerosis'. He adds that although by 1930 the terms 'coronary heart disease' and 'myocardial infarction' were not in common use nor had they been defined as major causes of death, the conceptual groundwork had been laid for the delineation of a major cause of death associated with degeneration and failure of the heart *due* to 'sclerotic' and 'fatty' changes in the arteries supplying blood to the myocardium and/or blockage of these vessels by clots.[6] As a consequence, the muscular failure of the heart could then be attributed mainly or solely to the state of the constituents of the blood or of the blood vessel walls. It is with a sense of irony that Bartley notes how in a period of massive economic depression:

> theories about diet, physical activity and other aspects of lifestyle could be used to account for excessive cholesterol, insufficient thrombolytic factor, absence of compensating collateral vascularisation, etc, according to which version of the theory is espoused. The heart will then be expected to bear the 'stress of modern life' as long as the personal health practices of individuals have kept their (particularly coronary) arteries in a healthy enough state. Thus the picture is completed, of a modern disease which, beginning at the time of the economic depression of the late 1920s–1930s, is about to become the commonest cause of death, a picture of a disease which—ironically—can allow it to be attributed to *rising standards of living*. (p. 298)

To all this he adds the ongoing controversy over death certification practices which are intimately linked to the persistent problems of diagnosing heart disease. For example, when certificating a death doctors may often be deterred from mentioning septicaemia or alcohol-related disorders because if these words appear on the death certificate they will attract the attention of the local registrar and then the death will be referred to the coroner. With this knowledge, and often to spare the bereaved relatives more emotional anguish, doctors often refrain from using such terms. However, even when an autopsy is carried out other influences intervene in the diagnosis.

Here, Bartley draws on the works of Atkinson (1978) who provides a penetrating insight into the process by which a sudden death gets defined as a heart-disease death.

> Towards the end, the coroner's officer asked the pathologist, 'Well, have you found anything for me?' . . . The pathologist had paused after the question and had picked up the heart of the deceased which he seemed to be examining closely . . . [he] looked up from his examination of the heart and said, 'Well, I'd like to give you "shock"—"shock" in the medical sense that is, because the shock of the operation is what really stopped his heart beating, but this coroner doesn't like "shock" does he?' The coroner's officer confirmed that this was indeed the case, to which the pathologist replied: 'I could give you "heart failure" then—how would that be?' 'That'll do me fine' replied the coroner's officer.   (Atkinson, 1978, p. 98)

In view of all this, and despite evidence to suggest that there are many who die of 'heart attacks' that have a pre-existing chronic illness, are unemployed, of particular social class, etc., Bartley asks the probing question, 'Why, one may ask, has it been the (largely unobserved, imputed) state of the coronary arteries which has been written into the orthodoxy of health education and the popular consciousness, rather than the unemployment and chronic illness?' (p. 307). He suggests that this definition of the problem with its attendant solutions carries out ideological work at two levels. First, it works at the level of explaining ominous changes in the health of certain groups in the community. Second, it works at the level of explaining individual deaths which take place 'suddenly', 'prematurely', and from suspicious and medicolegally ambiguous causes. The work that such explanations perform is taken to be part of the process by which medicine *individualizes disease and writes out social deprivation and inequality from the description of illness*. Bartley comments:

> Here it can be seen that once it had been assumed that the prewar poverty and inequality had been banished by the welfare state, new types of explanations were needed to account for the failure of class inequalities in health to diminish. The idea of coronary heart disease as caused by obesity and sloth in the newly affluent working classes fitted the requirements. *No further social change could be contemplated, now it was up to individuals to alter their behaviour.*   (p. 290; my italics)

However, there is another way to set the problem. For example, the assumptions about CHD as a category can be suspended to allow the problem to be posed in a different way so that it becomes not the 'epidemic of heart disease', but rather the failure of the health of men (particularly working-class men) in later working life to improve appreciably in the last 50 years. As Bartley suggests, 'This redefines the problem in terms of the experience of a social group, rather than in terms of a clinical entity' (p. 309). Framing the problem in this way *brings back in the social dimensions of health that established diagnostic classifications write out*. That is, issues of social structure now become important since these are taken to set limits and constraints on the health of particular groups in our society that are often beyond the control of the individual.

THE LIFESTYLE SOLUTION

This brief look at the social construction of CHD as an 'epidemic' parallels a range of historical developments within the world of medicine that has led to the doctrine of specific aetiology that concentrates attention on the minuscule details of what disease does in the human body. In doing so, this doctrine also deflects attention away from other causes in the environment and the individual's relationship to it (cf. Hart, 1988). According to Tones (1989), in a historical review of health education in England similar shifts in focus occurred once it was realized that the 'magic bullets' provided by medicine were less appropriate for dealing with the newly recognized problems of chronic degenerative disease. He suggests that preventive medicine sought to absorb health education as a device which might be used to prevent the incurable and cope with the intractable. This was to be achieved by influencing unhealthy lifestyles: 'Health education was now less concerned with raising awareness and campaigning for social action but almost entirely preoccupied with acquiring techniques to persuade people to modify their behaviour' (p. 267). Tones believes that in health education this approach reached its zenith in the late 1970s which is interesting because it was around this time that the contemporary HRF movement began to emerge as a force within PE. Against this historical landscape it is hardly surprising that the early instigators of this movement who were (and still are) predominantly (male) physiologists and psychologists focused their attention on the individual as the problem and the changing of lifestyles as the solution.[7] As Evans (1990a) comments:

> Although the HRF literature is both weighty and wide-ranging, its theoretical emphasis remains predominantly physiological and psychological. It gives high profile to fitness testing, measurement, and the monitoring and assessment of each individual's 'health'. In this physiological discourse, as in the 'softer' social psychological elements of the literature, health is conceptualised in a particularly individualistic fashion. In it we see that HRF provides the means of physical or psychological *repair*, it is a way of helping children to come to terms with the traumas of Western urban living, or a system of relief for stressed youngsters.   (p. 157)

At this point we need to return to the work of Lawson (1984) and his ideas on the issue of problem-setting. He suggests that one way in which problem-setting begins within a profession is when social trends or conditions are deemed ripe for opportunity. For example, an obvious trend to catch the eye of physical educators has been the changing cultural role prescriptions of women and the heightened interest in fitness and lifestyle. Within both these areas physical educators have been able to capitalize by expanding their offerings.[8] In terms of the opportunism associated with the latter the views of a leading advocate and popularizer of HRF in Britain are illuminating. In a special edition of the *Bulletin of Physical Education* devoted to HRF in schools, Almond (1983) in presenting a rationale for HRF argues that the medical profession have identified circulatory and heart disease as a major contemporary health problem and that an active lifestyle is a central preventive measure. Having added that physical activity is valuable in creating a sense of well-being and feeling good he comments, 'These points are strong indications that the physical education profession could play an important role in raising public consciousness about the value of exercise, being physically active as part of one's life style, and providing access to ways in which people can look after themselves' (p. 5).

Such comments reveal the way in which problem-setting within HRF has proceeded within the boundaries of a medical framework that was outlined earlier in this chapter. In relation to this, Tinning (1990b) argues that by constructing a rationale for HRF around 'encouraging and promoting an active lifestyle', and 'making the most of oneself', that Almond, along with others involved in the HRF movement, has constructed solutions to problems that have been defined by the medical profession and others (such as the fitness industry) who have a vested interest in physical activity as a marketable commodity. The consequences have been similar in that the net effect of this opportunism has been to locate the 'problem' of health at the level of the individual which has led to a selective blindness regarding other structural issues such as social class, gender, and race that also impact upon health.

Here, the work of Lawson (1984) provides us with further insights. He argues that once problems have been selectively framed and named, then attention is directed towards their solution. As such, problem-setting is a form of *social editing* that eliminates a range of possible problems from consideration while foregrounding others that are to become the focus of attention. As Lawson states, 'In other words, problem-setting determines the research questions that are asked, as well as those that are not; these questions determine, in turn, the profession's knowledge base' (p. 51). Consequently, problem-setting is itself a political act which is ultimately linked with power, control, and what counts as legitimate knowledge in the profession as newcomers are socialized to see the world and frame a range of problems in particular ways (also see Sparkes 1989a, 1991a). The political nature of problem-setting can best be understood by considering the manner in which it channels attention towards specific issues while deflecting attention away from others that might act to disturb the *status quo* in our society.

PROBLEM-SETTING IN THE CONTEXT OF INDIVIDUALISM

The process of problem-setting brings certain issues into view while selectively ignoring others. According to Tinning (1990b) this process 'is significant not only in what it defines as a problem but also in what it chooses not to define as a problem' (p. 7). In this section I hope to illustrate how having defined the problem within an individualistic framework that the HRF movement has selectively focused its attention on one particular aspect of Figure 13.1. That is, it has concentrated upon individual health choices at the expense of social and physical environment issues. For example, Mr Len Almond, talking on *The Education Programme* screened on BBC 2 in the autumn of 1988, stressed the need for pupils in schools to take more responsibility for their own health. He emphasized: 'In the long run it is up to the individual to learn to be more responsible and take control of their activity patterns'.

Similarly, Biddle (1989), having acknowledged that social and environmental issues along with genetic endowment can impact upon health, suggests that when health *through physical activity* is considered that individual choice is paramount. He argues, 'Although absolute levels of fitness and health that are achieved will be influenced by a great many factors, activity levels, within normal human limits, are largely determined by personal choice' (p. 64). These statements imply that individuals are capable of controlling their activity patterns and levels of activity and that they have a responsibility to do so in order to attain and maintain health. They provide interesting examples of how the dominant discourse of HRF has defined problems within the framework of *individualism*.[9]

At this point it is necessary to consider the nature of individualism in order to appreciate how problems formulated within its framework act to selectively ignore a range of important issues in relation to health. Individualism, or liberal-individualism as it is sometimes called, has been with us in one form or another since the time of the ancient Greeks and is one of the most pervasive ideologies in Western culture (see Ketcham, 1987; Lane, 1988; Turner, 1988). According to Naidoo (1986), the essential core of individualism rests upon the belief that individual free choice is both an accurate account of the *status quo* and the most desirable goal to aim for in social affairs. However, individualism is a complex beast and there are many strands operating within its boundaries that contain a range of ambiguities. For example, according to Bellah *et al.* (1985) it is concerned with the dignity of the individual, the right to think for ourselves, to make our own decisions, and to live our lives as we see fit: 'Our highest and noblest aspirations, not only for ourselves, but for those we care about, for our society and for the world, are closely linked to individualism. Yet . . . some of our deepest problems both as individuals and as a society are also closely linked to our individualism' (p. 142).

Tinning (1990a) agrees that most of us would have little quarrel with the apparent concerns of individualism for individual autonomy, independence, and equality of opportunity. However, he goes on to make the important point that the ideological influence of individualism does not end there since it goes further to support the more questionable notion that an individual is fully responsible for his or her own actions and life situation. Consequently, individualism as an ideology works as a system of beliefs that is central to the process of producing meanings and ideas in our society relating to numerous issues such as health, wealth, and poverty. For Smith and Stone (1989), individualism as a metatheory contains the age-old notion that individuals are ultimately responsible for their status in systems of social inequality. While their work focuses upon how Americans view the causes of wealth and poverty their analysis has important implications for how health is conceived in Britain. They comment:

> In capitalism, opportunities are readily available to all those who are willing to work hard, and socioeconomic mobility and standing hinge on the possession and expression of acquired personality characteristics such as drives, skills and motives. Moreover, the logic continues, because virtually all people have the opportunity to acquire and develop these traits, those who do are justly rewarded with wealth, while those who do not are deservedly penalised with poverty . . . The attribution of causal responsibility for wealth and poverty follows accordingly and rests squarely on the shoulders of the individual, not social structures, subcultures or other forces. Commonly mentioned causes of wealth include such well-known traits as exceptional effort, hard work, initiative and the willingness to take risks . . . whereas laziness, lack of thrift, and 'loose' morals are frequently voiced causes of poverty. (p. 94)

Just substitute the words 'health' for 'wealth' and 'illness' for 'poverty' to illustrate how individualism operates in the domain of health. In essence, this aspect of individualism allows social problems to be defined as individual problems and Hargreaves (1986) has noted how, within the world of PE, the discourse of individualism has consistently operated to accomplish 'the virtual disappearance of the social structure, that is, social processes and social phenomenon are radically individualised, reducing them to the attributes of persons and the interactions between them' (p. 165). In short, as Ingham (1985) argues with regard to the prevailing emphasis on lifestyle, the personal aetiology of illness is elevated over the societal–structural aetiology of illness.

He goes on to say, 'It is an idea and/or policy which is riddled, in both senses of the term, with voluntaristic assumptions that *a priori* define problems as personal and not as problems of milieu, structure, or egregious and invalidating ideologies such as racism, sexism, or ageism' (p. 50). According to Ingham:

> The fusion of new right ideology and right-thinking common sense thus promotes a lifestyle which exhorts us to save our hearts by jogging in the arsenic filled air of Tacoma. If jogging is not for you, then there are other routes to fitness—routes which conveniently ignore the fact that millions of people who hover around and below the poverty line cannot afford ten-speeds, tennis racquets, and memberships in health fitness centers. And as an active rather than passive lifestyle, it exhorts us to burn off calories while denying State dependents the food they need to survive.   (p. 50)

This is not to deny that many individuals can and do take responsibility for their health under certain circumstances. However, as Tinning (1990a) emphasizes, 'different individuals have different degrees of power at their disposal to control aspects of their life situation, by virtue of their sex, class, racial background, economic circumstances and so on' (p. 11). Consequently, it is important to recognize the many socially constructed limitations that operate to constrain the individual's choice in relation to health. For example, the Black Report in 1980 on *Inequalities in Health* found social class differences with regard to health (also see Townsend and Davidson, 1982; Whitehead, 1987). More recently Wilkinson (1988) has argued that research undertaken since this report suggests that these social class differences in health remain. He notes:

> Perhaps the most striking feature of class differences in health is how broadly based they are. All the main causes of death—with the single exception of breast cancer—show the lower classes at a disadvantage. This disadvantage occurs in every age group. But it is not only the *incidence* of fatal diseases which shows a class bias. There is also evidence, at least among victims of cancers and heart disease, that case-fatality rates are also higher among the lower classes ... In other words, as well as determining who gets a disease, inequalities also determine their chances of dying once they have got it.   (p. 210)

Ultimately, as Mitchell (1984) reminds us, 'working class people experience more ill health than middle class people, not through choice but because ... they are exposed to a health damaging environment over which they have little control' (p. 98). Gender differences have also been identified in relation to health and well-being (cf. Verbrugge, 1985), and Scraton (1987) has commented on the limited access to 'space' that working-class women have in their daily lives. She argues that sport and social settings are dominated by men and male groups. Also, working-class women experience material constraints which, 'together with a lack of access to private transport, further inhibits their movement. Middle-class young women have greater opportunity for participation in social and sporting activities. Not only do they have economic support, but also parental help to transport them to the gym club, swimming pool, youth club etc' (p. 165).

Therefore, it would seem that many groups in our society have less freedom of choice than others to pursue a 'healthy and active lifestyle' and that their lives and experiences are structured in such a way as to increase their chances of suffering illness. The leading figures within the HRF movement who have adopted the traditional and the educational approaches have been deafeningly silent on such issues. In relation to Figure 13.1 their attention has been almost exclusively focused upon health choices since for them structural issues are not defined as central to the problem.

PROBLEM-SETTING AS SOCIAL EDITING: SOME CONSEQUENCES OF INDIVIDUALISM

Framing the problem in terms of the individual and her or his lifestyle has consequences that may not be intended by those who adopt this position within the HRF movement. It is here that individualism as a potent ideology does its work behind the backs of people without their conscious awareness. These consequences are serious and need to be addressed. At the most obvious level the structured inequalities in health that we have mentioned are glossed over and the blame is laid firmly at the feet of individuals. That is, if you become ill it is your fault because you have chosen not to adopt a healthy lifestyle. In its crudest form this becomes *victim blaming* of the worst kind. Hyland (1988) summarizes the situation well:

> Of course, we all value individual freedom of choice and it is hard to deny that individuals obviously can take responsibility for their own health. Serious and dangerous errors arise, however, when this personal emphasis comes to be divorced from the social framework which gives it meaning. The upshot is that health comes to be regarded as being *purely* an individual matter, and illness is explained in terms of 'blaming the victim'. For many such 'victims' the appeal to autonomy is false and insincere for it diverts attention away from the class, gender and racial inequalities which, for a large proportion of the population, makes real choice impossible. More importantly, this approach displays a wilful disregard for epidemiological evidence which clearly demonstrates that health and illness are socially constructed . . . and that individual lifestyles pale into insignificance beside the structural inequalities which militate against healthy living.   (p. 26)

According to Nelkin and Gilman (1988), *blaming* has always been a means to make mysterious and devastating diseases comprehensible and, therefore, possibly controllable. They observe that even when in the past disease was routinely assumed to be caused by 'God's will' or 'occult influences', people still looked for the individual behaviours that were to blame for divine intervention, judgement, and retribution. Yet, even in our modern society diseases are never fully understood and so people continue to blame and make *moral judgements* about the misfortunes of others. They remind us that:

> We still point the finger of blame. In a situation of communal anxiety, locating blame for disease is in effect a strategy of control . . . In effect, placing blame defines the normal, establishes the boundaries of healthy behaviour and appropriate social relationships, and distinguishes the observer from the cause of fear . . . Categories of blame often reflect deep social-class biases. Illness is frequently associated with poverty and becomes a justification for social inequities . . . Inevitably the locus of blame is also tied to specific ideological, political and social concerns. Blame is in effect a social construct, a reflection of the worldviews, social stereotypes and political biases that prevail at a given time . . . Several categories of blame can be found in this popular discourse: disease has been attributed to particular racial groups or social stereotypes, to individual lifestyle, to immoral behaviour, or to those perceived as sources of power and control.   (pp. 362–3)

The ways in which explanations of disease become a means to define appropriate and moral behaviour is an important issue. Throughout the twentieth century concepts of morality have frequently been translated into questions of lifestyle and as already mentioned 'lifestylism' has been a central strand within the dominant discourse of HRF. As a consequence, moral judgements regarding lifestyle are often made. For example, Biddle (1987) writing in a chapter called 'Motivation and Lifestyle' comments, 'We all know people who lead "healthy" lives because they take the trouble to care about themselves. Others often leave their health to chance or simply don't care' (p. 4). The implicit message is that those who lead 'unhealthy' lives choose to do so and are morally lax. Here, as with the work of Almond (1983, 1988), concepts of health are translated into questions of lifestyle based on the assumption that health is a matter of choice and can be predominantly controlled by changes in behaviour.

As a consequence, explanations of disease can be used as a means to define appropriate and moral behaviour. Furthermore, blaming the individual for illness deflects attention away from structural issues and limits the responsibility of the larger society. It also legitimates within the kinesiological and health sciences discrete responses to holistic problems in such a way that Ingham (1985) argues, 'We tinker with the biological and psychodynamic individual rather than the socioeconomic and political structures' (p. 51). He goes on to say,

> research in physical and health education occurs within an institutional framework that favors the analysis of personal factors and discourages the analysis of social factors ... Given voluntaristic and behaviourist assumptions, and given discrete specializations, it is not surprising that the problem of lifestyle is not being addressed as a political concept by those of us in kinesiological and health science.   (p. 53)

As mentioned earlier, ideologies can work behind the backs of people in ways that they are unaware of or do not intend. As such, those who emphasize changes in lifestyles as a central solution to health need to become aware that this focus may actually militate against people gaining genuine knowledge and understanding regarding the determinants of health and illness (cf. Rodmell and Watt, 1986). Indeed, when lifestyles are continually over-emphasized there is a very real danger that those advocating such a stance might unwittingly be engaging in what Crawford (1977) has called the *politics of diversion* that serves the interests of powerful groups in our society.

For example, in discussing the political reluctance in a conservative political climate to associate cancer with exposure to industrial pollutants or occupational carcinogens Nelkin and Gilman (1988) comment, 'Attributing cancer to lifestyle has popular appeal because it appears to enhance individual control over the disease without threatening social or political institutions' (p. 372). Similarly, with regard to occupational illness, Quinlan (1988) notes how management in a range of industries attribute workplace injury to ignorance, apathy, or carelessness on the part of the workers. He argues that this is an attractive strategy to management because not only does it deny 'a fundamental clash of interests between employers and workers over occupational health but also because it endorses a paternalistic and delimited managerial response to addressing the problem' (p. 193). The concentration of management upon the worker as an individual belies a broader understanding of the power structure and dominant value systems of the workplace and legitimates remedies that involve minor modifications to the work environment by management. The point to be made is that once a problem is framed and named in a person-centred way then the political consequences are likely to be institutional reproduction and the preservation of existing operations and systems. That is, the *status quo* is maintained.

Clearly, as Tinning (1990a) argues, any recognition of the broader social structures which limit individual power is unpopular with the dominant power groups in a society. For example, it is in the interests of governments and industry to claim 'that a person's health is simply the outcome of his or her personal choice, and to fail to give credence to such adverse social conditions as unemployment, dangerous work environments (e.g. working with asbestos), chronic poverty and so on' (p. 11). For any government to admit otherwise would involve them in having to face some challenging and expensive issues that might not be politically popular. For example, Wilkinson (1988) suggests that the task of reducing inequalities in health should not be seen as simply a matter of reforming one or two aspects of working-class life, or alternatively, of getting rid of all differences in an attempt to create uniformity in the way people live: 'Rather it is a matter of reducing the inequalities in freedom, power, education and money which determine the disparities in the extent to which the way people live is a reflection of their choosing. Essentially, the range of choices open to people must cease to be dominated by their position in society' (p. 211). Such an approach would clearly disturb the *status quo* and would challenge the vested interests of many groups in our society.

Unfortunately, in recent years within the ongoing 'conservative restoration' (Apple and Teitelbaum, 1986) and with the emergence of the New Right in the field of education, the ideology of individualism has been reinforced in powerful ways.[10] Indeed, Rentoul (1989), commenting upon the 'Thatcher Revolution', suggests that we now live in a 'me and mine' society. Likewise, Tones (1989) points out that the present right-wing government is ideologically committed to the notion of individual responsibility that promotes the idea that if the poor and unemployed are unhealthy, it is their own fault and that they should change their unhealthy habits and even unhealthier value systems. Those that disagree with government views are destined for a hard time and Tones speculates that the demise of the Health Education Council in 1987 and its replacement by the Health Education Authority (HEA) may have had something to do with the former's irritating habit of disagreeing with government views about the measures needed to improve the health of the nation. According to Tones the HEA is 'organizationally much more closely wedded to the National Health Service as a special health authority and is thus more directly under the control of the Minister' (p. 266).

The political and cultural climate that has emerged in Britain during recent years has tended to vilify and erode the role of the state or any collective action in the management of people's lives. Furthermore, as Smith and Stone (1989) remind us, a continued emphasis on individualism provides no basis for solidarity among those who are poor. Instead, it encourages them to try to improve their fortunes and seek upward mobility through personal efforts and dog-eat-dog competition even though many of these people cannot pull themselves up by their bootstraps because they are already rooted in the social prophecies of poverty. As such, we need to be mindful of Ingham's (1985) concerns that much of the current research by kinesiological and health scientists might be acting to promote half-truths about well-being that 'wittingly or unwittingly, gives support to new right thinking and right-thinking ideologies that can emiserate the lifestyles of the poor' (p. 51).

So where does all this leave us? Should we, if it were possible, simply abolish individualism? I think not since, as I mentioned earlier, individualism is a complex beast that contains many ambiguities and contradictions. We have every right to admire those who strive and work hard to achieve excellence, and we have every right to value individual autonomy, independence, and equality of opportunity. To do otherwise would lock us into a system that defines mediocrity as its highest level of aspiration. Furthermore, we need to recognize and continue to address the issue that a significant portion of socially caused illness is, at some level, associated with individual, at-risk behaviour which can be changed to improve health. Consequently, as Crawford (1977) comments, 'A deterministic view which argues that individuals have no choice should be avoided' (p. 675).

To be more aware of individualism is not to banish it but rather to understand how it can shape the way we see the world and thereby influence the manner in which problems are set so that close attention is given to some issues and not to other equally important issues. Tinning (1990a) sums the situation up well:

> So we need neither to embrace totally nor reject individualism, but rather we must recognise how it has become compromised and ambiguous, and work towards a better understanding of the dialectical relationship between individual and society. By this I mean that individual action (what we do as individuals) is both influenced by society and, at the same time influences society.   (p. 11)

Having recognized this we are in a better position to understand the limitations and consequences to any particular way of framing problems and we can then recognize the need to reflect upon and set problems in different ways.

PROBLEM-SETTING WITHIN AN ALTERNATIVE FRAMEWORK

Towards the end of the 1980s another strand of thinking emerged within the HRF movement that questioned the manner in which problems had, until then, been framed by the traditional and educational approaches. Those involved in this strand have engaged in cultural and social critiques that have provided powerful insights into the ways in which health is socially constructed in our society and drawn our attention to some of the limitations inherent in the contemporary HRF movement, particularly with regard to individualism.[11]

In terms of our concern for problem-setting the important point to note is that as we enter the 1990s an alternative frame for problem-setting has entered the arena. As with other forms of problem-setting, it is a value-laden process that articulates a set of missions, goals, objectives, and personal visions regarding issues of health. Terms such as emancipatory, transformative, social justice and equality are central to the discourse in this alternative framework. While once again it is difficult to pull together the different views contained within this emerging strand of the HRF movement it seems that it has framed the problem in such a way as to incorporate and emphasize the social and physical environment as a major determinant of health (see Figure 13.1). With regard to Figure 13.1, Tones (1988) acknowledges that our experiences of health are determined significantly by our health choices but goes on to argue:

> Of equal relevance—indeed many would argue of greater importance—is the environment in which we live and work. Our health will be determined to a greater or lesser extent not merely by the physical environment but also by our socio-economic

circumstances. The effects of a deleterious environment—the impact of poverty, unemployment and other forms of disadvantage—have been thoroughly documented. (p. 29)

This newly emerging approach within the HRF movement has chosen to focus upon many of the issues that are overlooked within the traditional and educational approaches. Indeed, in many ways this particular focus has come about as a reaction to the perceived oversights of the other approaches. Consequently, Colquhoun (1989a) in drawing upon the work of Crawford (1986) comments, 'emancipatory health education promotes a collaborative, community or participatory approach to health and environmental issues which breaks free of the purely individualistic conception of health and illness' (p. 5). Others, like Ingham (1985) see the lifestyle concept as seriously flawed since it offers an implausible panacea for the relational and distributive problems of advanced capitalism: 'It is flawed, specifically in the area of health care, when it incorporates an assumption that voluntaristic adjustments in lifestyle can substitute for State intervention in alleviating structural impediments to well-being' (p. 46).

In Tones's (1986) categorization this most recent approach may be seen as *radical*. While this approach recognizes much of value in the other two approaches, it questions both the effectiveness and uses of a focus on lifestyles and on changing individual behaviour *without changing the social and economic environment*. Such an approach, according to Lawson (1984), sees individuals as transparencies by means of which systematic, societal problems may be apprehended: 'The root problems, in this perspective, are contradictions in institutional structures, and the intervention should be aimed accordingly at the institution, rather than at the person' (p. 57). That is, the radical approach emphasizes the social context in which health is constructed and is concerned to energize the public and bring about environmental change. As Beattie (1984) comments:

> Its key feature is to educate for an understanding of the ecology of the politics of health, to increase awareness of the forces within the social, economic and legal environment which constrain the choices any individual can make in matters of health; and to improve 'political literacy' in these areas, through study of those features of public policy that determine health. (p. 13)

Clearly, in terms of Figure 13.1, the radical approach gives closer attention to the avenues of agenda-setting and critical consciousness-raising with a view to changing the social and physical environment. Of these two strands it is the later that is the most problematic since as Tones (1989) argues, in seeking to stimulate public awareness through the process of critical consciousness-raising with a view to facilitating community action, 'Such action is supposed to pressure government to carry out actions which are not merely inconvenient but often ideologically unacceptable: for instance the alienation of powerful lobbies such as the tobacco and alcohol interests' (p. 262).

The radical approach is explicitly political and attempts to empower the community by modifying people's beliefs in their capacity to influence their destiny and by providing them with the skills to do so. Drawing upon the work of Freudenberg (1984, 1981), Tones (1986) has suggested that a major task for radical health educators is to become politically active so that they can involve people in collective action to create health-promoting environments. Furthermore, these health educators need to be trained to help people organize so that they can change health-damaging institutions, policies, and environments. Therefore, it is not surprising that a strong emphasis is placed upon the political dimensions of health since, as Cribb (1986) argues, 'There has recently been a growing recognition that politics and health are inseparable, that questions of health care policy cannot be treated separately from conflicting theories of distributive justice' (p. 104) Indeed, he suggests that since the fundamental determinants of health and health care are political that the fostering of 'political literacy' is a prerequisite of effective health education programmes.

Ultimately, the prime goal of the radical approach is social change which, it is believed, can best be achieved by a focus on the community rather than the individual. In this framework the problem is defined as the social structure and the solution is social change via empowerment. As a consequence, the radical approach to empowerment differs from that of the educational approach. With regard to the latter, Tones (1986) notes how the 'personality' characteristics of self-esteem and perceived locus of control have informed self-empowerment strategies that 'seek to facilitate decision-making by modifying the individual's self-concept and enhancing his or her self-esteem. Attempts are made to achieve this by equipping people with a variety of 'lifeskills' which not only modify self-image but also prove useful in their own right for the attainment of *specific* goals' (p. 9). Therefore, decision-making skills are central to notions of empowerment in this approach. Such a stance is problematized by advocates of the radical approach. For example, Colquhoun (1989a) emphasizes that:

> Unfortunately, we may foster the skill of decision-making but the empowerment model does not allow us to create the context of the decision-making. A young, single parent for example, might decide that a daily jog would improve his/her health yet may not be able to afford the equipment needed, baby sitters, travelling and so on. Emancipatory health education would encourage individuals to focus on the context of the decision by concentrating upon the idea of advocacy . . . Advocacy is a key element in the new public health and is concerned with redefining the relationship between people, products and settings . . . to encourage enabling strategies which allow individuals to recognise and break free from the constraints of their health.   (p. 6)

This advocacy, according to Baric (1988), can include rebellions against the system, the creation of public pressures to change it, the readjusting and redistribution of power, and the initiation of social reforms. In short, direct challenges to the *status quo* can be initiated. Tones (1989) also notes that advocacy is a key strategy in health promotion, but uses the term in a narrower sense to refer to representations made by a change agent on behalf of a client group, especially in the context of community development. He uses the term 'lobbying' to refer to a complementary strategy that includes those activities by individuals or pressure groups designed to influence political decision-making. Neither tend to be seen as 'educational' activities and as such they are often neglected in this approach. Therefore, the radical approach sees empowerment in a wider context and as part of a community development strategy— that is empowerment is conceptualized in *community* terms. Wallerstein and Bernstein (1988) in drawing upon the work of Paulo Freire define empowerment as:

> a social action process that promotes participation of people, organizations, and communities in gaining control over their lives in the community and the larger society. With this perspective, empowerment is not characterized as achieving power to dominate others, but rather power to act with others to effect change . . . Empowerment education involves people in group efforts to identify their problems, to critically assess social and historical roots of problems, to envision a healthier society, and to develop strategies to overcome

obstacles in achieving their goals. Through community participation, people develop new beliefs in their ability to influence their personal and social spheres. An empowering health education effort therefore involves much more than improving self-esteem, self-efficacy or other health behaviours that are independent from environmental or community change; the targets are individual, group and structural change. Empowerment embodies a broad process that encompasses prevention as well as other goals of community connectedness, self-development, improved quality of life, and social justice.

(p. 380)

Clearly, the radical approach incorporates a range of concerns that differ from those of the traditional and educational approaches. This is particularly so in terms of its emphasis on the political dimensions of health. Consequently, although the three approaches considered are not mutually exclusive there are definite tensions between them. However, as Tones (1986) reminds us, it would be misleading to think of them as inevitably exclusive or antagonistic. Each of them has a different emphasis that influences the process of problem-setting within their particular framework and this has political consequences in terms of the definition of appropriate solutions.

CONCLUDING REMARKS

At the beginning of this chapter I signalled that it was difficult to make sense of the many strands of thought contained within the HRF movement as it stands today. I think that the task will become even more difficult as we move into the 1990s and our awareness of issues pertaining to health becomes more subtle and complex. In view of this, a greater interest in the process of problem-setting can provide us with valuable insights and develop our awareness of these subtleties and the part that we play in their construction. My review of the traditional, educational, and radical approaches and their impact upon the HRF movement is necessarily partial and incomplete since the development of this movement is ongoing and ever-changing.

For example, the radical approach has only recently impacted upon the HRF movement and its influence upon future developments is difficult to predict. In a sense it is the 'new kid on the block' and this approach will itself be subjected to critical scrutiny as we enter the 1990s. Some concerns have already been noted. For example, Tones (1986) warns, 'it will be apparent that the use of critical consciousness-raising techniques will not necessarily safeguard the principle of voluntarism. Radical health education may be quite as coercive as a victim-blaming preventative model in so far as it seeks to perpetuate a particular political view of society' (p. 8). Furthermore, their emphasis upon structural issues can seem overly deterministic and act to deny the power of human agency. On a more general level, Lather (1990) notes that in terms of liberatory pedagogies there is often a failure to probe the degree to which 'empowerment' becomes something done 'by' liberated pedagogues 'to' or 'for' the as-yet-unliberated. Finally, advocates of the radical approach have yet to articulate a clear vision of the form that HRF programmes might take when developed within their framework. As a consequence, PE teachers have been provided with few guidelines as to how the issues raised by the radical stance might be addressed within the school curriculum.

At other times the antagonisms that some advocates of the radical approach have for the other two approaches leads them to dismiss much that is relevant and useful.

For example, Colquhoun (1989b) suggests that 'psychology is leading the physical education profession up a theoretical blind-alley and certainly its potential for informing social change is severely limited' (p. 121). The assumption here seems to be that psychology as a domain of study is an homogeneous entity rather than something that is heterogeneous, multifaceted, and diffuse. There are many strands of thought within the discipline of psychology and it would be something of an overstatement to claim that they all will lead us up a blind alley. As such, advocates of the radical approach need to be wary of throwing the baby out with the bathwater concerning issues of health. As Evans (1989) recognizes, to challenge the ideology of individualism 'is not for a moment to suggest that motivation, an individual's psychology, responsibility or attitude of mind, does not matter much in the achievement of health. Our work as teachers would be futile if we accepted such a claim' (p. 189).

The point we need to remember is that all approaches have their blind spots, their strengths and weaknesses. As I have attempted to indicate, each approach is engaged in a process of problem-setting that takes place within a particular conceptual framework that leads to attention being focused on some issues and not others. As Lawson (1984) reminds us, professionals frequently have different conceptions of problems because they possess different values, 'suggesting that problem-setting is a value-laden process. Its products—missions, goals, and objectives—represent personal ideals about the kind of future a profession should create' (p. 48). That is, all approaches to health are value-laden and contain some particular political view of society, with some approaches being more up-front about the political dimensions inherent in their approach than others.

Quite simply, a value-neutral stance is not possible because health educators cannot realistically avoid subscribing to certain key issues. Educators do not operate in a value-free and uncontaminated setting and health issues can no longer be viewed as apolitical and ahistorical in nature. This being the case, then, as the HRF movement enters the next decade it cannot afford to leave issues of value unexplored since, according to Hyland (1988), such a strategy would be disingenuous because 'not only does it *not* promote freedom of choice and independence in learners, it also effectively obscures the value base of health education thus concealing the inculcation of values behind a cloak of spurious objectivity' (p. 24). Once this cloak is thrown aside then the value dimensions of the various approaches to health can be subjected to close scrutiny and drawn into the realms of ethical, moral, and political debate.

A greater understanding of the process of problem-setting also allows us to conceive the problem from different vantage points and thereby become more aware that there is no one single answer to many of the complex issues relating to health as a multidimensional phenomenon. It also makes us aware that today's problems may not necessarily be tomorrow's. Here it is interesting to consider Tones's (1989) summary of recent World Health Organisation documents on health promotion that he believes reveal a new focus for health education.

1   it is less concerned with preventing *specific* diseases; more concerned with promoting generally healthy lifestyles and promoting feelings of wellbeing;
2   it is more concerned to provide *support* for healthier lifestyles than with exhortation and attitude change;
3   it is concerned to avoid victim-blaming and with raising critical consciousness about environmental conditions and stimulating community and government action;

4   it is not concerned to create *compliance* with medical prescriptions but with promoting collaboration and co-operation between medical practitioner and consumer; it is less concerned with promoting 'proper' use of health services than with 're-orienting' the services to meet consumer needs;

5   it is, above all, concerned to *empower* communities and individuals; to promote greater self reliance and control. Health education seeks to facilitate choice not to coerce into healthy choices defined by others; a major goal is, therefore, to remove barriers to healthy choices.   (p. 268)

How the HRF movement locates itself within this framework will be of vital importance as it enters the final decade of the twentieth century. The tensions between the approaches that I have considered will form a powerful undercurrent within the continuing debate and it remains to be seen what direction the HRF movement will take in the future and the kind of impact it will have on the school curriculum. One thing is for sure, there is much to be gained from those involved devoting some of their valuable time to the process and products of problem-setting. As Lawson (1984) stresses:

> Both researchers and practitioners can use problem-setting to become more reflective and reflexive in their work: reflecting upon their inevitable selectivity in framing and naming, and acting reflexively to make necessary changes. Whether completed individually or collectively, the results are the same: continued learning in the profession ... improved professional effectiveness, and elevated professional status. When these rewards are weighed against the high costs of ignoring problem-setting, its importance to the profession becomes difficult to overestimate.   (p. 58)

Those involved in the HRF movement simply cannot afford to ignore the process of problem-setting if they truly wish to understand the complexities of health in the lives of young people. The debate has begun and I think that we can look forward to the 1990s with great interest.

NOTES

1   Other terms in use besides health-related fitness include health-based PE and health-focused PE.

2   This is not to suggest that 'health' has not always been an issue within PE in some form or other. The historiography provided by Williams (1988) illustrates how the therapeutic stance of the early twentieth century has now been supplanted by a concern for prevention.

3   A common response from my own students when I put forward any form of relational analysis is to define it as irrelevant. The usual question I am asked is, 'What has this got to do with teaching kids in schools?' It is also interesting that I feel the need to begin this chapter with an attempt to legitimize critique as a form of analysis to the reader. I suspect that a more orthodox commentary would not require such legitimation.

4   This is not to imply that critique as a form of analysis has a monopoly on challenging taken-for-granted assumptions. Many key issues have been raised by those operating within a psychological and physiological framework and such work has challenged common-sense views regarding, for example, the relationship between health and fitness. However, these perspectives have not focused their attention specifically upon the issue of ideology and the manner in which this can operate to serve the interests of some groups at the expense of others. In this sense, the questions raised by critique are of a different kind.

5   In this chapter I limit my comments to problem-setting in what Bernstein (1986) has called the primary site of meaning production. As a consequence, my attention is given to the

literature on HRF as it has appeared in journals and books since these are readily available for those who wish to deconstruct my own preferred reading of these texts.

6   This is not to imply that the people from certain groups are not dying in greater numbers than was previously the case. The point I am making relates to the manner in which these increases have been 'explained': that is, how the problem has been defined within a specific socio-historical context so that some potential causes such as environmental pollution, unemployment, or poverty are not focused upon in detail or even considered.

7   The male domination of the HRF movement to date mirrors the gendered nature of a career in education generally. The voices of women are noticeable by their absence within the official discourse of HRF and there is a real danger that we are being provided with a masculinized and patriarchal view of health. As a consequence, there is an urgent need for a feminist critique of HRF. My own awareness of the problems women face regarding health issues within the context of patriarchy has been significantly influenced by Kitty Sparkes and more recently Jessica Sparkes.

8   This is not to deny that there is a place for such opportunism in terms of the micropolitical battles that physical educators have to engage in within schools as they compete for limited resources. Elsewhere, I have advocated that PE teachers need to develop a range of rhetorics as short-term strategies to defend their subject (see Sparkes, 1990a, 1990b, 1990c, in press; Sparkes *et al.*, 1990).

9   A critique of individualism within health education and PE has featured in the work of Colquhoun (1989a, 1990a, 1990b), Evans (1990a, 1990b), Evans and Clarke (1988), Hyland (1988), Kirk and Colquhoun (1989), Regis (1990), Sparkes (1989b, 1989c, 1989d), Tinning (1990a, 1990b). Colquhoun, Kirk, and Tinning incorporate individualism within the ideology of healthism that also links to the ideologies of mesomorphism and technocratic rationality. For the purposes of simplicity this chapter will focus only upon the ideology of individualism since it is taken to be the bedrock upon which many other 'isms' are built.

10   For a more detailed consideration of the impact of the conservative restoration upon education in general see Hargreaves and Reynolds (1989) and Whitty (1988, 1989). For its impact upon PE see Evans (1990b), and Sparkes (1990a, 1990b, 1991b).

11   Key advocates of the radical approach that has impacted upon the HRF movement in the United Kingdom include David Kirk, Derek Colquhoun, and Richard Tinning of Deakin University, who have developed many of their ideas within the context of Daily PE in Australia.

REFERENCES

Almond, L. (1983) A rationale for health related fitness in schools. *Bulletin of Physical Education* **19**, 5–10.

Almond, L. (1988) A health focus in physical education. *Health and Physical Education Project Newsletter* **16**, 2–3.

Apple, M. (1982) *Education and Power*. London: ARK Paperbacks.

Apple, M. and Teitelbaum, K. (1986) Are teachers losing control of their skills and curriculum? *Journal of Curriculum Studies* **18**, 177–84.

Armstrong, N. (1987) Health and fitness programmes in schools: a physiological rational. In S. Biddle (ed.), *Foundations of Health-Related Fitness in Physical Education*, pp. 19–27. London: Ling Publishing House.

Atkinson, J. (1978) *Discovering Suicide: Studies in the Social Organization of Sudden Death*. London: Macmillan.

Baric, L. (1988) The new public health and the concept of advocacy. *The Journal of the Institute of Health Education* **26**, 49–55.

Bartley, M. (1985) Coronary heart disease and the public health 1850–1983. *Sociology of Health and Illness* **7**, 289–313.

Beattie, A. (1984) Health education and the science teacher: invitation to a debate. *Education and Health* **2**, 9–16.

Bellah, R., Masden, R., Sullivan, W., Swindler, A., and Tipton, S. (1985) *Habits of the Heart: Individualism and Commitment in American Life.* Berkeley, CA: University of California Press.

Bernstein, B. (1986) On pedagogic discourse. In J. Richardson (ed.), *Handbook of Theory and Research for the Sociology of Education*, pp. 205–39. London: Greenwood Press.

Biddle, S. (1987) Motivation and lifestyle. *The Turnaround Lifestyle System*, pp. 4–13. New Jersey: Cambell's Institute for Health and Fitness.

Biddle, S. (1989) 'Innovation without change' and the ideology of individualism: a reply to Sparkes. *British Journal of Physical Education* **20**, 64–5.

Black Report (1980) *Inequalities in Health.* Report of a DHSS Working Party chaired by Sir Douglas Black. London: DHSS.

Brandt, A. (1988) Aids and metaphor: toward the social meaning of epidemic disease. *Social Research* **55**, 412–32.

Colquhoun, D. (1989a) Emancipatory health education and environmental education: the emergence of the new public health. *Australian Journal of Environmental Education* **5**, 1–8.

Colquhoun, D. (1989b) Health related fitness and individualism: continuing the debate. *British Journal of Physical Education* **20**, 118–22.

Colquhoun, D. (1990a) Images of healthism in health-based physical education. In D. Kirk and R. Tinning (eds), *Physical Education, Curriculum and Culture: Critical Issues in the Contemporary Crisis*, pp. 225–51. London: Falmer Press.

Colquhoun, D. (1990b) Emancipatory health education and the potential limitations of health based physical education. Paper presented at the AIESEP World Congress, Loughborough, July.

Crawford, R. (1977) Are you dangerous to your health: the ideology and politics of victim blaming. *International Journal of Health Services* **7**, 663–80.

Crawford, R. (1986) A cultural account of 'health': control, release, and the social body. In J. McKinlay (ed.), *Issues in the Political Economy of Health Care*, pp. 60–103. London: Tavistock.

Cribb, A. (1986) Politics and health in the school curriculum. In S. Rodmell and A. Watts (eds), *The Politics of Health Education*, pp. 100–20. London: Routledge & Kegan Paul.

Dewar, A. (1990) Oppression and privilege in physical education: struggles in the negotiation of gender in a university programme. In D. Kirk and R. Tinning (eds), *Physical Education, Curriculum and Culture: Critical Issues in the Contemporary Crisis*, pp. 67–99. London: Falmer Press.

Evans, J. (1989) Health related fitness: a suitable case for treatment? *British Journal of Physical Education* **20**, 189–90.

Evans, J. (1990a) Ability, position and privilege in school physical education. In D. Kirk and R. Tinning (eds), *Physical Education, Curriculum and Culture: Critical Issues in the Contemporary Crisis*, pp. 139–67. London: Falmer Press.

Evans, J. (1990b) Defining a subject: the rise and rise of the new PE? *British Journal of Sociology of Education* **2**, 155–69.

Evans, J., and Clarke, J. (1988) Changing the face of physical education. In J. Evans (ed.), *Teachers, Teaching and Control in Physical Education*, pp. 125–43. London: Falmer Press.

Freudenberg, N. (1981) Health education for social change: a strategy for public health in the US. *International Journal of Health Education* **xxiv**, 1–8.

Freudenberg, N. (1984) Training health educators for social change. *International Quarterly of Community Health Education* **5**, 37–51.

Hargreaves, A. and Reynolds, D. (1989) Introduction: decomprehensivization. In A. Hargreaves and D. Reynolds (eds), *Educational Policies: Controversies and Critiques*, pp. 1–32. London: Falmer Press.

Hargreaves, J. (1986) *Sport, Power and Culture.* Cambridge: Polity Press.

Hart, N. (1988) *The Sociology of Health and Medicine.* Lancashire: Causeway Press.

HMSO (1928) *The Registrar General's Statistical Review of England and Wales for the Year 1926.* London: HMSO.

Hyland, T. (1988) Values and health education: a critique of individualism. *Educational Studies* **14**, 23–31.

Ingham, A. (1985) From public issue to personal trouble: well-being and the fiscal crisis of the state. *Sociology of Sport Journal* **2**, 43–55.

Ketcham, R. (1987) *Individualism and Public Life: A Modern Dilemma*. Oxford: Blackwell.

Kirk, D. and Colquhoun, D. (1989) Healthism and physical education. *British Journal of Sociology of Education* **10**, 417–34.

Kirk, D. and Tinning, D. (1990) Introduction: physical education, curriculum and culture. In D. Kirk and R. Tinning (eds), *Physical Education, Curriculum and Culture: Critical Issues in the Contemporary Debate*, pp. 1–21. London: Falmer Press.

Lane, L. (1988) Individualism, civic virtue, and public administration: the implications of American Habits of the Heart. *Administration and Society* **20**, 30–45.

Lather, P. (1990) Staying dumb? Student resistance to liberatory curriculum. Paper presented at the annual meeting of the American Educational Research Association, Boston, MA, April.

Lawson, H. (1984) Problem-setting for physical education and sport. *Quest* **36**, 48–60.

Mitchell, J. (1984) *What is to be Done about Illness and Health?* Harmondsworth: Penguin.

Naidoo, J. (1986) Limits to individualism. In S. Rodmell and A. Watt (eds), *The Politics of Health Education*. London: Routledge & Kegan Paul.

Nelkin, D. and Gilman, S. (1988) Placing blame for devastating disease. *Social Research* **55**, 361–78.

Quinlan, M. (1988) Psychological and sociological approaches to the study of occupational illness: a critical review. *Australian & New Zealand Journal of Sociology* **24**, 189–207.

Regis, D. (1990) Self-concept and conformity in theories of health education. Unpublished Ph.D. thesis, University of Exeter.

Rentoul, J. (1989) *Me and Mine: The Triumph of the New Individualism*. London: Unwin Hyman.

Rodmell, S. and Watt, A. (1986) Conventional health education: problems and possibilities. In S. Rodmell and A. Watt (eds), *The Politics of Health Education*, pp. 1–15. London: Routledge & Kegan Paul.

Scraton, S. (1987) 'Boys muscle in where angels fear to tread'—girls' subcultures and physical activities. In J. Horne, D. Jary, and A. Tomlinson (eds), *Sport, Leisure and Social Relations*, pp. 160–86. London: Routledge & Kegan Paul.

Smith, K. and Stone, L. (1989) Rags, riches, and bootstraps: beliefs about the causes of wealth and poverty. *Sociological Quarterly* **30**, 93–107.

Sparkes, A. (1989a) Paradigmatic confusions and the evasion of critical issues in naturalistic research. *Journal of Teaching in Physical Education* **8**, 131–51.

Sparkes, A. (1989b) Health-related fitness: an example of innovation without change. *British Journal of Physical Education* **20**, 60–3.

Sparkes, A. (1989c) Health-related fitness and the pervasive ideology of individualism. *Perspectives* **41**, 37–45.

Sparkes, A. (1989d) Health-related fitness in England: a deconstruction of the official discourse. Paper presented at the AIESEP World Convention, Jyväskylä, Finland, June.

Sparkes, A. (1990a) The changing nature of teachers' work: reflecting on governor power in different historical periods. *Physical Education Review* **13**, 39–47.

Sparkes, A. (1990b) The emerging relationship between physical education teachers and school governors: a sociological analysis. *Physical Education Review* **13**, 128–37.

Sparkes, A. (1990c) School governors and physical education in the 1990s: on the need for effective advocacy. *British Journal of Physical Education* **21**, 236–8.

Sparkes, A. (1991a) Towards understanding, dialogue and polyvocality in the research community: extending the boundaries of the paradigms debate. *Journal of Teaching in Physical Education* **10**, 103–33.

Sparkes, A. (1991b) The changing nature of teachers' work: physical education, school governors and curriculum control. In N. Armstrong (ed.), *New Directions in Physical Education 2: Towards a National Curriculum*. Champaign, IL: Human Kinetics.

Sparkes, A., Templin, T., and Schempp, P. (1990) The problematic nature of a career in a marginal subject: some implications for teacher education programmes. *Journal of Education for Teaching* **16**, 3–28.

Tinning, R. (1990a) *Ideology and Physical Education: Opening Pandora's Box*. Deakin: Deakin University Press.

Tinning, R. (1990b) Physical education as health education: problem-setting as a response to the new health consciousness. *Unicorn* **16**, 81–90.

Tones, K. (1986) Health education and the ideology of health promotion: a review of alternative approaches. *Health Education Research: Theory and Practice* **1**, 3–12.

Tones, K. (1988) The role of the school in health promotion: the primacy of personal and social education. *Westminster Studies in Education* **11**, 27–45.

Tones, K. (1989) Health education in England: an overview. In C. James, J. Balding, and D. Harris (eds), *World Yearbook of Education 1989: Health Education*, pp. 260–78. London: Kogan Page.

Townsend, P. and Davidson, N. (1982) *Inequalities in Health: The Black Report*. London: Penguin.

Turner, B. (1988) Individualism, capitalism and the dominant culture: a note on the debate, *Australian & New Zealand Journal of Sociology* **24**, 47–64.

Verbrugge, L. (1985) Gender and health: an update on hypotheses and evidence. *Journal of Health and Social Behaviour* **26**, 156–82.

Wallerstein, N. and Bernstein, E. (1988) Empowerment education: Freire's ideas adapted to health education. *Health Education Quarterly* **15**, 379–94.

Whitehead, M. (1987) *The Health Divide: Inequalities in Health in the 1980s*. London: Health Education Council.

Whitty, G. (1988) The New Right and the national curriculum: state control or market forces? *Journal of Education Policy* **4**, 329–41.

Whitty, G. (1989) *Towards a New Education System: The Victory of the New Right?* London: Falmer Press.

Wilkinson, R. (1988) Health, inequality and social structure. In M. Keynes, D. Coleman and N. Dimsdale (eds), *The Political Economy of Health and Welfare*, pp. 207–20. London: Macmillan.

Williams, A. (1988) The historiography of health and fitness in physical education. *PEA Research Supplement* **3**, 1–4.

Name index

Subject index

(Where numerals are in **heavy** type, this represents a subject covered by a chapter.)